MW01094956

"In *The ServiceMaster Story*, Al Erisman gives us both a quality business school case study and a much-needed seminary course in faith and business. While I've met Bill Pollard and know something about the company, this ninety-year history of its leaders and leadership transitions gives a realistic picture of the challenges and rewards of committing a company to the mission of honoring God, developing its people, pursuing excellence, and growing profitably. ServiceMaster has led the way in recognizing the dignity of all work (washing the floors, emptying garbage, cleaning up hospital operating rooms, etc.) in ways that contributed to the life and growth of every employee and served its customers well. The book is filled with wisdom. One of my favorites is from Ken Wessner: 'That's our job; that's our responsibility: to build winning teams with ordinary people.' I took away some creative ideas for my own work and renewed encouragement that God continues to build his kingdom through the everyday work of everyday people."

—**Katherine L. Alsdorf, Vice President**
Global Faith & Work Initiatives, Redeemer City to City
Board Member, The Theology of Work Project
Co-author of *Every Good Endeavor*

"ServiceMaster has long been held up as a model company founded on Christian principles, with its first objective 'To Honor God in All We Do.' This objective was demonstrated in the company's long-standing efforts to serve its frontline employees in the industrial cleaning industry with dignity and respect, and to serve its customers with excellence.

"But is it possible for a business founded on such overt faith-based values to continue to exemplify those values as it grows, changes leadership, acquires other companies, expands globally, goes public, and faces significant market challenges? In this book, Al Erisman takes us through the history of ServiceMaster, focusing on the impact of its leaders on the financial performance and cultural identity of the company from its founding through today. In it, he captures the stories and people of a remarkable organization that has changed significantly over time and continues to have something to teach us."

—**Denise Daniels, Professor of Management, Seattle Pacific University**
Co-author of *Working in the Presence of God*
Executive Producer, Faith & Co.; Board Member, Theology of Work Project

"Albert M. Erisman charts a powerful and in-depth chronological journey through the pages of *The ServiceMaster Story*. This story clearly illustrates what is possible when leaders choose to build an enterprise on Christian principles, elect to keep first things first, and experience the favor that follows when faith is put into action. This book is sure to accelerate the business as ministry movement that is swelling across this country and around the world. But I also believe that the truths captured in the tenures of each ServiceMaster leader will inspire, challenge, and even convict Christian leaders wherever God has called them to serve. The lessons here are too rich to miss."

—**Tami Heim, President and CEO, Christian Leadership Alliance**
Leadership career with Macy's, Borders Books, and Thomas Nelson Publishing

"Al Erisman captures the complexity of building a thick culture that is animated by a thoughtful Christian ethos while operating in the realities of a market economy. The exemplary work by the leaders of ServiceMaster to create a coherent culture that is based on a Christian anthropology and an understanding of power and leadership that flows from that—but is set in a pluralistic organization, competing in the market every day—demonstrates the difficulty of building a sustainable culture beyond the voice of a set of founding leaders.

"In this book, I am reminded that the mixture of financial realities, human gift-edness, macroeconomics, customer preferences, and technology all require a level of strategic insight and adaptation that is extremely difficult to sustain, but it is a high calling and worthy of one's life work. This book also captures the extraordinary responsibility of leaders to grapple with their decisions because of the profound impact they have on every member of the organization. I found this book inspiring, challenging, and thought-provoking."

—Don Flow, Chairman and CEO, Flow Automotive Companies

"'If you don't live it, you don't believe it.' The almost immortal words of Marion Wade, founder of ServiceMaster, have echoed through the generations of the company's history. Bringing a lifetime of senior business experience to bear on his study, Al Erisman has served all of us very well, reading critically and listening carefully, all the time judging ServiceMaster's business practices in light of its corporate commitments and its deepest desires for the way business ought to be done with the way the business has been done. For years it was a model of what a company can be and should be, under the pressure of financial performance in service of shareholder expectations—an albatross around every corporation's neck—the company's prized integrity was severely challenged. What stands out is the way that Wade's vision was sustained for so long, and the extent that it is remembered almost a century later. From beginning to end, this book is a fascinating window into why that was and why it is still true."

—Steven Garber, Professor of Marketplace Theology, Regent College
Author of *Visions of Vocation*

"*The ServiceMaster Story* is an inspiring account of the legacy of a once-great company, whose history is examined in fine detail. Fascination and instruction await you here if you have your eyes set on building a better world, whatever your ideology, religion, philosophy, or values."

—Prabhu Guptara, Executive Director
Relational Analytics Ltd., Cambridge, UK

"This is an important story of large-scale servant leadership that proves that making money—lots of it—and changing the lives of people for the better are more than compatible; they are inextricably linked. Values-driven organizations win. But leaders have to believe this for it to happen. The ServiceMaster story of servant leadership is still proving this to be true."

—James L. Heskett, UPS Foundation Professor Emeritus
Harvard Business School
Author of *The Culture Cycle*

"Anyone who may have studied the autobiographical accounts of Chester Barnard's *Functions of the Executive* or Alfred P. Sloan's *My Years with General Motors* will see in *The ServiceMaster Story*, as told by Al Erisman, a clearly presented body of evidence of what enables a complex organization to persist through thick and thin. The four foundational principles of Marion Wade endured, even as the enterprise experiences changed. 'To honor God in all that we do,' 'To help people develop,' 'To pursue excellence,' and 'To grow profitably' are aspirations that apply to any business and clarify what it means to lead, as well as what it means to organize human activity in pursuit of some common organizational goal. Business enterprise is built by and for people who are owners, employees, suppliers, and customers. As honorable and practical as the last three principles may be, it is the first principle—'To honor God in all that we do'—that serves as the means to resolve any conundrum that anyone anywhere in the organization or in its community may experience in the conduct of the business.

"Erisman carefully documents the consequences of deviations from the founding principles as pursued by various elements of the evolving organization. This is a story of joy and suffering in the context of a business. Most importantly, perhaps, the gift of this rendering of the story of one enterprise that gives credence to the wisdom, dedication to purpose, and the grace of Marion Wade and his successors as characterized in the book is the confirmation of what human enterprise is all about. *The ServiceMaster Story* is an engaging account and an object lesson that should be required reading in business schools around the world."

**—David Gautschi, Dean Emeritus and Joseph Keating Professor
Gabelli School of Business, Fordham University**

"This book is fascinating reading purely for its anecdotal style. But the book goes on to lay down markers that will prove to be very helpful for Christian entrepreneurs who would want to lay down values for their own start-ups. In my part of the world—South Asia—some Christians are likely to misread success stories purely in terms of a 'prosperity' version of the gospel of Jesus. This book makes it clear that it is not so. Erisman has made it a point that failures, the need for accountability, discipline, and forgiveness are all part of running a company that attempts to follow a biblical model. I will heartily recommend this book to a number of Christian entrepreneurs in my own country of India."

**—L. T. Jeyachandran, Chief Engineer, Civil (Retired)
Department of Telecommunications, Government of India**

"This book is a must-read for Christian marketplace leaders. It speaks eloquently to the difference that leadership makes and in this case a progression of leaders—from Marion Wade to Ken Hansen, Ken Wessner, Bill Pollard, and Carlos Cantu. When ServiceMaster focused on its four core values, centered on God's heart, the company prospered both in profits and for people. During that era, ServiceMaster sustained a corporate culture that generated more than a Return on Investment; it generated a Return on Involvement. Without these values, ServiceMaster lost the organizational cohesiveness that had brought such marketplace strength. There are lessons in these pages for every organization seeking to honor God through the marketplace."

—Chuck Proudfit, Founder and President, At Work on Purpose

"Al Erisman marvelously captures ServiceMaster's fascinating and impressive story. Its culture was intentionally thick with Christian faith, values, and purpose. Its leaders vigorously worked at doing what they believed, while laboring that others might (believe and) do likewise. The story is not simple or easy, but it breathes with the confidence that people, work, the workplace, and profit really matter to God."

—Mark Labberton, President, Fuller Theological Seminary

"A must-read for all CEOs! Through his research and deep insights, Al Erisman does a masterful job highlighting important lessons for all companies that want lasting success. As the CEO of several successful firms, I can personally attest to the power of company culture."

—Gloria Nelund, Chair and CEO, TriLinc Global
Former CEO, U.S. Private Wealth Management Division, Deutsche Bank

"Integrating your faith and work is challenging enough, but doing it in a publicly traded company takes it to a whole new level. How do you lead a company accountable to the shareholders, manage a diverse global workforce, and grow it profitability, all consistent with Christian principles? Beyond the theoretical, Al Erisman explores these and other important questions using the real-life example of ServiceMaster."

—The Honorable Edmund C. Moy
Director of the United States Mint (2006–11)
Director of multiple public companies

"Many in our churches now understand that there should be no sacred/secular divide and that all of life should be lived under the lordship of Christ. This includes the world of work. But there remain questions as to whether one can excel in work using Christian principles, especially in the tough world of business. Therefore, there is a need for actual models of companies that are doing well, while consciously adhering to Christian values. Thank God there are such companies. In our part of the world, I think of the Nehemiah Reinforced Soil Company in Malaysia and the Far East Organization, Singapore's largest property developer.

"Al Erisman has given us a well-researched and honest study of ServiceMaster, another company that overtly stated their commitment to God as part of their primary objectives. Here are the four key tenets of the company: 'To honor God in all we do,' 'To help people develop,' 'To pursue excellence,' and 'To grow profitably.' Erisman's study shows how the values encapsulated by these four main tenets helped the company grow, and he is quick to point out the inherent tensions between the tenets and the strengths and weaknesses of the company's CEOs. Indeed, the company could not escape the rapid changes happening in the world of business and has now changed the four main tenets for an updated one. The reference to God is now covert, though the underlying values remain the same. For now. Erisman's book should be required reading for all who attempt to bring Christian values into the marketplace. Clearly, it is not an easy mission, but the story of ServiceMaster shows that it is possible."

—Soo-Inn Tan, Graceworks, Singapore

The
ServiceMaster
Story

The ServiceMaster Story

Navigating Tension between People and Profit

Albert M. Erisman

The ServiceMaster Story: Navigating Tension between People and Profit

Hendrickson Publishers Marketing, LLC
P. O. Box 3473
Peabody, Massachusetts 01961-3473
www.hendrickson.com

ISBN 978-1-68307-263-8

Kind permission granted by Seattle Pacific University and the Institute for Business, Technology, and Ethics for the use of *Ethix* interview material.

Printed in the United States of America

First Printing—January 2020

Library of Congress Control Number: 2019952414

CONTENTS

FOREWORD

In this foreword, several former ServiceMaster leaders offer their perspective on the company and what it meant to them to be a part of it. Their perspectives here will set the tone for the rest of the book.

Our objectives—to honor God in all we do, to help people develop, to pursue excellence, and to grow profitably—have had a great influence on my development and the way I have sought to serve and live my life. For me, the ServiceMaster years were a continuing learning experience as I was mentored by those I worked with, served, and led. It was a time of rapid growth for me as a person and for our business. I am indeed grateful to Al Erisman for writing this book. He has captured both the spirit and soul of the company I knew.

C. William Pollard (1977–2003)
CEO (twice) and Chairman

It was early May of 1963. I was looking forward to my college graduation and my wedding in June. I needed a job. I talked to my senior class advisor and he gave me a good lead. It seems he had invested some of his savings with a man named Marion Wade. Mr. Wade had given him debentures that would later become ServiceMaster stock. I learned later that my senior class advisor had greatly benefitted from this transaction. He encouraged me to call a fledgling company called ServiceMaster. I called and was put in contact with Ken Wessner, a vice president with ServiceMaster.

He came to my college apartment to interview me. At the end of the interview I remember him saying not to look at this as just a job, but he thought it could be a career for me. I certainly didn't think of it as a career then, but forty years went by and I retired in 2003. This book covers the period of time that I had the privilege of working at ServiceMaster.

The leaders of ServiceMaster—Marion Wade, Ken Hansen, Ken Wessner, Bill Pollard, and Carlos Cantu—were my bosses, my mentors, and later became my good friends. I look back on these wonderful years, realizing these men were not just good businessmen, but they were also loyal husbands, good fathers, and great life models for me, men of integrity, possessing great character.

When I started, I had no idea I would spend forty years in this great company. We were encouraged to recruit our friends who were looking for opportunity. Little did I know that working with so many of my friends as teammates, we would develop a way of life. Working hard, learning our jobs, and teaching and mentoring others taught us leadership.

It was an amazing journey and career from all aspects. One of the greatest unanticipated bonuses of my career was that many ServiceMaster customers became lifelong friends! I am so grateful for my career with ServiceMaster.

Chuck Stair (1963–2003)
Vice Chairman (retired)

Al Erisman has written not only a business book with lasting leadership, management, and business lessons of leading with purpose and passion, and a wonderful history of what was named "the most respected company in the world" by the *Financial Times*, but he has also written a love story of leaders who shared a love for God, the people they worked with, and the company.

Having spent twenty-five years with the company's four tenets—"To honor God in all we do, to help people develop, to pursue excellence, and to grow profitably"—I came to know that these were not only a way of working, but also a way of living. With the starting point that *all* people are created in the image and likeness of God, it set the foundation of inclusion. When I left ServiceMaster and went on to lead other companies, I took these objectives with me, and they will remain in my leadership DNA.

Patricia Asp (1978–2003)
President, Compass Executives

This book is about *real* faith in the workplace. You'll learn how people at all levels of leadership at a rapidly expanding Fortune 500 company lived out, every day, that company's first objective: "To Honor God in All We Do." The ServiceMaster story is unusual, because it finds that the key to success in business grows from the leaders' commitment to live out their faith in the workplace.

Among the extraordinary people who led ServiceMaster through decades of double-digit growth, two men most impacted my faith and leadership: Marion Wade and Bill Pollard. I never met Marion Wade, but my life has been forever impacted by his quote (and commitment to the motto), "If you don't live it, you don't believe it." His approach was much simpler and straightforward than so many of today's faith-in-the-workplace seminars that spend a great deal of time on political correctness. When I served at ServiceMaster, there was no concern about political correctness—just a diverse group of men and women doing their best to live out the four objectives.

Bill Pollard's investments in my life made me the man I am. He led me as a student when he was my church youth group leader. He mentored me during my non-ServiceMaster career and served as my boss while at ServiceMaster. Most of all, Bill has been my great friend. Bill taught me (and thousands of others) by being an example of what it means to honor God in the workplace every day. He is the most brilliant man I have ever known, yet Bill is humble and eager to teach others. He has always been an excellent example of real faith in the workplace.

I am not a prosperity gospel devotee, but I do know that 2 Chronicles 26:5 (KJV) played a big role in ServiceMaster's success: "As long as he sought the LORD, God made him to prosper." If you are interested in living out your faith in your workplace, read this book! You'll save time and money wasted on just another business seminar—and you'll prosper from what you learn.

Rob Keith (1985–2001)
Former Group President, Management Services
Led Management Services at Aramark
after that division was sold (2001–04)

This book captures the essence of achieving success in the service business. ServiceMaster embodies what servant leadership is about, which was evidenced by the success of our CEOs in leading the company. They understood the work and the impact it had on the personal development and the lives of our associates.

While I never met Marion Wade, I did meet "the Kens" [Ken Hansen and Ken Wessner]. My interactions with them gave me a sense of the history and culture of ServiceMaster and the role the four objectives played in the growth and success of the company. I did serve under Bill [Pollard] and my father [Carlos Cantu], and it was evident they understood that the effectiveness of our four objectives was measured not only by the financial success of the company, but more importantly by the impact on people's lives. They were role models in living what they believed.

ServiceMaster acquired the majority of the companies that comprised the consumer services business, with Terminix being the first major one. These acquisitions theoretically presented a challenge as to how they would be integrated culturally. In actuality, they all assimilated and thrived. What each of these businesses had were leaders who knew the work and the connection it had to the service worker. In addition, they were in some form or fashion already practicing the four objectives. It wasn't a stretch to know what ServiceMaster was about.

I consider myself fortunate to have worked in the same organization as my father and to have witnessed close-up his vision, leadership, and practical application of our four objectives. I periodically run into current and former ServiceMaster associates, and to this day some will share with me a story about an event or encounter they had with my father and how that impacted their career and/or life. On a personal level, it gives me great pride to hear these stories as his legacy lives on. On a professional level, it proves that humble servant leadership stands the test of time.

I am grateful for my time at ServiceMaster and appreciative of all on the ServiceMaster team who helped shape me and my career.

Albert Cantu (1986–2006)
Former President and COO, Terminix International
Founder, Cantu Enterprises Holdings

"The story will be told in the changed lives of people" was a statement heard often at ServiceMaster. Fortunately, my life was one of those changed. I first met Bill Pollard during an interview in the fall of 1987. I came prepared to learn about the vision and strategies that would perpetuate the company's great success and how my experience and skills might contribute. I also came needing to understand the company's unique culture and whether I could comfortably fit in.

Bill's very first question was whether I had ever fired anyone. It threw me off guard, which is one of Bill's many talents, but it eventually led to a fascinating discussion about the company's four objectives, and (as this book so vividly describes) the tension that sometimes existed in trying to keep them in balance. I heard several incredible success stories involving the development of people. But we also discussed ServiceMaster's responsibility to provide appropriate returns to its shareholders, and how that occasionally required a painful parting of ways with individuals or businesses.

When I left ServiceMaster over twenty years later, I was committed to exploring opportunities both inside and outside of business, and to bringing the best of ServiceMaster with me wherever I went. Since leaving, I have served as pro-bono president and chairman of an inner-city Catholic high school in the heart of Chicago's troubled South Side. I have found the best of ServiceMaster to be relevant to our efforts in faith-based education, as we strive to overcome economic challenges and develop six hundred young men to their full and unique potential.

What did I see as the best of ServiceMaster? It started but did not end with the company's objectives and culture. Initially concerned about whether I would fit in, I ultimately embraced them and they changed my life. We made mistakes, but I do believe our "batting average" was relatively high as a result of our focus.

To Honor God in All We Do. Recognizing that in a world of gray, there *is* a fundamental right and wrong, and that leaders are accountable for doing the right thing, especially when it is hard and no one is watching.

We are human and sometimes we fail. But failure is not hypocrisy, unless it is intentional.

To Help People Develop. Recognizing a responsibility to help people develop. Not just enabling them to *do* their best, but to *be* their best. A dramatic difference. Building on their strengths and developing their weaknesses. Providing them with the opportunities, tools, and mentoring they need to grow. I benefited significantly from the mentoring, opportunities, and support I received from all those I worked for, including Bob Erickson, Bill Pollard, Carlos Cantu, and Jon Ward; but also from those who worked with and for me, such as Mike Isakson, Scott Cromie, Ed Dunn, Deb O'Connor, Eric Zarnikow, Jim McMahon, and so many others. I am forever grateful.

To Pursue Excellence. Recognizing that in any service business (including education) relentless pursuit of excellence is a mandate. Success requires us to regularly exceed expectations. "Good enough" never is.

To Grow Profitably. Understanding that profits are the means that enable the pursuit of the end goals of the organization and its people.

"ServiceMaster's Best" went beyond a strong culture. It included exceptional *vision*, which enabled several successful transformations of the company—from a franchised cleaning business, to a provider of housekeeping management services to hospitals, to the extension of management services to other functions and industries, and to the acquisitions-enabled expansion that helped ServiceMaster become the world's leading provider of home services.

The company also demonstrated exceptional *creativity*, as illustrated by the change from a corporation to a master limited partnership, which was almost unprecedented for an operating company. This was very complex, but over time it saved more than a billion dollars that was reinvested in the business or returned to shareholders. Another example was the unique and complex structure that enabled the company's game-changing acquisition of TruGreen and a large pest control business from Waste Management, in exchange for a minority equity interest in ServiceMaster's nonpublicly traded Consumer Services subsidiary.

Finally, *exceptional service delivery* by well-trained and motivated service workers led by talented and committed operating leaders. Nothing was perfect, including ServiceMaster. There are things that I wish we had done differently or better. But overall, it was a remarkable company and a life-changing experience.

Ernie Mrozek (1987–2008)
President and Chief Financial Officer (retired)

"The executive who is concerned only with current success is going to pass from one crisis to the next, until his head is reeling."

"I did try to build a business that would live longer than I would in the marketplace that would witness to Jesus Christ in the way the business was conducted."

"Don't expect to build a super company with super people. You must build a great company with ordinary people."

"If you don't live it, you don't believe it."

—Marion Wade

"Managing multiple objectives is like pulling an elastic exercise strip to the point of tension. It's hard to do, but you had better hold on to both ends. If you don't, the tension will be released, and you will get hit on the head!"

"Anything worth doing is worth doing poorly—to get started."

"Sometimes you need to move sideways, like a crab."

—Ken Hansen

"I've never hired a gentleman because he was a Christian, and I've never not hired one because he wasn't. But we do insist that a man be of high moral caliber."

"I am *pleased,* but not *satisfied.*"

"We need to help a person *be* before we help them *do.*"

—Ken Wessner

"One should not expect or promote financial success or gain from seeking to honor God."

"My leadership responsibility was not about me or my feelings. It was about what should be done for our business and for our people."

"People work for a cause, not just for a paycheck."

"The awesome responsibility of leadership. . . . A leader has only one choice to make—to lead or mislead."

—Bill Pollard

"In order to be an effective leader, I had to be prepared to serve. That required being constantly willing to listen and learn from every relationship."

"People develop when they catch a vision and take responsibility for making it happen."

"Leadership must help anticipate future opportunities and prepare the organization for change."

—Carlos Cantu

1

An Unusual Company

Can a business be successful if it focuses primarily on the growth and development of its employees? What if those employees are manual laborers? And what if that company is publicly traded and global? For many years, ServiceMaster forged this path, creating success for both the employees and the business.

From 1929 through 2000, five leaders of ServiceMaster built on the work of one another to create an unusual business, rooted in the value and dignity of its front-line workers. When most of the service business was competing on the basis of low-cost labor, with an annual turnover of 100 percent to 300 percent per year, ServiceMaster created a career opportunity for those who did the work—beyond a job and a paycheck.[1]

As the company grew from a few people working from a home office in 1929 to a $6 billion global, publicly traded company by 2000, each leader refined and sharpened what had come before. They pushed back on one another and worked collaboratively. The results, by many measures, were astounding.

Along the way, in 1985 and 1995, ServiceMaster was honored by *Fortune* magazine as the number one service company in the United States. In 1998, it was recognized as one of the twenty most respected companies in the world by the *Financial Times*. Its third CEO, Ken Wessner, was elected to the Health Care Hall of Fame—the ultimate in customer recognition—for his leadership in the housekeeping work ServiceMaster provided for hospitals. For a long period of time, the company set a target of promoting 20 percent of their front-line workers to leadership positions. In 1988 and 2000, Harvard Business School created two case studies about the company.

Between 1970 and 1999, the company experienced growth in revenue and profit every quarter and every year—which was the result of many decisions and details coming together to create this success. Understanding how this accomplishment worked requires understanding the details that matter, but there is a big picture conclusion. The success of these leaders was rooted in a set of principles that centered on serving God in the marketplace, on integrity, and on the dignity and worth of every service worker and the work that person performed. The leaders of this era saw their work as more than a job or a stepping stone to the next position; they saw it as a mission and a passion, and a response to a deeply held belief. The financial performance and customer satisfaction that ServiceMaster generated was a result of these commitments. Although some critics[2] suggested the workers were valued in order to produce these results, they didn't seem to look deeply enough at what was really going on. This commitment often showed itself in unexpected ways for a company at this level of accomplishment.

Dave Aldridge had earned his MBA degree, and was working as a manager at ServiceMaster. Like other leaders, he participated in We Serve days, during which senior company leaders worked as front-line employees to experience the physical and emotional experiences of those they led.

> The hospital was opening a new wing, and I was helping to prepare the birthing suites. I was on my hands and knees cleaning baseboards. An excited group of nurses who would be serving in this new area walked through. As they walked by, I looked up and said "hello," and no one responded. I wanted to cry out, "Hey, I have my MBA, and my wife is a nurse!" But the reality was, no one cared or thought I was worth acknowledging.[3]

How did this service help Dave and other such leaders, and why would ServiceMaster require this of its executives? For many companies, managing labor-intensive work is simply a cost issue. ServiceMaster, however, wanted those who were leading people to understand firsthand what the work was like and how it felt to be treated as if they were invisible. It shaped their management.

Dave went on to say of this experience, "I have learned about the 'heart' of our business and about the feelings and emotions of the routine and mundane that are often involved in serving others."[4] This was not just a lesson in humility but was deeply rooted in what the company was trying to do.

In addition to knowing what this kind of service work is like, the company researched how to create a better work environment. It is rare that a company like this has a research department, but ServiceMaster wanted to find the best techniques for performing tasks and the best tools for the jobs. The company also wanted to support its employees in finding meaning and purpose in their work. At the hospitals, for example, they would bring doctors and nurses in to talk with their service workers, helping them to see the connection between their cleaning work and the health of the patient.

Equally unexpected is James Heskett's story. In the mid-1990s, he was a Harvard professor, visiting ServiceMaster in preparation for writing a case study on the company. He wrote:

> At one Board meeting, the case writer observed Chairman Pollard, having spilled coffee on the boardroom carpet prior to the meeting, down on his hands and knees cleaning up the mess with chemicals brought from the

laboratory. Just as surprising, directors in conversation over their continental breakfast hardly appeared to notice. It was the ordinary or expected thing at ServiceMaster for a leader to be serving.[5]

From early in the company's history, successive leaders laid out what they thought was the right way to run a business. They believed strongly enough in this mission that they were not distracted by short-term pressures. That started with seeking to understand both the dignity of the workers and the dignity of the work they did. This included servant leadership. Heskett, who wrote extensively on the service industry, said that ServiceMaster "has broken the cycle of failure, and has basically reengineered jobs, provided training to people, and attempted to deliver a level of self-esteem that many workers have never had in the past."[6]

To be clear, early ServiceMaster leaders did not set out to "break the cycle of failure" in the service industry. The foundation, laid early in the formation of the company, was more simply to value the people because it was the right thing to do. While achieving these results in the service industry is unprecedented, it is clear that what ServiceMaster accomplished is not limited to this industry. When people are part of a company that recognizes each employee as a person, rather than a unit of production, they respond positively. Supporting meaning and purpose for the employee brings ownership and passion to the work, which results in greater customer satisfaction. The lessons from this story can offer valuable insight for any business.

The exact way ServiceMaster went about its mission is specifically due to those leading the business. Starting from a foundation of Christian faith, these five leaders of ServiceMaster were rooted in an understanding of the value and dignity of every person and a commitment to the highest level of integrity. This is also what helped them separate foundational principles from practices that might need to be adapted as circumstances and business climates changed. This rootedness allowed them to hold on to the core, even when times became turbulent.

This book traces the history, challenges, and the developing understanding of what it is to run a company rooted in the value of the individual worker. Each leader built on what the previous leaders had done, adapting the company along the way.

An amazing part of the story is the way these successive leaders added something to the company in just the right order. An ethical foundation for the business, along with an idea for the business, was laid first, even before building a strong financial foundation. Then the business structures were put in place. After the business structures were in place, processes and systems were added to allow the company to operate efficiently and in the right way. With this platform, the company was able to achieve significant growth through the acquisitions of other companies, adding to the three layers of this foundation. Over the period of 1929 to 2000, the company followed this path. At each stage, the various leaders adapted to changes in culture and the economic environment, refining what had gone before while also building upon it.

There was no grand plan for the ServiceMaster leaders to build the company the way they did. Each successive leader connected a deep understanding of what had gone before with their own insights and skill set for achieving further growth. In addition, they found a fascinating way of operating through this growth. Each new leader was empowered to do new things, but he was also challenged to remember what his predecessors had done earlier. They referred to this unique way of working together as "shingles on a roof." Overlapping, covering, encouraging, and challenging occurred as previous leaders stayed engaged in the ongoing work of the new leader. It took significant humility for each of them to build while continuing to listen.

Cumulative Effects of the Different Leaders

In 1929, Marion Wade founded the company. Coming out of the Depression, he simply needed a job and an income for his family. He had only an eighth-grade education, but his practical foundation in ethics caused him to think about business in a way that always directed him to do the right thing. He had been, and continued to be, a front-line worker through much of the early stages of growth, and he carried this experience with him for the rest of his life. He also was an inventor, and his discoveries provided both the ideas and the discovery mind-set that continued as a foundational element of the company. He adopted the goal, "To Honor God in the Marketplace." Rooted in his own Christian faith, it meant to be accountable beyond himself to do things in the right way, to treat people in the right way, and to value every person made in the image of God. He became known for his statement, "If you don't live it, you don't believe it," reflecting his goal of connecting words with actions. His story and work are developed in chapter 2.

Despite all of these significant contributions to the company, Wade didn't have strong financial skills and the company could not grow without such skills. Wade recruited a man named Ken Hansen to join the company in 1946 and fill in what he was unable to do. Hansen also came without obvious credentials, since he had studied philosophy and theology and was an interim pastor when he was recruited. But he had a knack for business that allowed him to structure and grow the business, while his faith and his training allowed him to interact on a very deep level with the ethical and philosophical foundation that Marion Wade had built. Ken led the process of incorporating and naming the company, Wade, Wenger and Associates at first.

Ken put the financial systems in place. In 1962, he took the company public after he had been named CEO and Marion had changed his position to chairman. The company grew rapidly, and Hansen went back to the University of Chicago to get an MBA so he could acquire some new tools for his challenging work. In 1957, the company was at about $1 million in revenue when Ken took the lead, and it grew to $70 million by the time he stepped back from the CEO role in 1973. Ken had a bias for action and frequently said, "Anything worth doing is worth doing poorly, to get started." Practically oriented, he didn't want to spend too much time studying, but rather learn quickly when things didn't work. In our modern tech world, this is called "fail fast." His story and work are developed in chapter 3.

Working together in a collaborative fashion, Wade and Hansen recruited Ken Wessner to join the team in the mid-1950s. Wessner quickly demonstrated a skill for processes. He developed and created a structure around the business of managing the cleaning of hospitals, which grew to become a substantial part of the overall business by 1973 when he became the third CEO. He also created training and educational programs that were supportive of both the person doing the work and aspiring leaders.

But his processes were not at the expense of people. In fact, he deeply owned both the ethical and business foundations of his predecessors, working closely with Wade and Hansen. He expressed several key things that had been done in practice but had never before been clarified. One was his frequent statement about people in the organization: "Training is not so much about what we want people to do, but rather what we want people to be."[7] He also clarified the four objectives of the company that had been lived but not written down before:

- To Honor God in All We Do
- To Help People to Develop
- To Pursue Excellence
- To Grow Profitably

He loved to talk about the inherent tension between these objectives that forced discussion and creativity toward finding good solutions to any issues of the company. Under Wessner's leadership, the company revenues grew to $700 million. Ken Wessner's story and contribution to the company are the subject of chapter 4.

In 1977, Ken Hansen and Ken Wessner together hired Bill Pollard, a lawyer by training and practice, as executive vice president. Bill, like his predecessors, brought a strong Christian faith into the work. He quickly owned the four objectives, speaking about them with Wall Street leaders within a year after joining the company. But since he lacked experience as a front-line worker, he spent his first six weeks at ServiceMaster performing cleaning tasks such as mopping floors.[8] Urged by Ken Wessner to help the company find its next growth curve when Bill became CEO in 1983, he used his legal skills to begin acquiring other service companies. Bill's unique skill set made this path possible, as did the strong foundation built by the earlier leaders. It became his passion and mission to provide a work environment for other service workers, so that they too could see dignity and value in the work they did. The acquisitions also created the imperative to train and develop the people in acquired companies, from front-line workers through leaders, in this new way of operating. By this time, Marion Wade had died, and Bill worked closely with both Ken Hansen and Ken Wessner through his leadership period. He frequently made the statement, "People want to work for a cause, not just a living." By 1993, ServiceMaster was a $3 billion global company. The story of his leadership is developed in chapter 5.

In 1986, the first major acquisition that Pollard made for ServiceMaster was Terminix, where Carlos Cantu was the CEO. Carlos was a thoughtful leader, and he worked closely with Bill through the years. Carlos saw the value of the ServiceMaster way early in the acquisition process, but grew over the years in his understanding and application of these objectives. In 1993, Bill and the board of directors determined that Cantu was ready to step into leadership of the company. In 1994, both Ken Hansen and Ken Wessner died.

Cantu and Pollard now worked together with the goal of continuing acquisitions, assimilating those that had come before, and identifying the next growth curve. By 1999, the company revenues had grown to almost $6 billion, but the assimilation work was still in progress. Cantu was tough, as the previous leaders were, but also compassionate. Mike Isakson recalled a time with Cantu when he had not achieved the financial goals for his part of the business. Cantu put his hands on Mike's shoulders and said, "You should be disappointed, but not discouraged."[9] Unfortunately, in the spring of 1998 Cantu was diagnosed with a serious illness and he did not respond to treatment. In late 1999, he had to step down from his position. His story is the subject of chapter 6.

For the next period (slightly more than one year), Bill Pollard returned to the CEO leadership position. He outlined two possible future directions for the company, worked on assimilation of acquisitions, made additional acquisitions, and worked with the board in hiring the next CEO. This transition is the subject of chapter 7.

Adapting to Reality

Two practices from this part of the story bear careful attention. Both deal with the reality of operating a company in this way, where day-to-day practice may not always align with the plan. First, the leaders of the company were not perfect. They all talked clearly about their own mistakes and shortcomings. Ken Hansen said it clearly in his little book *Reality*:

> I have had failures. Some have been failures of judgment. Some of motives. The first type of failure should be faced openly (not covered up) and then put in one's memory bank for future reference, but not dwelt upon. The second requires forgiveness in order to be healed. I'm grateful for forgiveness; forgiveness by God, by family, and by friends. Failure and risk-taking seem to be woven together in this life, in which we have limited knowledge and mixed motives in doing what we know ought to be done.[10]

Bill Pollard added to this in his own writing:

> People are not perfect. Some will abuse privilege, steal, lie, or "innovate" only in areas where they personally benefit at the expense of others. That is the risk of empowerment, but one worth taking. The best way to minimize the imperfections and guide the soul of your firm toward responsible behavior is to never ignore or cover up instances of abuse. People must be encouraged to recognize their failures, correct them, learn from them, and then move on. In the process, the leader must remember not to shoot the messenger who brings bad news.[11]

It has always been true that even great people are prone to mistakes, but that doesn't need to define a person in the real world. As David McCullough said when speaking of Thomas Jefferson, "He was an exceedingly gifted and very great man, but like others . . . he could also be inconsistent, contradictory, *human*."[12] The test of ServiceMaster was making its mission work in the reality of truly human people.

The second practice is managing the inevitable tension between the four objectives. All of the early leaders—from Marion Wade through Carlos Cantu—spent time talking about this tension. Ken Hansen created a vivid picture of this when he likened managing these multiple objectives to pulling an elastic exercise strip to the point of tension. "It's hard to do," he said, "but you had better hold on to both ends. If you don't, the tension will be released, and you will get hit on the head!"[13] There will be times when financial needs suggest that the ideals of valuing the worker need to be put aside. There is always a time where pressure for excellence might be challenged by financial realities. The high standard of honoring God in all they did created tension in the nitty-gritty reality of the business. But because there was tension, there was the need to hold on to both, ignoring the easy path of picking one over the other.

In 1989, a model of a balance beam (like a teeter-totter or seesaw) was created, centered on a triangular fulcrum labeled, "To Honor God in All We Do." Three blocks were on top representing the other three objectives. Holding the beam in balance meant it was not possible to simply focus only on the finances, the people, or excellence. They all had to work together. This training tool was another way to acknowledge the reality of the tension and relationship between these objectives. These recognitions are fundamental to learning from this story. What they did was not easy, and it was carried out with real, imperfect people in a real pressured world of business.

Post-2000

As the company entered the new millennium, it faced the challenge of finding a new leader with the sense of passion and mission for the "soul of the firm." Bill Pollard's book of the same title, *The Soul of the Firm*, came out in 1996 and described how the ServiceMaster objectives had shaped the way people did things in the company. This was the uniqueness of the company. In fact, Bill Pollard later compiled a set of talks he had given to the board over the years, helping those who hadn't worked in the company to understand the vital role of this soul, or culture, particularly around the four objectives.

Not everyone on the board bought into this. Greg Leith told of the time he was in a meeting with Bill and one of the other board members in the late 1990s, and he watched a debate between the two of them. Bill was arguing that companies can have a soul—not in the same sense as a person, but in the way in which the company operated. It was the power of a strong culture. The other board member thought this was not the case and that companies did not have a soul. In the selection of the new leader, how strongly was the soul weighted and how readily is that soul assessed in a new candidate?[14]

After significant deliberation and search, the company made the decision to hire the next CEO from outside. The board saw the opportunity to bring in some new ways of thinking. While previous leaders had come from outside, none had stepped into the top position without a period of time working under the incumbent CEO, absorbing and understanding the unique culture. Perhaps Bill's concern over the sense of soul was not as important as other factors, as seen through the lens of the rest of the board. New leadership led to a significant turning point in the company.

What happened after 2000 and where is the company today? At the time of this selection process, the business world was being rocked by the "dot com" impact, the events of 9/11, and a recession. In 2001, Jonathan Ward was hired and there have been five subsequent CEOs since he left in 2006. ServiceMaster continued, going private for a time, and then public again in 2013.

This period after 2000 can be viewed in two ways. One is to see it as a difficult part of the story where the company continued but lost its uniqueness. Another way to see this, however, is as a way of understanding the importance of the practices in the early part of the story. When something is changed, what happens?

While the four objectives were still stated, the focus shifted toward profit. The balance beam was forgotten. Pieces of the company were sold. Changes were made in the service offerings; and in 2007, the company was sold to a private equity firm for a time. In 2013, ServiceMaster again became a publicly traded company and was recognized in 2015 as one of the top service companies by *Fortune* (though not number one). But in its current form, it is now a very different company, with a different set of objectives. The sharp focus on the front-line worker is no longer a key part of company objectives or writings. Understanding this part of the story is important, because it shows what happens with a company when one "soft" area is modified. That is the subject of chapter 8.

Postscript

In spite of the changes in the company starting in 2001, traces of the old ServiceMaster, with the focus on the employee, are still there. They are a part of many of the franchises within the company, where these "small business leaders" carry on the work often as second- or third-generation leaders. Today on the home page for many of the franchise leaders in ServiceMaster Clean, the original objectives are clearly displayed. But that is not the only way the early days of ServiceMaster live on. ServiceMaster's influence extends far beyond the walls of the company today. Business leaders who had a role in ServiceMaster in the past are now part of other organizations or lead their own companies. Many of these business leaders carry on their understanding of what they learned from their time with ServiceMaster, including holding on to the four objectives. Honoring and supporting front-line workers is deemed the right thing to do by these leaders, and it creates good business. Current stories from leaders still running ServiceMaster franchises, and from people who are working in other organizations after their lives were shaped while at ServiceMaster, are in chapter 9.

What Can Others Learn from ServiceMaster

Any business, even any organization, can learn from the history of ServiceMaster. An educational institution, a government organization, a church, and many other organizations set goals, manage people, manage finance, and accomplish results. *The ServiceMaster Story* offers insight to both the leadership and the workers in these organizations.

Business cannot be reduced to a single profit motive. Some argue that the profit motive drives a company to care for its employees, because when employees are motivated, the company makes more money. This fails for at least two reasons.[15] First, employees know when they are being manipulated, and the response is not a sense of purpose and mission but of betrayal. Second, it can be difficult in challenging times to maintain the focus on the employee. It takes courage to hold on to principles when the world seems to be falling apart.

When employees are truly empowered and have this sense of purpose, it is amazing what can happen. Pollard again said this well, "When there is alignment between the cause of the firm and the cause of its people, move over—because there will be extraordinary performance."[16] Barry Schwartz showed, from a psychological point of view, why work with a purpose changes everything for the worker.[17]

None of this is to say that profit is unimportant. Again, Bill Pollard expressed in his writings what had developed over the long history of the company.

> Profit is a means in God's world to be used and invested, not an end to be worshipped. It is an essential source of capital. It is a requirement for survival of the individual, the family unit, and any organization in society, whether it be a for-profit or not-for-profit organization. No organization can survive with continuing deficit.[18]

Or as Don Flow, owner of Flow Automotive, put it,

> We have to have a profit . . . but profit is not the goal. I don't know a healthy person who gets up in the morning and looks in the mirror and says I live for my blood. But I don't know a person alive who doesn't have blood. Blood is like profit—necessary to live, but not the reason for living.[19]

In some privately held companies, we can see practices similar to what ServiceMaster did, worked out over a shorter period of time. The stories of Flow Automotive[20] and Broetje Orchards[21] are two such examples. Related practices have been worked out in publicly traded companies for a while, as illustrated by AES[22] and Herman Miller.[23] And there is some similarity between ServiceMaster and Costco.[24]

The distinctions at ServiceMaster as a publicly traded company are: the long period of time in which this way of operating was tested, challenged, and dealt with change; the number of successive leaders who maintained this focus; the type of labor at the service level that was carried out; and the deep roots in Christian faith that kept the anchors in place. In his book *Evangelical Christian Executives*, Lewis D. Solomon observed that, after

1999, "the firm found it hard to live up to its saintly standards."[25] It is hard. That is why the commitment to a way of doing business must be deeply rooted over generations of leadership. This is the key factor that keeps a company from being buffeted by the challenges of the market.

What Christians in Business Can Learn

The ServiceMaster story provides a case study of how faith and work can be connected in our world of business. Although the goal of honoring God in the workplace has been a growing discussion over the past few decades, ServiceMaster serves as a reminder that this work was being done long before many modern proponents of the movement were born.

This story also shows that connecting work and faith is possible for all kinds of work. In a recent article in *Christianity Today*, Jeff Haanen quoted a pastor of a working-class church as saying, "For us, work isn't about thriving, it's about surviving."[26] The story of ServiceMaster helps us see that an understanding of purpose can bring meaning in daily work to all those who labor. This indeed is what it means to thrive.

Haanen went on to say that the blue-collar worker has been forgotten by the work and faith movement. While it is true that many leaders of the work and faith movement today focus on business leaders, the *Service-Master Story* provides an important statement that Christian faith can be, and has been, deeply connected with the work of labor.

Marion Wade, the founder of the company, observed this truth a long time ago. In his book he quoted a poem, introducing it with the statement,

> I don't know who the author is but he certainly knew what he was talking about when he wrote:[27]
>
> Every mason in the quarry, every builder on the shore,
> Every chopper in the palm-grove, every raftsman at the oar,
> Hewing wood and drawing water, splitting stones and cleaving sod,
> All the dusty ranks of labor in the regiments of God
> March together toward His triumph, do the task His hands prepare:
> Honest toil is holy service; Faithful work is praise and prayer.[28]

The ServiceMaster story also shows us that a business is about carrying out work in a meaningful, effective way. Workers are important, integrity is important, excellence is important, and profit is important. Sometimes Christians see their businesses as a platform for other agendas, whether influencing culture or proclaiming their faith, ignoring how the work they do is of value to society. The products and services themselves bring value to the societies where the business operates. Good business done to the glory of God has always been a part of God's plan. God's instruction to the people of Jeremiah's time is a reminder of this: "Also, seek the peace and prosperity of the city to which I have carried you into exile. Pray to the LORD for it, because if it prospers, you too will prosper" (Jeremiah 29:7).

It is also interesting to see what ServiceMaster did not do. There is very little focus on political lobbying, very little about imposing Christian faith on workers. No doubt some of this happened, but it was not the focus and was generally corrected. Dave Baseler told this story:

> When I joined ServiceMaster, Bill said to me on my first day at work, "Dave, I know you will have opportunities to share your Christian faith with other workers. If you choose to do that, it's possible that someone might complain about this. If they come to me, my first question will be, 'Is he doing his job?' If the answer is 'yes,' then I have another shot at them. But if the answer is 'no,' then I'm going to come to you and tell you be quiet about your faith until you *are* doing your job." As time went on, I hired a man who was an outspoken Christian, and I told him the same thing. As it turned out, people complained, and said he wasn't doing his job. I told him to be quiet about his faith. Ultimately, I ended up letting him go.[29]

Rather, the Christian faith was the foundation from which leaders at all levels worked to provide value to society rooted in creating opportunity for workers, working with integrity, being accountable beyond themselves, seeking excellence, and growing profitably.

Bill Pollard often says, "There are no Christian companies." That is true. But there are companies that seek to operate from a foundation of Christian faith for the good of all. ServiceMaster was a special example of this.

2

The Marion Wade Years

In 1944, Marion Wade was moth-proofing a closet in Wheaton, Illinois, when the chemicals he was using exploded in his face. "All I could think of at first was that I was lucky to be alive," he wrote later, "lucky even though the doctors believed I would probably lose my vision."[1] He was the owner of a small business, conducting his own research, supporting sales, and doing some of the actual work himself. In this case, he had been using a process created and tested in a laboratory at Northwestern University. Heating the chemicals was part of his process, which is what had caused this explosion.[2]

For most of the next year, he was in and out of hospitals. Vernon Anderson, who worked for him, was able to carry on the business. For Wade, however, there was the larger issue of having to think about a life without sight. He figured out that he might be able to carry on the business as a salesman while others, like Vernon, did the actual work. "Resigning myself to the new life I would have to learn to live, I waited in darkness for the day when the doctors would tell me I could get going again."[3]

As a person always on the go, this forced sabbatical gave him time to think. Reflecting on his life and on his status as a businessperson, he realized he was not satisfied. As a Christian, he wondered about the importance of his business, recognizing that sometimes "the Lord lets accidents happen for reasons of His own." He thought about the apostle Paul, who had an accident of his own when he was knocked off a horse, an accident that had transformed Paul's life. "I was already a Christian," Wade said, "and now I figured that if my accident was God's way of getting through to me on some point, he would eventually let me know."[4]

The doctors finally concluded that Wade would not be blind after all, but he would still have a long recovery. During this time, he gained a vision for what God wanted him to do. No, he didn't leave his business to become a missionary. Rather, he decided to look at his business another way. "I was trying to personally honor God, but I never tried this with my company. I had been trained in the school of competition that attests that religion and business can't mix."[5] He asked God to give him insight on this new direction. After months of inactivity, bandages, and quiet time, eventually he was able to return to work—but it took almost a year. This period changed his life and his company.

"When I finished that prayer, I caught myself smiling. I was truly full of joy. I didn't feel relief. On the contrary, I realized I had taken on a great responsibility and I was very much aware of it. But I had purpose now. I had meaning. I had direction."[6] And so Marion Wade began the rebirth of his company, which later became ServiceMaster.

Marion Wade was a most unlikely candidate to lay the foundation for a global company. He had a difficult childhood with an alcoholic father, and he dropped out of school in the eighth grade with a passion to play professional baseball. These challenging times shaped his character and impressed upon him the importance of hard work. On top of this, his mother taught him about integrity. Later, he had an encounter with Jesus Christ that further shaped his life.

By the time of the accident in 1944, he had already been in business for himself for fifteen years, although this small company had not yet been incorporated. Despite this humble beginning, however, Marion's personal and business experience influenced products, services, practices, and values that remained an integral part of the multinational, publicly traded company known as ServiceMaster for the rest of the twentieth century and beyond.

Early Days of Marion Wade

In 1898, Marion Wade was born in Pocahontas, Arkansas, and was the youngest of four sons. His father—a tall, handsome, well-educated man—had been a partner in a dry goods store that failed. Unfortunately, his father seemed to fail along with the store. His drinking problem created tension and conflict in the home where Marion grew up. He described his mother as a small, attractive, austere, and immaculate woman who was quiet and patient. As she was an excellent seamstress, her work provided the support for the family.

Marion recalled being with his mother when she worked her trade into the evening when his father would come home drunk. He watched helplessly while his mother tried to calm his father and put him into bed. "She was never argumentative with him, nor was she with my brothers and me," he said. But when he would go out to play, she would remind him to "remember whose son you are."[7] This admonition would keep him out of fights for fear of making more work for his mother, who might have to repair a torn shirt.

In 1905, the family moved to McAlister, Oklahoma, with the hope of providing a fresh start for Marion's father, but it was more of the same. So, the rest of the family got to work to provide their living. Mom was a dressmaker, and the boys did odd jobs. Marion recalled meeting the 5:30

a.m. train from Oklahoma City, walking through the cars and selling newspapers while the train was at the station.

An incident stood out for him from this early time that forever shaped his view of honesty. Marion noticed that some people left current edition magazines in the station as they boarded the train, so he scooped them up and sold them on the train along with his newspapers. When he told his mother about the extra money he had made selling the magazines, she was not pleased. "Those magazines didn't belong to you, and you have no right to sell them. Don't ever do it again."[8] Even though he realized he could continue selling the magazines behind his mother's back, he so valued her approval that he never did.

By the time he was ten years old, Marion had gained a great deal of street smarts. After his father beat him and threatened to shoot his dog, the young Marion had enough. He made a plan to run away with his friend Wingy, and they sold the dog to get money for a train ticket. Arriving in Fort Smith, Oklahoma, in the late afternoon, Wingy turned to Marion and asked, "What do we do now?" Marion's response was quick and to the point: "Let's find jobs."[9] They split up and started looking. Marion soon found a possible job at Western Union, but it would require a bike. No problem, he thought, and headed out to find a way to buy one. But that all changed when he ran into his brother Maurice, who was working there. In no uncertain terms, Maurice reminded him that their mother would be very worried. He wired her to say that Marion would be home the next day, and then he arranged a place for the boys to sleep and sent them home on the train in the morning.

As he approached home, Marion realized that he still had a problem with his father and wondered what his father would do. When his father saw him approaching, he demanded he come in the house. Marion's first instinct was to run away again. But his mother intervened, invited him in, fixed him something to eat, and provided his protection. Marion made two decisions in that moment. He committed to not do anything else that could cause his mother misery. And since his father's drinking was the root of all the problems, he decided to never drink because of the conflict it could create at home.

Marion's mother soon made the decision to leave his father. She took the family to Oak Park, Illinois, where Marion's Uncle George and Aunt Florence lived with their five children and his grandfather. This provided a stable home where Marion gained some strong adult role models. He learned respect and discipline to go along with his ability to work hard. He learned about the Bible from nightly family Bible readings and church attendance. He also learned about baseball and the Chicago Cubs. Discipline, the Bible, and baseball would provide a major foundation for his life. But in those early days, baseball was the one that won out. He admitted:

I was obsessed by the game. Although I couldn't memorize the Bible verses that had been assigned at last week's Sunday School class, I could rattle off a play-by-play description of any Cubs game anyone cared to mention. Although I never mastered the multiplication tables, I could calculate what each player's hit was doing to his batting average while the ball was still in the air.[10]

That said, he acquired a lot of life lessons from baseball, and he would eventually build his business around what he learned from the sport:

- Play as a dedicated member of the team, which is the only way to be important to the team.
- Take care of a problem when it arises, before it gets out of control.
- Talking about baseball is a good entry to business discussions. (When he sold life insurance, he always started the conversation with baseball.)
- Sacrifice. In baseball, a bunt means giving yourself up for the good of the team.

Although Wade's book, *The Lord Is My Counsel: A Businessman's Personal Experiences with the Bible*, draws lots of business wisdom from Scripture, it has many baseball stories as well.

In 1912, at age fourteen, Marion Wade finished grammar school and got a full-time job. He took a course in business arithmetic at the YMCA, but baseball became his passion and he played at every opportunity. As a fourteen-year-old, he was told he was too small to play baseball with the "muscle-bound" teamsters with whom he worked, and he was left to watch. But one day, they were short a player and allowed him to participate. He hit a home run in his first at bat, and then became a regular until another hard blow was struck. In 1914, Uncle George died and the family could no longer afford the home in Oak Park. They soon moved to a smaller house on the west side of Chicago.

Again, Marion Wade found opportunity in the face of difficulty: there was a group of boys closer to his age in his new neighborhood, and they formed a semi-pro baseball team. This allowed him to play baseball and earn extra money at the same time. His mother was concerned about the money that came from playing baseball, fearing he was gambling. But knowing of his love of baseball, she let him play as long as he kept at his work that helped provide for the family. He also had to attend church on Sunday mornings. He complied, though he was already on his way to the baseball field before the final "amen" was completed.

If anyone had asked Marion Wade at this time what he wanted to do for a living, he would have answered that he wanted to play professional baseball. He played semi-pro with the Chicago Braves, attracted attention from scouts, and was one of two players to be selected for a professional tryout. When he was not selected, he was told he would definitely get the chance the following year. Unfortunately, that opportunity evaporated when the United States entered World War I. After his brother's death in combat, Marion enlisted with the Marines in 1918. He was sent to Parris Island, where he endured combat training, even though the war ended shortly after he joined.

He took a chance on a minor league contract after returning from the service, but the bank responsible for paying the players folded, and the banker committed suicide. He decided to return home, broke. When he arrived home, his fiancée, Lil, was there to meet him, and they were married a few weeks later. Though he tried baseball one more time, his passion had dwindled. He was now responsible for both his wife and his mother, and he needed to earn a living. It was time to get a real job.

Finding Work

He decided to pursue a career in sales because he wanted his income to depend on individual performance rather than "sweating out a raise every other Christmas."[11] It was a way he could turn hard work into economic opportunity. But life would not get any easier for Marion Wade. Hardships can defeat some people, like Marion's father, or can make them stronger. These shaping events for Marion Wade seemed to harden his resolve.

For four years he sold life insurance. While making a reasonable income, he was looking for more out of life when a colleague invited him over to his house. The colleague had a second business, selling aluminum pots and pans by holding demonstration meetings in homes. It was a new product and a wide-open opportunity, so Marion jumped on board. His wife helped him learn how to cook so he could demonstrate the product, and his business started to grow. Unfortunately, so did the complaints about the poor product he was selling.

At the same time, he heard about the opportunity to sell for another company he thought would be better. With little cash reserve, he and his pregnant wife, along with their three-year-old daughter, moved into a basement flat—a "horrible place"—while he tried to get the work with the new company off the ground. "And then tragedy struck that sank me to the lowest point of my life."[12] In March 1926, he had spent the last of his money on food for a luncheon demonstration in a nearby suburb. The weather was horrible, and he made the trip "out of terror and desperation." The demonstration went well, and he got nine appointments for sales calls the next day. When he returned home, he discovered that his wife had been rushed to the hospital. The baby had died, and Lil was in difficult shape. Although he was distraught over their loss, he resolved to go through with his sales calls the next day, needing to prove to Lil that he was not a failure.

The next day, he finished with $450 in his pocket. Returning to the hospital, he shared the success with Lil and then vowed never to get in this position again. Both Lil and his work improved, and he was promoted a year later to a sales manager role with the branch in St. Louis. He jumped at the opportunity to get his small family out of the basement flat and out of Chicago with its painful memories of loss and struggle. He was then promoted to manage the office in Cleveland, where his fortunes continued to improve. "I was not a Christian at the time, and had no idea that tragedies, like blessings, can be a part of God's plan for a man."[13] Although it looked like he was on his career growth plan, God had a different idea for Marion Wade.

A key factor in the success of the kitchen product sales came from the fact that the same product was not available in stores. But the company created a new strategy, where they decided to offer an inferior product at a lower price in the stores. This both undercut the sales because of the lower price and gave the product a bad reputation. After complaining to management, Wade found himself out of a job and on his way back to Chicago. Looking back on that time, Wade was grateful for the turning point that ultimately led him to what he considered his calling. But it didn't seem that way at the time.

It was 1929 and Wade was looking for a new opportunity. He heard about a company that was moth-proofing homes. While he initially knew nothing about moths, he was intrigued enough to learn. His study of moths helped him see that they had nothing to fear from most of the products on the market. "The only way you could kill a moth with a mothball," he said, "was to hit him over the head with one."[14] Moths have no sense of smell. When he was asked why these products are in the stores if they don't work, the only answer he received from the company was, "Because people buy them, and stores sell them."[15]

While this looked like an opportunity, the new company was not hiring. It was, however, selling franchises, but Wade had no money. Never one to give up, he devised a different approach. Instead of purchasing a franchise, he proposed to the company that they finance a car so he could have transportation and that he would work on commission. They took the offer. But after working on this arrangement for a few months, he arrived at the company one day and found it locked. The company had gone out of business and his car was repossessed. The stock market crashed in 1929, and this was a chaotic time.

The Start of the Company

Once again, Marion took this setback as an opportunity. He convinced a friend, also a moth-proofing salesperson, to join him in creating a business. They would provide the service of moth-proofing homes, using the same product the previous company had used. He looked for a car to aid the business, but the cheapest he could find was $90 and he didn't have the money. He and his business partner decided to sell locally, where they could walk. They spread out through the neighborhood going door to door. After knocking on a number of doors, Marion encountered a couple that needed his services. When asked how much it would cost, he responded with a price of $90. That allowed him to buy the car and broaden his sales territory. Starting in 1929, Wade kept a journal with entries every day, showing a key event from that day. A picture of the 1947 journal is shown in the 1971 annual report.[16]

One other important event happened in this time period. Because he was struggling, his mother urged him to go to the Moody Church with her, where he heard a sermon that, he said, "made a Christian out of me."[17] Yet it was more a Sunday event at this point. Only later, after he had the accident, would he learn what it meant for God to be in control of his business. Like so many other Christians, even today, he believed that God cared about his life, but business was somehow separate and certainly up to him.

He became dissatisfied with the product he was using for moth-proofing, because it didn't work very well. Then in 1932, when he was working in a home in Evanston, Illinois, he got into a conversation about moths with the lady of the home. She asked him lots of good questions, and he told her that no research had been done on a truly effective product for killing moths. "If I could get into a laboratory," he told her, "I would certainly do the research myself."[18] She remembered a friend who had a lab at Northwestern University. A couple of phone calls later, he was talking with a professor who headed the biology lab. The professor gave him free rein in the lab and full cooperation. Although it is astounding to picture this would-be baseball player with an eighth-grade education leading a scientific research project at a prominent university, this is what happened.

After several months of experimenting with dozens of different materials, he found a solution. He called the product Fumakill, and for many years it paid the rent for his fledgling business. "The sales he lost developing Fumakill were substantial, but he was sure the time spent in development would be worth it."[19]

Wade learned a powerful lesson on leadership while working in the lab—a side benefit he was not expecting. While the moth was still in the cocoon, it would begin to quiver and then struggle to get free of the cocoon. He soon discovered that if he reached out to help it escape the cocoon, it would never fly. It had to go through that struggle to gain its wings. He began applying this observation to leadership development. As he sought to teach people how to grow and develop, he often had to step back and let them work it out for themselves.[20]

It wasn't long before a new opportunity presented itself. While he was moth-proofing a home, a woman asked him for a recommendation for cleaning rugs. He had been burned by recommending someone in the past, so he had made it his policy not to provide recommendations but to simply suggest looking at the Yellow Pages. This time, however, the question stuck in his head. Like moth-proofing, he knew that the current processes for cleaning rugs didn't work very well. The process of sending carpets out to be cleaned was difficult and time consuming. Something was needed to allow these carpets to be cleaned in place.

Recalling his success with moth-proofing, Wade decided to research this one himself. This time, however, he acknowledged that God had guided him to this conclusion. He studied the magazines from the chemical industry, and he came across a new mordant (an oxide that combines with a dye or stain and thereby fixes it in a material), which was designed to get deep into the fabric during the dying process. The chemical company that had created this product was not interested in creating a better cleaning agent for rugs, but it was happy to let Wade experiment. He then began experimenting with a mixture of the mordant and various detergents, trying to find something that did a good cleaning job on rugs.

His testing process was unusual. While on a later moth-proofing job, another customer asked Marion about rug cleaning. He described the process he had been developing. "I warned her that I still considered it experimental. I was confident that it wouldn't harm her rugs, but I wasn't sure how good a job it would do."[21] It did an excellent job.

He succeeded with a formula that he said "appeared to be exceptionally effective."[22] Because of the success of this new product, rug cleaning became a big part of his early business. In May 1937, he serviced his first on-location customer.[23]

After the Accident

After the accident in 1944, Marion Wade had a new sense of purpose for his business. He continued to work hard and to be curious, not satisfied with existing solutions. He still had a small company, but he now saw business differently. It was not just about making money, or even simply earning a living, but about honoring God in his work. He also reflected differently on his products. Thinking back to the days when he had sold life insurance, he realized that products brought real value to families. So did the high-quality aluminum cookware he sold for a time. And now he was thinking about his moth-proofing and rug cleaning work in the same light. Doing excellent work in these areas brought real value to people. Many Christians in business think about *how* they do their work, but he was thinking about the value of the work itself.

He also began to see the Bible as bringing practical insight to his work: "The whole purpose of reading the Bible and keeping it in mind was to learn how to conduct ourselves in our daily affairs."[24] Reading the Bible this way was revolutionary for that era. For many Christians, the Bible was either about the afterlife or the way to live in the present life, but Wade held on to both. Thus his reading of the Bible also changed the way he saw his business.

He looked around and saw other businesses that had been started by Christians, but the Christian values were not embedded deeply. These companies left their biblical foundations when leadership changed, as the commitment became diluted due to growth, or when they encountered difficult times. What could he do to build a company with a long-term commitment to live out the principles of the Bible—not just for his lifetime, but for lifetimes beyond? "I pledged that there and then I was committing myself to Him entirely—myself, my home, my business—day and night."[25] But this did not make him passive. "I don't expect miracles. I don't intend to sit back and expect You to run everything, but I want You to tell me how to run things and to send my way the men I will need to do the job." But he wanted something more. "I wanted to have men working with me who would know what the Lord had done, and was doing, so that as the Lord was receiving me into His glory, I would be able to tell Him that His company was still working for Him."[26]

Other things were changing as well. After World War II, wall-to-wall carpeting became increasingly popular. Previously, people had to pull up their wall-to-wall carpet and send it out to be cleaned. Because it was wool, many times it came back shrunk and couldn't be properly reinstalled. Wade's early work in creating a new cleaning process worked perfectly for this new wall-to-wall carpeting. Apparently, Wade was the first person to clean carpet on the floor so it didn't have to be sent out and then reinstalled. The basic process he invented for cleaning carpet on the floor is still the one used today.

When the war ended, there was a growing need for new homes for returning troops and their families. With this need, new opportunities emerged that Wade went after with a newfound energy.

Developing the Business

Wade was careful, however, to take full advantage of these new opportunities. He soon realized that if his business didn't grow, someone else would step into the opportunity. This meant he needed to hire more people to expand his business around this new product.

The timing was perfect, since a number of his former Bible school classmates were coming home from the war. By hiring a dozen of them, he accomplished two things: he was able to grow the staff and hence the business, and he rooted this growth in helping his people gain a deep understanding of what the Bible had to say about doing business to the glory of God. When asked why he was hiring so many people, he said he couldn't do much with his work on the new cleaning solution because there was so much moth-proofing work to do. "He hoped that the new men would be able to lighten his load so he could complete the development of the cleaning solution and expand the business further, giving the new employees opportunity to grow with the company."27

It wasn't, however, just this extra help that was important. In studying the Bible, Wade came to believe that when people worked for the Lord it raised their effort. As the apostle Paul wrote in Colossians 3:23, "Whatever you do, work at it with all your heart as working for the Lord. It is the Lord Christ you are serving." In addition to being good for the worker, this extra effort was also good for his business.

In May 1945, Wade moved his business from his home to an office at the corner of Belmont and Austin in Chicago. Marion and his staff gathered for prayer each morning around the potbelly stove in the back of the shop. With an increase in the number of customers and an increase in staff, Wade now needed help in leadership for his developing business. One person he had his eye on was Ken Hansen.

To understand this connection, we have to back up a few years. In the winter of 1942–43, a blizzard hit Chicago and the Wades decided against traveling to their regular church on Sunday. On a particularly stormy day, they walked to Bethel Community Church, a local church they had seen in the neighborhood but knew little about.28 Ken Hansen, a recent Wheaton College graduate, was preaching. Because of the bad weather, only a few were in attendance, but Ken preached for an hour, "and he seemed to be telling us everything he knew."29 The ensuing conversation tells us a great deal about both of these men.

After introducing himself, Marion told Ken, "That was quite a sermon. It made me think of how this hog raiser found a way to keep himself from going broke. When he called the hogs to feed them and only a few showed up, he didn't give them everything he had." "When Ken saw I was joking," Marion later said, "he got the point and grinned."30 The Wades decided to continue to go to that church.

While Hansen was only an interim preacher, Wade noticed that he threw himself into the position. Every time someone moved to the neighborhood, Ken Hansen was there to meet the truck and introduce himself.

He recruited the Wades to help build the Sunday school program, and the two men got to know each other. When Hansen said he knew he was meant to work for God but wasn't sure it was as a pastor in Chicago, Wade invited him to consider a career in business. But Hansen was not ready for that move—not yet. Hansen finished his assignment at the church and went away to work for the Christian Service Brigade, and the two did not see each other for two years.

In 1946, another type of business opportunity emerged. When fire damaged a downtown hotel, Wade put in a bid to do the cleaning and restoration. Winning the contract to do this work created a third type of business for his developing company: bug killing, rug cleaning, and now disaster recovery. While this was not a formal product line until much later, it set out a range of work that would become the foundation of the company. That year, the company did about $45,000 in business.[31]

It was about this time that the company began to formalize its commitment to serving God through business, with a stated objective: "To Honor God in the Marketplace." This statement represented the company for a number of years.

As a result of the disaster recovery work, Marion Wade worked closely with Bob Wenger, a mediator called in by the insurance company to assess what could be salvaged from the ruins of the hotel. Through their work together, they became friends. When Wenger let Wade know he was planning to leave that insurance company, Wade started to explore whether Wenger would also have an interest in joining his growing company.

Although there was no question about Wenger's competence, there was a question about his faith commitment. Wade said:

> I explained how I had come to dedicate the company to the Lord. I defined my religious convictions, assured him that I had no trouble mixing religion and business, and that if he did, I had the wrong man. Bob, a Catholic, assured me that he had absolutely the same convictions that I had.[32]

In those early days, Wenger played a vital role in the company in two quite different ways. First, he had a great set of contacts—today we would call him a networker. Kuno Laren, another long-time ServiceMaster employee who would later be involved both in taking the company public and as a board member, recalled,

> Bob was so well connected. If there was a fire in a hotel in Chicago, he knew exactly who to call so that the company could participate in the cleanup. We got the name and made the contact before the last fire truck left the site. We got a lot of new business through his contacts.[33]

But Wenger was also a man of "deep pockets" for the struggling company in those early days. When things got tight for payroll, Wade would ask

Wenger for help. "They did these deals on a handshake," Laren said, "without paperwork."[34]

Meanwhile, Hansen's tenure at the Christian Service Brigade was coming to a conclusion, and he called Wade for a meeting. Marion filled Ken in on his accident and time in the hospital, the return to work, and the growth of the company. Then Marion offered Ken a job to help him lead the growth of the business. Hansen prayed about the opportunity. He said that it sounded "challenging" and seemed like he would enjoy working with Wade. Hansen later said that Marion had asked him, "Do you want to keep working with small groups of people and affect a few hundred people, or do you want to join me and potentially affect millions?"[35]

Wade saw potential in Hansen, based on his work as an interim pastor and their friendship. It soon became evident that Ken had a great deal of talent for the work, although his initial job description from Marion was a little rough around the edges: "You start to learn the business by going out on production jobs. Then you can move into sales. This experience will equip you for real leadership. After that, you can step in where you are needed most."[36]

Hansen advanced rapidly, demonstrating a real gift in finance, an area that was not Wade's strength. Wade showed both his character and his informal approach to finances with this next job description for Hansen: "Pay our bills promptly. Give the men the best wages possible. Pay them first. If there's anything left over, you get paid, and if there's anything left over after that, I'll get paid. And do what you can to keep the sheriff away."[37] An informal business environment, however, would soon give way to Hansen's more structured way of doing business, finance, sales, and organization—but the principles remained.

Growing the Business

On January 1, 1947, Ken Hansen (working with Wenger and Wade) wrote the incorporation papers for the company, officially named for the first time as Wade, Wenger and Associates. Each of the employees who had been with Wade for a period of time received stock in the company. It was Wade's way of saying that they were part of a team and that every member, while having different gifts, was vital to the team. At this point, the company had ten employees and an annual revenue of about $125,000. By 1948, revenue had grown to $200,000.[38] That was the year they opened their first branch office in Milwaukee, Wisconsin.

Because of the growth, the company moved its office to 6472 W. North Avenue in Chicago in 1949. They moved again in 1951 to an abandoned brewery, hoping to have enough space to grow and develop the business for the next ten years.

In 1952, the company established its first franchise,[39] which was sold to Rhea Young in Seattle.[40] The company provided training, chemicals, and tools for a franchise fee. They then collected a portion of the revenue. Franchising became a foundational element for the company because it allowed those with entrepreneurial capabilities to develop and grow their own businesses. In 1953, the company attracted an $80,000 investment from a group in Detroit, and they began licensing their cleaning systems.

Also in 1953, while Marion was on vacation on Prince Edward Island in New Brunswick, he met a twenty-one-year-old man named Thane McNeal. Thane had just lost his father, had family responsibilities, and was "struggling for survival." Wade offered him the opportunity to join the company, saying, "You supply the man, I will supply the future." Wade asked McNeal to take part in a six-month training program in Chicago, and he sent him a one-way train ticket to Chicago. A few years later, when the company was more successful, McNeal asked for a meeting with Wade and raised the question of the one-way ticket. McNeal said, "Wade started to cry, and then he laughed and said, 'I could only afford a one-way.'"[41]

Though the company was scrambling for resources at that time, Wade still had a clear dream about the company. McNeal recalled Wade saying, "I have a dream that someday I will be able to get up in the morning and drive a while to have breakfast with company people. Then drive further and have lunch with others. And that this process will go on for days and weeks." This was far from the case in these early days, but "before Mr. Wade passed away, this dream became a reality."[42]

In 1954, Ken Wessner was hired and went on to enjoy a long career with ServiceMaster, ultimately becoming their third CEO and chairman. We will hear a great deal more about him. Wessner recalled that when he was hired the company had three goals:

1. To Honor God in the Marketplace
2. To Provide a Good Living for Many People
3. To Help People to Grow[43]

Over the next ten years, the company grew significantly from this humble beginning to achieve revenues in the millions. Wenger had decided to leave the company and take an opportunity on the East Coast, though he continued on the board for a time. While Marion Wade had a strong hand of leadership in this period, more and more of the responsibility came to Ken Hansen. The concept of "shingles on a roof," overlapping leadership using the best of the skills of each person, was begun during this time and continued the rest of the century. It took strong trust and respect to make this work, with each person willing to acknowledge the strengths of the other. Marion and Ken modeled this brilliantly. Ken brought the business and financial insight to the company, and Marion continued to provide the foundation of his passion for people and for the work. They often worked together when hiring new employees for the growing company.

It was critical to Wade to live out what he believed, matching what he believed with what he did. He often said, "If you don't live it, you don't believe it."[44] A banner with this statement continues to be displayed in offices today with Marion Wade's name.

In 1954, Marion Wade began to feel ill, and his doctor recommended a complete physical exam. The result was not promising. The doctor said he had hardening of the arteries, and he "should not make long-range plans."[45] Because of his strong faith, Wade was not afraid of death. But he wanted to do what he could to take care of himself, and that meant reducing anxiety. No doubt this began the planning process for Ken Hansen to take over the company three years later. Wade also wanted to put the company in position for long-term success, and that meant taking care of himself by going on a strict diet and reducing his stress levels. To do the latter, Wade decided to play more golf. While his doctor opposed this decision initially, Marion convinced his doctor that golf was relaxation, not stress, and he lived that out.

Wade was very bullish for the future of the company. In a 1956 interview in *Fortune* magazine, he said, "I have my first line of executives at about forty years of age, another line about thirty-five, and another in their late twenties. As each group takes over, I think they will continue to follow the path the Lord has charted for us." The article went on, "That path, Wade's economic adviser tells him, will lead to $50 million gross revenue in 1961." Although that number was not achieved until 1971, it was indeed achieved.[46] Then Wade began the preparation for handing off the company.

> I had men capable of running the company better than I could run it myself. I had trained them, of course, but they had their own God-given talents which they were using excellently. . . . Though I habitually referred to the company as "my company," this was more out of affection than possession, for the company was partially owned by practically everybody who worked for it, and ultimately it was owned by the Lord.[47]

In 1957, Wade handed over the day-to-day leadership of the company to Ken Hansen, and he took on the role of chairman of the board. This didn't mean he disappeared from the scene, however, as we see the "shingles on a roof" continuing under Hansen's reign and beyond. Foremost among the duties for the new chairman was speaking before customer and employee groups for the purpose of gaining and strengthening commitment. Wade was by far the company's most effective spokesman. As Hansen once put it, "Marion was a magician on the platform."[48] In spite of this speaking ability, Wade was reluctant to close deals and so that fell to Hansen. The two also worked together on strategy and key hires.

Foundational Elements for ServiceMaster

During this period of leadership, Marion Wade put in place key directions that profoundly influenced what ServiceMaster would become. In reflecting on these, it is important to note the time period. Although we hear very little about women in leadership from Marion Wade, for example, we need to remember the times.[49] And he was learning on the job. His humble statement was: "Don't expect that you'll become a business genius and every decision will bring in a fortune for the company!"[50]

It is important, however, to observe the big-picture goal of some of his initiatives and then watch the way later leaders adapted the practices while preserving the larger goals. The most obvious foundational element is seen in his collection of products and services. Bug killing, on-site cleaning, franchises, and disaster recovery were all a part of the story to this point. All of these areas, and some complementary services, were ultimately a part of the growing ServiceMaster portfolio, though pest control and disaster recovery were forgotten for a time and reintroduced later.

Other successful areas were also rooted in the foundation Marion Wade laid. These include his commitment to the following principles:

- To Honor God
- To Value and Develop People
- To Engage Families
- To Pursue Excellence
- To Learn from Mistakes
- To Deal Fairly with Competitors
- To Stand for Values
- To Go beyond Profit in Defining Long-Term Success

All of these were an integral part of Wade's own personal life and experiences. Although this list was not formalized by him, each commitment was lived out in a unique way and built into the foundation of his company.

To Honor God

Wade believed that his company belonged to God and should therefore be built to last beyond his lifetime. To make this a reality, Wade sought to incorporate his faith into all aspects of his work. We will see this as a vital part of every practice he put in place.

He was also committed to hire and retain the people he believed would best carry on this commitment, understanding that wise hiring was critical.

> It is only when a man has the high purpose of living for the Lord that he remains constant as an individual who is constantly growing. As Service-Master continued to grow, I was always on the lookout for young fellows like that.[51]

> When I am interviewing a man who is seeking a position with our company, it is my policy to question him about his personal habits, including the use of alcohol and tobacco. I wouldn't risk having a man working for me who had so completely lost his freedom of choice that he couldn't say no to a personal habit.[52]

After people were hired, Wade found it equally important to ensure that they continued their focus. He told of one person of another faith who expressed how he felt that Wade's mixing his religious beliefs with business was offensive. When Wade met with the person, he told him he was sorry he felt that way, but he then reminded him that the company that hired him had not changed, so perhaps it was the employee who had changed. He went on to say,

> If you find my talks offensive, I won't mind if you leave the room, but if you find the company's policies offensive maybe you ought to leave the Firm. I know you're doing a good job, so I hope you'll stay. I know you've got your convictions, but remember that I have mine. As long as we both live up to them, we can work together.[53]

The employee stayed, and they continued to work together. This was Marion Wade's attempt to do what Jim Collins wrote about much later in his book *Good to Great*:

> Most people assume that great bus drivers (read: business leaders) immediately start the journey by announcing to the people on the bus where they're going—by setting a new direction or by articulating a fresh corporate vision.

> In fact, leaders of companies that go from good to great start not with "where" but with "who." They start by getting the right people on the bus, the wrong people off the bus, and the right people in the right seats. And they stick with that discipline—first the people, then the direction—no matter how dire the circumstances.

Modern labor laws would not allow the particular approach to hiring that Wade took, but his bigger goal was clear. How could he get the right people on the bus to move toward his mission? Later leaders adapted their hiring practices, but continued to talk about honoring God.

To Value and Develop People

Wade learned to empower employees by giving them more responsibility and authority in their work.

> In my opinion, the essential point in the delegation of authority is that though it presents the chance to fail, it also gives a man a chance to exercise his ingenuity and judgment so that he does not fail. Without this risk, there can be no growth. It is my experience that people learn to manage by managing.[54]

Often, he would return to the story of his work with moths and the laboratory discovery to remind others that learning and growth take place through struggle. One must be careful not to help someone too much, and failure can be the means of growth.

In the context of service work, however, there is an added challenge in valuing and developing people. This particular area of work may appear to lack the "dignity" often associated with "professional" work. This is why Wade began the discussion of this topic in the early days of the company. We will see that later leaders developed and refined this message.

One day, a man Marion knew from his cookware days came to see him, and he offered Wade a job as director of sales training with his company. At the time, Marion was on his hands and knees cleaning.

> I thanked him and said "no," explaining I had gone into business for myself. He said, "Marion, why are you groveling around in all that dirt when you could be making many times more than whatever you're earning now and have a job with some dignity besides?" I knew he meant well, so I let it pass.[55]

This experience, however, laid the groundwork for executives engaging in the cleaning work of the company to understand both the work and the response workers often receive when doing manual labor.

As the company began to grow, Wade reflected on a person who walked away from the job because his wife didn't believe the work was dignified enough for him. "A job has only as much dignity as the man gives it, and the best way to dignify a job is to dedicate your efforts to the glory of the Lord."[56] The hard work he had done since he was quite young was something he truly believed in. He exemplified what Barry Rowan, currently EVP and CFO at Gogo, said much later: "We don't derive meaning from our work; rather, we bring meaning to our work."[57]

To Engage Families

From the early days, ServiceMaster engaged whole families in their work, particularly with the franchise owners. This was reflected in Wade's comments,

A man in business for himself can't always choose his own working hours, and if his wife is the type to whom having dinner on time every night is a matter of life or death, there is going to be trouble. A good wife tries to make herself part of her husband's business. Maybe she can cover the phones or keep the books till he can afford to hire for these positions.[58]

He went on to describe how executives seeking to hire people would often go to their homes. Wade told of having dinner with families when he was discussing a job, even reading bedtime stories to the children and helping wash dishes after dinner.

In twenty-first-century Western culture, these practices seem quaint at best, laden with gender stereotypes.[59] We must deal with the mark of past stereotypes that persist in the business world. It is difficult to realize how normative such practices were at the time.[60]

Yet if we can look past the detail of these practices, we see an important foundational goal of ServiceMaster that came from this time. From its early days, ServiceMaster was not thinking about 9–5 jobs, but work that was a part of a whole integrated life, engaging the family. Many of today's ServiceMaster franchise owners are second- and even third-generation owners, with husband and wife engaged together, using their skill sets rather than stereotype roles, and even the children participating. They are truly family businesses.[61] Many of the events of the company engaged the whole family. For many years, pictures of the CEOs in the boardroom included the wives of the leaders.

To Pursue Excellence

Regarding excellence, we have already seen that Marion Wade was not satisfied with the moth-proofing solutions of his day and so he invented new processes. He was not satisfied with the carpet-cleaning agents of his day and so he invented new treatments. The research foundation he had laid in the company continued to provide improvements for the rest of the century.

In addition to finding new solutions, leaders had a passion to deliver value to customers. They wanted to listen to their customer, and then hold themselves accountable to produce results. This was disciplined work that characterized all of the leaders, and spread throughout the organization. Their commitment to the highest level of integrity was part of this passion for excellence. Later, when the company formalized its objectives, "To Pursue Excellence" was one of them.

To Learn from Mistakes

Wade readily admitted his own shortcomings, and vowed to learn from them rather than pretend he was perfect. "We learn from our mistakes and we grow by them. Without this risk, there can be no growth."[62] This failure applied to hiring decisions as well. "To be sure, we have made a couple of mistakes, and with such disastrous consequences that I now consider it my prerogative and my duty to learn as much as I can about a man before sending him out to represent a company that is dedicated to the Lord."[63]

To Deal Fairly with Competitors

Wade argued,

> There is no room for contention in the world of business competition. The businessman who spends his time worrying about the fellow down the street is merely taking that much time away from his own company, time that could be invested in improving his own products and services to the point where the competition couldn't compete. The Bible has a prescribed obligation to "Let nothing be done through strife."[64]

The real spirit of competition, then, should be in fulfilling one's own potential, not in thwarting somebody else's. "We should compete with ourselves, never be satisfied."[65] Cal Flaig, Franchise Sales and Support for ServiceMaster, recalled hearing Wade say, "The greatest competitor you have is yourself."[66]

To Stand for Values

Responding rightly to others became a hallmark of Wade's work. He illustrated what this meant to him by the following example of dealing with a supplier. The supplier had made a mistake in estimating a project and stood to lose a large sum of money. When Wade and his team learned of this, they renegotiated the contract and the supplier was able to salvage some profit from the work. The supplier said that no one before had ever treated him or his company that way. When he asked why they were such "nice people," Wade explained that, while they did try to be nice, it went deeper than that. He then shared the "Golden Rule" and the foundations of his faith with the supplier's representative.

Sometimes Wade appeared a bit naive. Integrity was deeply a part of who he was and he assumed others were just as ethical.

> I was ignorant of the extent to which some salesmen would go to close a deal. Customer-stealing, commission-cutting, minimizing the importance of the small print—all of these were tricks of the trade I learned after becoming the victim of them several times.[67]

He returned to his favorite sport for his solution:

> If I managed to survive, it was mostly because baseball had made me
> fast on my feet and I enjoyed the competition more than I despised the
> double-dealing. I was willing to work longer and harder than the next
> guy.[68]

His attitude helped as well. He quickly learned that a business needed a
long-term plan. It didn't work to create short-term gains that sacrificed
the long term.

> The executive who operates his business only on a short-range basis, who
> is concerned only with current success, is going to pass from one crisis to
> the next, until his head is reeling.[69]

Yet a modern businessperson might smile in thinking about one particular way he resolved the dilemma of a cheating business partner. To accelerate the growth of their cleaning business, Marion had the idea to work
with the rug department of the local department store. When a salesman
from Wade's company identified a need for cleaning services, the customer
would call the department store to handle the order and Wade would send
out the cleaners. As an incentive, the department store received a percent
of the sale. Unfortunately, it was not long before the department store discovered the potential of this business and opened its own cleaning department. Wade eventually discovered this when a customer complained about
the poor work the customer thought had been done by Wade's company.
His response is telling.

> Our first reaction was the normal one—we hit the ceiling. Not only was the
> store violating our agreement, but they were actually doing the cleaning
> of many jobs our own salesmen had sold. It was a bad situation. But we
> realized we would need to resolve this in a Christian manner, and Paul
> had written, "Recompense to no man evil for evil."[70]

His solution to the problem is equally surprising.

> We got in touch with the store management and told them we wouldn't
> be able to do business with them anymore. But rather than leave them in
> a jam with a backlog of new orders coming in every day as a result of a
> customer canvass we had made, we said we'd go along with them for six
> months, which was the time we thought they would need to expand their
> own rug-cleaning department to the point where they could handle the
> whole thing themselves. And that is the way we settled it. He extended his
> concern to others to include someone who had just taken advantage of him.
> Few would go this far, but it characterized Marion Wade.

Dick Armstrong, who had a long career at ServiceMaster (from the late 1960s to 1998), recalled Marion's strong sense of trust. More than once, he said, Marion would tell this story to illustrate his attitude.

> A professional golfer who had just won a tournament was walking back to the clubhouse when a woman came up to him. She looked pretty disheveled. She said, "Oh, congratulations. Do you know about my son?" Then she told him a story of how her son was in an accident some years ago, and she's been not able to save the money for him to get surgery he needs. And so, on the spot, the golfer writes out a check. When the golfer got back to the locker room, someone came up to him and said, "I saw you talking to Mabel. You didn't fall for her story, did you? She doesn't even have a son." The golfer wiped his hand across his brow and said, "Oh, I'm so glad she doesn't have an injured sick son."

And then Marion would say,

> If you're going to be the kind of guy that I believe God wants you to be, caring for others, sometimes you're going to be taken. Keep doing the right thing. Don't let that stop you.[71]

Another story of Wade's straightforward approach to ethics is seen in an encounter with a department store rug buyer. When Wade asked for help in setting up a meeting with the store president, the buyer asked for a kickback. Wade responded,

> "Well OK, if you think you've got it coming, but let's talk with the president first and see if it's OK with him." He told me to forget it as I knew he would. But I'll never know how such a man can live with himself under the eyes of God. . . . Dishonesty is dishonesty, no matter when and where it occurs or on whose part. Honesty is not relative; it is absolute.[72]

This commitment to the highest level of integrity became another vital part of the objectives of the company for the rest of the century.

To Go beyond Profit in Defining Long-Term Success

Although Marion Wade cared about profit, he had a bigger goal.

> Naturally, we all want our companies to make a profit. We have an obligation to the stockholders to keep the company in the black. We have a responsibility to our employees to keep the money coming in, so we get paid. But if bigger and bigger profits are all we care about every year, then we run the risk of losing our spiritual perspective.[73]

It was also clear that Wade was not the one to lead in the financial area. As Richard Hattwick wrote following an interview with Ken Hansen, "The key to growing profitably was good financial controls. This was not an area of strength for Marion Wade. Consequently, he delegated [financial] responsibility to Hansen."[74]

Here, Marion Wade explains what constituted true success for him:

> I was not asking for personal success as an individual or merely material success as a corporation. I do not equate this kind of success with Christianity. Whatever God wants is what I want. But I did try to build a business that would live longer than I would in the marketplace that would witness to Jesus Christ in the way the business was conducted. We are in short pants now, but some day we will wear the long pants.[75]

> How a business is run is much more important than whether it runs. Some businesses should not be in business today just because of the way they are run. I like the definition of success I found in Webster: "the favorable termination of a venture."[76]

The key to this understanding of success is that it is not measured only by profit but involves a broader scope of objectives. Although some of these objectives could not be readily measured, they were used as talking points in reviews.

This view of success didn't mean that Marion avoided nice things or scorned financial success. But he didn't want financial success only for himself; he wanted to make sure that others did well also. Dick Armstrong explained it this way:

> Shortly after I joined the company in 1964, Marion asked me to go to lunch with him. I was surprised because I was just the staff assistant to a regional manager, and he was chairman of the board. When he picked me up in his new Cadillac, and he got a new one each year, I said, "This is a really nice car." He responded, "Someday all of you will be driving cars like this. You guys are going to make history." But when he said this, he was not talking only about economic growth in the company, but growth in a company built on Scriptural principles. The right kind of growth.[77]

Throughout the century, growing profitably remained an objective for ServiceMaster, but it was always treated as a means to supporting the other goals of the company. Though not formalized until 1973, the version of the company objectives that emerged were deeply rooted in Wade's philosophy of business.

Final Comments

Marion Wade served as chairman until his death in 1973. After his death, his influence continued to be felt as the company grew and developed under Ken Hansen's leadership and beyond. Although today

ServiceMaster is a very different company, it continues to give tribute to its founder on its home page.

Wade was recognized for his work by the Illinois Business Hall of Fame; and in October 2014, Wade was selected for the American National Business Hall of Fame. With this honor, he joined one hundred thirty members of this elite group, which included Walt Disney, Andrew Carnegie, John Deere, and Thomas Edison. The hall of fame criteria focused on a person's corporate performance, leadership, and business ethics.[78]

In addition to his love of business, Wade loved people and sports and also became an enthusiast for the writings of C. S. Lewis. In 1974, his friends and family established an endowment at Wheaton College in his memory to support "The C. S. Lewis Collection." This is a repository that eventually included not only Lewis's items (such as his desk and a wardrobe that played an important role in the first Narnia book), but also materials from six other British writers, including J. R. R. Tolkien, known as "the Inklings." Later this was renamed "The Marion E. Wade Collection." In 1998, with the generous help of Wade's daughter Mary, the Wade Center began construction of a new limestone building on the Wheaton campus, fashioned after the style of an English manor house, which opened in 2001. In addition to the Lewis writings, the center has tributes to ServiceMaster and to Marion's short-lived baseball career.

At the opening of the Marion E. Wade Center, former friends and business colleagues sent letters in tribute to him. Many of those remembrances focused not on his business success but on his down-to-earth care for others in a business context. Here are three examples:

> We all knew that uppermost in the thinking of ServiceMaster leaders was the desire to pass on a value system. We discussed these ideas frequently— and the Wades made themselves available for younger people. We saw how Christianity looks when it is lived.—Sharon Cloud

> Mr. Wade still holds the top spot in my memory as the man that I respected most in my lifetime. His warm friendship during my years with ServiceMaster were very meaningful to me. His constant reminder to his co-workers was very simple: "If you don't live it, you don't believe it." He believed it and he lived it. His perseverance during the early days of Wade, Wenger & Associates was an inspiration to everyone. Marion E. Wade: A man of humility who achieved the highest form of success.—Robert S. Pierre

> He was kind to me as a new inexperienced young salesman. He was a warm senior executive. He gave me insight into myself that has allowed me to grow as a salesman, an executive, and as a man, husband, father, and Christian friend. Marion Wade changed my life.—E. F. Morgan[79]

In 1966, while still chairman of the board at ServiceMaster, Wade thought back on how he had begun it all in 1929. His company was now publicly traded, spread out across the country and across the ocean, and hired college graduates for its leadership positions. Its annual revenues exceeded $15 million. Overwhelmed by the wonder of what had happened, he remarked,

> If today I applied for an executive position with the company of which I am Chairman of the Board of Directors, I wouldn't even be granted an interview. My application form would be dismally brief.[80]

The leader with an eighth-grade education, who started a company because he needed to support his family, learned through a life-changing accident that he could serve God in business. He went on to create new and unique ways to think about products, purpose, and people—establishing a company that became ServiceMaster.

3

THE KEN HANSEN YEARS

Marion Wade may have started ServiceMaster and given it its soul, but Ken Hansen turned it into a business. Together they laid the foundation for a multinational, publicly traded company that was deeply connected to its roots as expressed in Marion Wade's first-stated objective, "To Honor God in the Marketplace."

The two men worked closely together between 1946 and Marion's death in 1973. They had in common a deep faith that penetrated everything they did, a strong work ethic, a strong sense of curiosity and possibility, and a deep sense of integrity. But they were completely different in so many ways. Ken was taller; Marion was short. Ken wore a bow tie; Marion dressed more traditionally. Ken was abrupt and to the point; Marion was a storyteller and a friend of everyone. Ken loved the numbers; Marion did not. Ken was raised in two-parent home; Marion by a single mother. Ken graduated from college; Marion had an eighth-grade education. Yet they became friends, respected each other's strengths, and filled in for each other's weaknesses.

The two leaders were able to play off each other in ways that seldom work for two strong-minded people. Often when a new leader takes over at a company, that leader wants to establish control, distancing himself (or herself) from the previous leadership. But while Marion Wade was CEO, Ken clearly and frequently deferred to Marion even when his ideas created new growth and direction for the company. When Ken became CEO and Marion the chairman of the board, Ken took the lead on innovation and decisions. Yet he readily engaged Marion Wade in decisions where he might have gone alone: key hiring and customer presentations, for example. And he learned from Wade's challenges all the way up to Wade's death in 1973. It takes strong and insightful leaders to engage in this way, demonstrating strength that was not threatened by the strength of another. This collaboration set the tone for a long-standing ServiceMaster practice called "shingles on the roof," leaders working together in a complementary way to fully utilize the skills of the other. That practice continued for more than fifty years.

Like Marion Wade, Hansen's resume would never have come up as a future hall of fame business leader, let alone someone to hire to help a fledgling business grow and develop. Yet between 1946 and 1957,

Hansen influenced and created a change in this small company that was truly astounding. It was only after Ken Hansen came on board, late in 1946, that the company was finally incorporated and named. Ken led both. Under Hansen's leadership, they began to operate outside the Chicago area as well. With revenue of slightly more than $50,000 in 1946, the company quickly grew to revenues of $349,000 in the next two years. While Marion Wade continued as CEO, he relied more and more on Ken Hansen's leadership. When Wade encountered some health issues in 1957, he remained as chairman of the board but appointed Hansen to lead the company as CEO. Hansen led the development of international operations by expanding to Great Britain in 1958, and he took the company public in 1962. As with Marion Wade, Ken's early life shaped his character and his work ethic. These attributes added to his natural bent toward business.

Ken Hansen's Growing Up Years

Ken Hansen was born in Chicago on August 17, 1918, as the first child of Gustavus Adolphus and Anna Emily Hansen. His brother Glen was born two years later, and his sister Audrey was born in 1926 after the family had moved to a new home in Elmhurst, Illinois.[1]

In the summer of 1928 the family moved again, this time to Wheaton, Illinois. Their house in Wheaton was close to Wheaton College, and soon the parents made some extra income by providing rooms for students from the school, girls at first. This started a relationship between Wheaton College and ServiceMaster that continued through the rest of Hansen's life. The family also started regularly attending College Church in Wheaton.

By the time Ken was in junior high school, he was working hard after school doing odd jobs and helping to support family needs during a time when his dad was having difficulty landing a steady job. Then came high school, and Ken began taking an interest in football, girls, English literature, and poetry. Perhaps this was the foundation for his later love of literature. In his senior year, Ken was inducted into the Scholastic Athletic Honor Society.

After high school, Ken got a job in Chicago as a messenger boy for the Northern Trust Company. In this year of transition, he "came to the reality that his life of seeking pleasure after work was heading down a road away from God. Early one morning after 'a night out,' Ken came home and in the quiet of his bedroom confessed his sins and asked God to forgive him and save him."[2] Ken's life changed after that early morning encounter with God. He enrolled in classes at Moody Bible Institute, while in the fall of

1937, he took "Survey of Accounting 1" at the University of Chicago as a "student at large." He earned a grade of B in that class.[3] A year later, Ken enrolled as a freshman at Wheaton College. He worked to support himself through school as an attendant in the men's athletic supply room.

When Ken enrolled at Wheaton, his parents decided to "take in boys, instead of girls, so that Ken would have the experience of dorm life in his own home." In his senior year at Wheaton, one of his roommates was Billy Graham, and their friendship continued for the rest of Ken's life. "Two other boys, Don Hoke and Phil Foxwell, also were a part of the 'dormitory' life in his own home," and they also became lifelong friends.[4] The young men who lived upstairs in Ken's house were known on campus as the "attic gang." Ken graduated in three years from Wheaton College in 1940, with honors, with degrees in religion and philosophy. In addition to his studies, Ken was active in yearbook staff, Christian Service Council, Publications Board, and Foreign Missions Fellowship.[5]

At Wheaton, Ken also met the love of his life, Jean Hermann. Jean's early life was spent in China where her parents were missionaries. Her parents had recently moved to Wheaton so she could attend Wheaton College. Near the end of their senior year, Ken and Jean made a commitment to get married, though the formal engagement didn't happen until Christmas 1941. They were married July 25, 1942.

After marriage, both Ken and Jean enrolled in Wheaton College's graduate school. During this time, they were also approached by Bethel Community Church, a small church on the west side of Chicago, to work at the church. In agreeing to come, Ken made it clear to them that he was not trained as a pastor, but he stepped into the work with both feet.

Ken was soon preaching on Sundays and was often referred to as their "interim pastor." The church grew as God was clearly working in the lives of people. One of the visiting couples to the church was Marion and Lil Wade. Marion saw something in Ken and tried to convince him to come to work at his company. As already seen in the previous chapter that it took a while for Marion to convince Ken that a business career could be his ministry. Marion Wade observed:

> He was serving the church as interim pastor, but this didn't prevent him from doing the job wholeheartedly. The neighborhood was building up fast and every time a moving van pulled in, Ken was over there introducing himself. The church needed a Sunday School and Ken wanted to build it as rapidly as possible. Lil and I were able to be helpful in doing this. Soon we had more children than we could handle. During this time, Ken and I became well acquainted. I admired him as a person, I respected him as a Christian, and I envied his zeal. He never stopped. He was intensely curious about everything, deeply interested in people. I could see that here was a young man who was going places.[6]

Ken Hansen was not so sure that business fit his idea of a Christian calling. He knew he was meant to work for God, but didn't believe that meant as a pastor. Working in business was a long way from a typical Christian calling. Wade said, "I suggested to him that if he ever got the feeling that God wanted him to take a place in the business world, I would like to talk to him about it."[7] But Ken wasn't ready to do that, yet. He appeared to be leaning more toward overseas missionary work.

In supporting the ministry at the church, Jean got involved in the Pioneer Girls Club and Ken with the Christian Service Brigade program for boys. Soon a former classmate of Ken's at Wheaton College replaced Ken as the full-time pastor for this young and growing church. Ken agreed to serve as the General Secretary of the Christian Service Brigade. The organization was growing rapidly and needed Ken's leadership and organizational skills. It also required Ken to do a lot of traveling across the country as the ministry grew in many different locations.

They hit a transition in their lives when Ken and Jean had their first child in October 1944. According to Hansen, Kenny was "a wonderful little boy who came into this world with a severe handicap which is often called Down's syndrome."[8] Ken and Jean were advised to put Kenny away in a care facility, common practice in those days for children born with Down syndrome, but they said no. Having Kenny, however, altered Hansen's dream to go overseas in mission work. This care for those with disabilities remained an integral part of Ken's life throughout his business career. Dave Baseler later recalled that Ken had no tolerance for anyone who would make fun of someone else's limitations.[9] Interestingly, Marion Wade had his accident and came to the subsequent understanding that he could do business to the glory of God, also in 1944. That is when Marion became sure that the Lord wanted him to expand and grow his business and when he also believed that Ken should be a part of this. So, Marion continued to be in touch with Ken urging him to become a part of the company. Because of his family situation and his commitment to Kenny, Ken finally agreed to join Marion Wade late in 1946.

What did Marion see in Ken? Certainly, he saw the common commitment to serving Christ, a person willing to work hard, initiative that helped him grow his church. He saw entrepreneurship in the way he met new people in the neighborhood, helped them move in, and recruited them to his church. He saw solid character, a person of integrity, along with that intense curiosity. His one class in accounting, though not much, gave him financial insight that Marion did not have. But there was no MBA (that came later, it turns out), no obvious business experience, and no obvious financial skills. Perhaps it was an intuitive sense, but in any case, the two made quite a combination for growing the business.

The Hansen Family

Before describing Ken's influence on the company, we see him as a man of integrity and a family leader. The best definition of integrity is wholeness—that is, when a person is the same in any situation—and that fit Ken perfectly. He was the same person at home as he was at work. On the one hand, he was an incredibly generous and compassionate person. Keeping Kenny at home was a lifetime decision. In fact, the family moved to acreage in the country to provide a better environment for him. As recently as 1983, the life expectancy for someone with Down syndrome was twenty-five years; Kenny lived to age sixty-six, outliving both of his parents. When Jean died in 1988, Kenny continued to live with his father until he died in 1993. Kenny spent his final seventeen years with a caregiver until his death in 2010.

Ken and Jean's second son, Walter, was born in October 1946. In 1950, Ken and Jean invited two young brothers, Vince (eight years old) and Jim (almost six) Nelson, into their home because their single-parent father was no longer able to care for them. Vince had been in seven homes before arriving at the Hansen home, and learned to use a toothbrush for the first time after arriving. He remembers being sent to the dentist after arriving, learning he had a cavity in every tooth. Vince recalled, "I had not been socialized. We were feral boys."[10]

Vince arrived with his brother and an orange crate containing a few clothes provided by the school. Ken picked up the boys (with their orange crate) at their one-room apartment on the north side of Chicago, and they became an integral part of the family. James was the same age as Walter, so Vince was the oldest in the family; Kenny was six years old at this time. Ken and Jean's third child, Joyce, was born in January of 1951, Jeanne in 1952, and Linnea in 1954. Ken and Jean were both equally committed to caring for and raising their large family.

Although Hansen was a deeply generous and caring person, his hard-driving personality could be a challenge for some. Vince recalled him as the most disciplined and hard-working man he had ever met, but also as one who expected those around him to live up to those same standards: "On that small farm, even when I was eleven or twelve, I worked eleven to twelve hours a day during the summer. Ken would frequently use the word *arbite*, a Swedish word from his heritage meaning 'work.'" The discipline paid off, however, as Vince's school grades improved and he went on to a successful career, including twenty-five years on the ServiceMaster board of directors. But Vince also remembers that it was not a lot of fun.

Every year Vince and his brother would go off with their birth father for a one-week vacation, "and it always took Ken and Jean a few days to get us back into shape," he recalled. Ken and Jean worked together in lockstep, "very black and white," and "there was no daylight between them." They attended church in Wheaton every week, Sunday morning and Sunday evening, and had family worship around the dinner table every evening. Even if Ken was just getting home from a business trip, they still made time for devotions.

This large family often had even larger Sunday dinners with as many as sixteen people gathered around their large dining room table. Guests included visiting missionaries from church and frequently Marion and Lil Wade. Vince remembers that Marion always had a smile on his face and that he was a great story and joke teller—very much unlike the more serious Ken Hansen.

Developing the Business

The small company Ken joined in 1946 did carpet cleaning, disaster recovery, and moth-proofing. Carpet cleaning and moth-proofing were products of Marion's research, while disaster recovery was simply work Marion thought the company could do. These were not formal product lines yet, but Ken started the process of formalizing the business.

Together, Ken, Marion, and Bob Wenger were a vital part of the early growth. In such a small company, it was often difficult to distinguish the roles. In 1947, under Ken's leadership, the company was incorporated as "Wade, Wenger, and Associates." Marion Wade had been in business for eighteen years, but it took Ken Hansen to drive the incorporation. It is also worthy of note that Hansen, the mastermind behind the naming and incorporation, did not include his own name in the company name. When asked about this, he later said, "My name was in the title—it was in the 'and Associates' part!"[11] This willingness to work without fanfare and to create opportunity for others would continue to characterize Hansen's leadership.

Two weeks after the company was formed, Ken visited Milwaukee, made a few sales, and decided to open a branch there. Wade asked him to take charge of the branch, and he was given authority to employ two production people there and grow the Milwaukee business. Hansen began to spend two days a week in Milwaukee, leaving his Chicago-area home at 5:00 a.m. to make the trip. Most of that time was devoted to selling, and Hansen was ultimately able to get enough business to employ two crews. Once the Milwaukee business had been firmly established, Hansen was given the task of opening company-owned branches in other locations. Wade and Wenger helped with this task, but it was Hansen who spent the most time on the road.[12] His early travels demonstrate the discipline and frugality he applied to himself and not just to others. He rarely took a suitcase and washed his clothes by hand each night.

When Wenger received an attractive offer to head up the sales distribution for a large carpet company, both Marion and Ken supported him in this move. Bob agreed he would stay on the board of directors and be available for advice and counsel.

As part of the expansion of the business, the company began selling other franchises. They realized the best way to manage a growing company was through small, independent businesses that used the products and processes of the company, that embraced the same values and objectives, but that operated as independent entities. This was a first step in adding structure for growth to the small business. The larger growth process involved developing people for leadership, hiring, and recruiting, and ultimately creating more formal product lines. In 1950, Art Melvin and Ed Morgan were hired to sell franchises. Morgan went on to a thirty-nine-year career with ServiceMaster. The first franchise agreement was signed in 1952.[13]

The work of growing the company went beyond a mere job. In these early days, the Hansens and Wades lived next door to each other, which enabled them to have discussions at home and involve their wives as well. Ken recalled a difficult time of uncertainty when their wives were concerned about their future, as the four of them sat on the Wades' screened-in porch talking about business, as they often did. Hansen recalled, "The girls would get nervous. Then we would say, 'Don't worry, we're both door-to-door salesmen. If this goes bust, we'll go back to the street and support you.'"[14]

Wade quickly realized that Hansen had skills in finance: "He had talents which the Lord denied me, so between us we had a fine balance and our business grew rapidly. Ken had a real feel for finances, and I was happy to give him plenty of latitude."[15] The challenge Hansen faced in managing finances was that he also had the responsibility for growing the franchise business. This meant he had to figure out how to keep up with the financial reporting while traveling in those days before cell phones and e-mail. According to Richard Hattwick,

> He solved that problem by devising a simple formula which he could use in the field to keep track of the rest of the business on a daily basis. Once a day he would call the home office and ask for a few numbers from each of the other locations. Using his slide rule and the formula, he would then estimate profit for those locations. If the numbers indicated a potential problem, he could then arrange immediate remedial action.[16]

In the current business environment, executives are often provided with a computer-based graphical summary of key performance indicators, to readily get a picture of the state of the business. Hansen was doing an early version of this with his slide rule.

Under pressure to make the financial numbers work, Hansen sometimes pushed people a bit too hard, and this is where the partnership with Wade paid off. Wade said, "It was Ken's job to control expenses, and he started 'pushing' people in the organization to do so."[17] Marion reminded Ken that his actions and words could negatively affect his relationships with other people in the company. He could hurt the organization and be inconsistent with his witness as a Christian.

> Initially, Ken reacted negatively to this advice. However, during the next few months he spent time studying the Sermon on the Mount in chapters 5, 6, and 7 of Matthew and he realized the need for God to work in his life with respect to his attitude and his actions towards others. There needed to be a work of grace in Ken's life as he integrated his faith with his work, and Ken began seeing how he should treat others in the way God wanted him to and also get the job done of controlling expenses.[18]

The idea of holding conflicting objectives (treating others well *and* making the numbers) became a part of the DNA of the company.

Not everything went smoothly, however, for the new company. In addition to franchises, they established reselling relationships with retail companies that sold carpet and referred customers to Wade and Wenger for cleaning. Wade, Wenger and Associates became the point of sale for the rug-cleaning work of a number of retail companies. Wall-to-wall carpeting was becoming more the norm, where rugs were cleaned in the home using the new carpet-cleaning agents. This was the work ServiceMaster was doing with the retail outlets, though most of the rug-cleaning business still involved sending rugs out.

One day, one of their retail partners suggested they set up a factory to clean rugs that were still being sent out, promising to pass on their entire rug-cleaning business. Since the retailer offered a revenue target, Hansen ran the numbers and concluded this would be a worthwhile business. After finding the right building, they just needed to raise $25,000 to purchase and refurbish it.

Meanwhile, Marion and Lil Wade had decided they needed a bigger home for their growing family. Wade handled the sale of his current home himself. In the sales process, he showed prospective buyers both the strengths and the problems of his house. He hid nothing and was clear on the expected price. When he asked the final prospective buyer if he wanted to buy it or not, the person answered, "I've enjoyed doing business with you. I have never met a man before who was so forthright.

If you ever run into a business transaction where you need an investor, let me know."[19]

Wade told the buyer about the facility that would become part of the business, their financial projections, and their need to raise money to refurbish the building. The home buyer put $6,000 into the business immediately and then raised the rest from his relatives. "When I told our fellows what had happened," Wade recalled, "we were all sure this was God's way of letting us know that we were on the right track."

After receiving the money, they immediately began refurbishing the new facility. They were so eager to get started with the cleaning work that they began cleaning rugs while the building was still wide open on one side. Ken Hansen remembers sleeping on a pile of oriental rugs one night to protect them, because there was no way to lock the building.

But the project backfired. They soon discovered that the retailer's revenue commitment was not even close to reality. Ken and Marion then tried to build the business independently, but when the United States became involved in Korea, the War Production Board stopped the manufacture of key equipment. In the end, they had to declare that part of their business a total loss. Hansen, however, learned from this setback, handling it in his own style by doggedly pursuing the next opportunity.

Early on, Ken desired to delegate and empower others. It started as his personal way of operating, and the practice was later formalized in the company. In May 1954, George and Lu Holland purchased the forty-second on-location ServiceMaster franchise. They paid their hard-earned $500 and received a roto, a tank vacuum, a wall-cleaning machine, and a few chemicals. They agreed to pay 4 percent of their revenue back to the company.

George had been introduced to the business by Ken Hansen during one of his training sessions in Chicago. When Hansen taught marketing to them, it was not just a lecture in a classroom: they went into a neighborhood to sell door-to-door. After they had been let into a house, Holland recalled, "Ken was about halfway through his presentation, when he turned to him and said, 'Okay, George, now you take over. Finish the sale.'"[20]

That same year, Marion Wade began to show some signs of illness that proved to be serious. This meant that he needed to step back a bit from his involvement, which began the process leading to Ken Hansen taking over the company in 1957. One of the discussions between the two in this transition was about the name of the company. They decided Wade, Wenger and Associates "was quite a mouthful for the switchboard operator," Wade said, "when we grow big enough to have one." Both Marion and Ken decided independently on Wade Wenger ServiceMaster, Inc., derived from their goal to be "masters of service, serving the Master."

The company's franchise business continued to grow rapidly, and Ken Hansen was spending most of his time on the road. The company needed to add more leaders to the business, and in 1954, Ken Wessner joined the team. Revenues for the company that year were about $800,000.[21] It was not long after "Wes" (as he was called) came on board that Marion and the two Kens became a vibrant leadership team.

Ken Hansen Becomes CEO

In 1956, Marion Wade experienced a heart murmur that put him face-to-face with the prospect of death. He had said earlier that he wanted to have a company that lasted well beyond him, and now was the time to pay serious attention to that objective. Although he lived until 1973 and continued to play a strong role until his death, his health issues caused him to worry about the future of his company. In 1957, therefore, Marion Wade formally made Ken Hansen the CEO, while he continued in the role of chairman of the board. The transition—a huge event for many companies when the founder steps aside and hands the reins to a new leader—was almost a nonevent for ServiceMaster. This is because Ken and Marion had already been working together, and they continued to do so, only with different titles.

In spite of this low-key transition, the change marked a major event in the history of the company and led to a series of changes that added more foundation for growth. One change was the decision to phase out company-owned branches and rely strictly on franchises. Hansen believed the only effective way to deliver service was to use owner-operators, as their ownership would give them extra motivation. At that time, the company-owned branches were profitable and made a major contribution to covering company overhead.

So, Hansen worked out a break-even type model that showed the number of franchisees needed to cover all of the company's fixed costs. When that number was reached, he argued, the company should sell the branches to independents that would then become franchisees. Wade and Wenger were lukewarm about the idea and the three other managers opposed it, because the branches were so profitable at that time. But the two senior partners decided to trust Hansen's judgment and the decision to phase out the branches was made.[22] As market opportunities continued to grow in the cleaning business, both Marion and Ken concluded that more franchises and fewer company branches was the best future growth strategy. Ken Wessner was given responsibility to lead franchise growth.

The second change was a new service for hospitals. Lutheran General in Chicago was their first hospital customer in the United States, which launched the Hospital Services business. This business became the revenue leader for ServiceMaster for many years. It is not surprising that Marion Wade, Ken Hansen, and Ken Wessner all had a role in developing this business, although the leadership for this work ultimately fell to Wessner, which will be discussed in the next chapter.

The company also tried to launch a business for cleaning offices, but that approach was abandoned. In retrospect, the problem was a strategic error. They had targeted serving small businesses, but they learned these companies typically didn't realize what the service could do for their productivity and didn't feel they could afford it. Many years later, ServiceMaster would try office and industrial cleaning again, but focus this time on the large customer who could afford the service and who better appreciated the need for it.

Company Growth

To staff the growing company, it was necessary to attract talent that matched the company's strong work ethic, commitment to values, and the commitment to Wade's objective, "To Honor God in the Marketplace." In his language, "No employer ever finds enough of the right men."

Ken Hansen had graduated from Wheaton College and appreciated the Christian foundation he received there, so he proposed an advertisement in the *Wheaton College Alumni Association* magazine that simply stated, "If you feel God is calling you in business, get in touch with Marion Wade."[23] Wade was pleased with the outcome of the ad. In 1966, he reported, "Some fine young men came around to see us, and some of them are still here as executives."[24] This may have been the reason behind the persistent rumor at ServiceMaster that the only way to get ahead is to have a Wheaton pedigree. This was no doubt due to the fact that Ken Hansen and the two CEOs who followed him (Ken Wessner and Bill Pollard) were all graduates of Wheaton College.

As the years passed and the company grew, they had a real challenge: finding the type of people who could carry on the vision of the company, while at the same time including men and women who would come from a variety of backgrounds and beliefs while holding the values of the company. Over time, the company became more intentional about its inclusive stance.

Though the company was definitely guided by deep principles and values, these values were not clearly spelled out at the beginning but would need to be as it grew. One day in 1958, Ken Hansen arrived at the ServiceMaster office at 2177 North Way, called a meeting of those present and said, "I'm forty years old, and we have to talk about the kind of company we want to be." That launched a fifteen-year search process that culminated in the adoption of ServiceMaster's new strategy and a new set of corporate goals. That year, they began the discussion to become a publicly traded company. As the business continued to grow, there was a need for more capital. The Beadles family from Cairo, Illinois, agreed to make an investment in the business, and Tom Beadles agreed to come on the board of the company. Beadles would later have a major role in advising and helping Hansen and Wade with the financial structure of the company, especially when they decided to go public.

At that time, Ken Wessner began to play a stronger role in the growth of the company. Also that year, ServiceMaster opened its first international business in England. The 1960s would be a time of significant change for the company, stemming from both internal decisions and external forces.

Succession Planning Is Born

Because Marion Wade had a heart problem and Ken Hansen was showing signs of the same, Wade wanted to develop a succession policy. He and Hansen talked about the idea frequently, both at work and at home, since they were neighbors for a time. Wade began researching what other companies did, and he found a plan he liked at the United Silver Company. There they identified successor chief executives and put them at the head of the company before the CEO was ready to retire. The predecessor remained active in a support role, but the new person took the position. The book that he read about this plan used the term "shingles on a roof," which he obviously implemented. Wade and Hansen had already been operating in this fashion, but this is when they formally named the process.

At ServiceMaster, they began the process to find and train future leaders and give them "grooming experiences." Eventually from this pool they would select the next leader. But they didn't want to wait until it was too late and have to name the new person under pressure. An important factor in making this work was to be able to retain key leaders. This caused them to begin the process of creating a public stock offering so that the talented leaders could be provided with stock incentives to stay. At the time, Wade, Wenger, and Hansen owned the controlling interest in the company through their Class B stock.

Becoming a Publicly Traded Company

In 1958, they began exploring the idea to take the company public. In the early 1960s, the company moved its headquarters from an old brewery plant in Chicago to a new location and building in Downers Grove, Illinois. This became headquarters for the rest of the century. At the same time, they retained Kuno Laren, an investment banker, to advise Ken Hansen and Marion Wade regarding the possibility of a public offering.

Leading up to the time that the company was publicly traded, the revenue and profits had grown some (see Figures 3.1 and 3.2 below), but it was not enough to allow the leaders to develop the growth they thought was important.

In the spring of 1962, a public offering of the company stock was approved by the SEC. Kuno Laren agreed to market the stock, with the original plan to sell 140,000 shares. The general stock market was in a slump at that time, however, and they agreed to reduce the total sale objective to 60,000. They hired an underwriter to offer the new ServiceMaster stock to the public, but the underwriter had trouble selling the issue. The timing was particularly poor. ServiceMaster had some quarterly losses in three of the previous five years. The prospectus that was issued showed financials only for the previous quarter, which also showed a loss.[25]

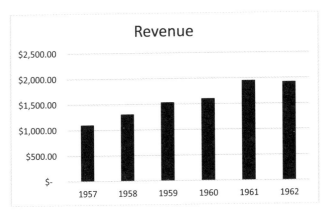

Figure 3.1. Revenue under Hansen prior to company going public (dollars shown in thousands).[26]

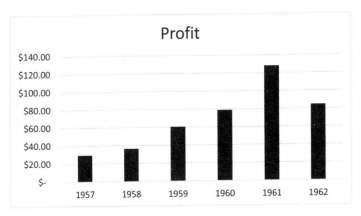

Figure 3.2. Profit under Hansen prior to company going public (dollars shown in thousands).[27]

Wade and Hansen decided to make the sales themselves, and within three days they had sold enough stock to employees and friends to make the underwriting a success. In addition to the public sale of stock, the company sold 250,000 subordinated convertible notes to existing shareholders. Ken Hansen also developed a plan to sell some of the company's shares to younger key leaders of the company, including Ken Wessner, Frank Flack, and Ed Morgan. Sears Roebuck, one of the major retail companies that referred cleaning work to ServiceMaster, became a shareholder of ServiceMaster and entered into further partnership by cross-selling agreements. By 1963, the company revenue was $3.7 million.

The New York underwriting firm was so impressed with the sales of stock that it asked Wade and Hansen to sell new issues of other companies. Flattered, they nevertheless refused.[28] These early shares would become valuable later: during its growth period, the company adopted the practice of having stock splits to keep the stock price affordable. Over the years, there were over fifty-five stock splits of 2-for-1 or 3-for-2. In 1993, Kuno Laren reported that $400 worth of original ServiceMaster stock had a value of $667,000.[29] When Laren reflected on Ken Hansen and his role in those early days, he said, "Ken was a great teacher. But he was also a great listener. He learned something from everyone he talked with."[30]

Ken Hansen was not blind to what this public offering meant. What had been a tightly controlled company was now open to public investment and influence. "We are now for sale every day," he acknowledged. The first annual report to shareholders as a public company was issued in the spring of 1963.

Research Department Formalized

In 1963, the research and development department was formally created. Its task was to help the company develop improved procedures, cleaning products, and equipment. This became another competitive advantage for ServiceMaster. They had used research to identify best practices and best cleaning agents back in Marion Wade's day, and now they were using it for competitive advantage. "The idea came out of Marion's fertile mind," said Ken Hansen. Prior to 1963, chemist Ray Haas was hired, but the company couldn't afford a full-time research person. Haas was a company salesman by day and then conducted company research at night.[31]

Testing Succession Planning

During this time, Ken Hansen became seriously ill, the first of a series of such illnesses. Perhaps it was because Hansen was CEO, taking the company public, and managing a big family. In any case, Ken Wessner recalled that Hansen was "hospitalized, and we really did not know if Ken was going to make it. . . . Marion took me into his office and talked with me very frankly and clearly."[32]

After Marion showed Ken Wessner the leadership transition between Moses and Joshua in Scripture, he said, "Wes, if Ken doesn't make it and the Lord takes him Home, I will be calling on you." Marion would not be able to come back and manage the business as he once did, Wessner noted, because of his own health. "But I remember the peace and joy in his life at this time. . . . Marion believed God had not led him here to mock him, but he knew there was a purpose and reason." Although Hansen recovered, the succession planning had been tested.

More Formalized Training

After his recovery, Hansen saw the need to have more formal business training in order to lead this growing, now publicly traded company. He enrolled in the executive MBA program at University of Chicago, on a weekend basis so he could continue his work. He completed his MBA degree with Beta Gamma Sigma honors from the University of Chicago in 1965.[33] This was a valuable experience for Hansen, and he saw the need to extend this kind of training to those at ServiceMaster.

Soon thereafter Hansen and Wessner, with the help of Ray Brown—a professor who taught MBA programs at the University of Chicago, Harvard, and Northwestern—developed a ServiceMaster graduate program for growing key leaders within the company. Brown also helped them develop a management skills program for younger managers.

Acquisitions

As a publicly traded company, there was an added reason to grow. Perhaps coming out of his MBA studies, Hansen embarked on accelerating growth through acquisition. In December 1965, the company purchased a tool-making company to supplement its development of new cleaning tools. In July 1966, Hansen made a more daring acquisition when he purchased a communications company and set it up as ServiceMaster Communications Systems, Inc. This company "designed, manufactured, and installed custom audio and video systems, including intercom and closed-circuit television systems for commercial and industrial use."[34] This particular acquisition was seen as a way of growing the company's set of services that could be offered to commercial and industrial companies.

External Events Affecting the Company

In 1964, two external events affected ServiceMaster in different and interesting ways. The first was the "space race," which was obviously not connected to what ServiceMaster was doing. But the space race ushered in the start of the technology revolution, creating a fear of job loss through automation. In 1966, the company placed an ad in *Popular Mechanics* magazine promoting ServiceMaster franchises, drawing on the "Space Age Count-Down," the threat of job automation, and the promise of a great job in the service business.

The ad headlined, "Don't Let the Count-Down Count <u>You</u> Out!" Then under "space age advice," it offered ten reasons to consider owning a ServiceMaster franchise, starting with "10" down to "1" on a sidebar designed like a rocketship, just like a countdown for a launch. Number 8 of the countdown asked a question that seems way before its time: "What's going to happen to *you and your job* as the Space Age 'computerizes' the work force?" Number 3 offered the answer: "The professional service industry is the largest single new-opportunity factor in the entire economy."[35]

ServiceMaster created other clever ads in this period as well, reflecting their desire to grow after going public. In the December 1964 issue of *Life* magazine, they featured a pitch to husbands: "What would your wife say if you gave her a clean house for Christmas? Ask her!" Not a company to waste good ad space, they slipped in another message as well in a small box in the corner of the page: "Note to any husband looking for a new career." Inside the box they made a pitch for purchasing a ServiceMaster franchise.

The second external event was Title VII of the Civil Rights Act of 1964, which prohibited employers from discriminating against individuals because of their religion. It stated that religion (or lack of religious belief) could not be a factor in hiring, firing, or any other terms and conditions of employment. The record suggests that, at this time, ServiceMaster began to focus more on values and commitment to hard work for their hiring and promotion needs, beginning a journey toward being much more inclusive. This may have contributed to the *Popular Mechanics* and *Life* ads for franchise owners.

Nonetheless, they continued to hire Christians in key leadership positions. The partnership with Allan C. Emery provides an example of the strong Christian orientation of ServiceMaster in this era. It was also a key growth step for the company.

Partnership with Allan Emery

After graduating from Wheaton College, Allan Emery worked with his father in the Boston woolen industry, ultimately running the family business.[36] He was highly respected in this industry, demonstrated by becoming president of Boston Wool Trade and the National Wool Trade Association. In 1964, however, the world began to shift toward finding low-cost labor offshore. He started down the road of selling the business, but he didn't really know what he would do with his life, since he was only forty-five years old. While he was on a trip to see a customer in the Chicago area, he decided to stop at Wheaton College for a dinner event and a chance to connect with old friends. In conversation with Ken and Jean Hansen, they told him that there was an opportunity with ServiceMaster.

Ken told Allan that he would be in Boston the following week and they agreed to meet there. Hansen had been looking for a way to expand his company in the Northeast and so he proposed a joint venture to set up a new operation there that would handle housekeeping for hospitals. He invited Allan to spend two days at the headquarters in Downers Grove, Illinois, to explore the possibility. Emery shared,

> I guess I went because I didn't want to hurt his feelings and because I had told the Lord I'd be available for His leading. I had no idea that cleaning hospitals was anything I would want. After seeing the operation and looking over their figures, I was to meet with Ken Hansen, Ken Wessner, and Marion Wade to give my decision. It would be a polite "no." I told the triumvirate that while I thought the project had real opportunity, I did not feel this was my area of experience. Not one to take no for an answer, Wade suggested we pray about it. He led in a beautiful prayer, and then Ken Hansen prayed.

This prayer seemed to break down the real reason why Emery was planning to turn down the deal.

> I saw myself as unwilling to accept this kind of work in spite of having told the Lord I'd go where He led. For the first time in my life, I saw myself as a stuffed shirt. I was under conviction. Ken Wessner then prayed, and I followed. When I finished, I said I'd take the job and set up a joint-risk operation. When I said this, I did what I had never done publicly as an adult—I wept. I was embarrassed and disbelieved my reaction. But I had peace, utter peace.[37]

He had become convinced, but he still felt the stigma of the service industry. After being president of a major international company, he wasn't sure about working for a company that provided janitorial services. This realization reached even deeper when he reported for work in Downers Grove. After meeting some of the other leaders, he was asked to buy three sets of green work uniforms. His first assignment was to work for two weeks as a houseman at a large metropolitan hospital mopping corridors, emptying trash bins, and cleaning ash trays. Although he soon realized he was not in the best condition for this type of physical labor, he made it through.

He learned something else about the business that changed him, as he came to see the challenge of the people in the organization.

The shock was not in the work but in the general rejection of me as a person because of my green uniform and the kind of work I was doing. Not a single person responded to my "Good Morning" except others in the Housekeeping Department. I had never before experienced the caste system.[38]

During this period, he made some wonderful new friends—in the housekeeping department. And he realized that this was the place where he could invest his life in people.

The joint venture with ServiceMaster, where each party had 50 percent ownership, was budgeted to lose money for two and a half years before turning a profit, and it met its business goals. In creating his new staff for the business, Emery found himself asking a different set of questions for job candidates. "How does he or she see people? Are people to be tools, objects to be exploited, or does this man see people as the objects of the love of God and sense his own responsibility to help develop them?"[39]

In 1968, Jim Huse joined Emery in the hospital business, launching a thirty-five-year ServiceMaster career. He recalled those early days in Boston in growing the business:

Allan was amazing. He had this incredible set of contacts throughout the Northeast that opened the doors. And the four objectives of ServiceMaster were the key to keeping these doors open. We worked with people who carried trash and cleaned up the operating rooms; people who were not used to being treated with respect. We helped them find dignity in their work. Turnover went down. Quality went up. It was a great business and what we brought to it made all the difference. We also had regular reviews with our customers, making sure we understood their needs and were delivering value.[40]

Emery had enjoyed the wool business—with its international flavor and interesting people—but now he said he was "excited" because the company was in the people business, focusing on helping employees, patients, hospital administration, and staff alike. He thought back to his struggle to sell his previous business and his concern about God's wisdom and faithfulness. He learned that the struggle was necessary "to make me leave [my] old security and to begin a new and wonderful ministry."[41] Although ServiceMaster later bought out the partnership, Allan Emery continued as a board member of the company from 1977 to 1986.

The Continued Evolution of the Objectives and Company Name

Amid all the growth in the company and its accompanying hiring and geographic expansion, the leaders continued to work out another important initiative for the company and its people. They needed a statement that would reflect the company's mission and purpose. To begin, they encouraged suggestions from the people of the company. Ken Hansen, in particular, struggled with what it meant to hold multiple ideas in tension. In his words,

> The struggle to define and reach our business goals was affecting all segments of our lives. We were changing for the good in our attitudes and actions as husbands, fathers, friends, and as businessmen. We were faced with the need for these changes as we wrestled with the apparently, but not necessarily, conflicting qualitative and quantitative goals in our business.[42]

Ken knew they needed to keep Marion's original goal, "To Honor God in the Marketplace." But they also needed a financial goal. Finally, Hansen was growing in his understanding of the role of the company—not just in completing tasks, but in growing people. "As I grew in a vital union with Jesus, I came to see that I was viewing people as a means to get work done. I viewed work as the end accomplished. I realized that I was reversing the positions of means and ends which the Bible teaches."[43]

By 1962, they had revised their 1954 goals and had now three goals: To help people to grow; to increase the worth of common stock; and to make a positive contribution to society related to growing people, growing financially, and honoring God through doing good work in the right way.[44] As they studied this further, they saw these were interconnected: the quantitative growth fed the qualitative growth. Again, from Ken Hansen:

> The quantitative growth—more customers and employees, more franchises and divisions, more revenue and profit—was essential in order to fulfill our qualitative goals. We accepted a stewardship responsibility for the men and women who were joining us in increasing numbers. These men and women expected growth opportunities.[45]

Before the end of 1967, as the company continued to grow, they decided to make another change in the name of the company—this time to ServiceMaster Industries, Inc. Now they presented six goals: To honor God, to be a good corporate citizen, to be market oriented, to deliver results to customers, to value people, and to grow profitably.

Honors for Hansen

In May 1966, Ken Hansen was awarded an honorary doctor of letters degree by Wheaton College in recognition of his leadership in business. Also receiving an honorary doctorate was Andrew Song, a 1949 master's graduate from Wheaton who headed the Chinese Native Evangelistic Crusade in Hong Kong.[46] It is interesting to note that Wheaton recognized a business leader and an evangelist on the same platform.

In 1967, Hansen was asked to serve on the board of trustees of the college. In addition to his work at Wheaton, he also finally had the opportunity to do some work as a missionary. On three occasions, Ken Hansen went to Nigeria and Ghana "to teach our pastors and missionaries biblical principles of time and organizational management," according to SIM missionary W. Harold Fuller.[47]

Challenging Continued Growth

The annual report for 1967 notes that, for the second consecutive year, the healthcare business had doubled in size. The total revenue of the company, including the franchise business, was $22.7 million with net income at $480,000. By early 1968, the company was serving in over one hundred hospitals.[48]

When the company needed more capital for the growth of the business, Ken Hansen engaged William Blair and Company to do a private placement of convertible debentures. Again, Ken was personally involved in selling added shares to New England Mutual Life Insurance Company and, through his friendship with George Bennett, to State Street Investment and Harvard University. In addition to this important work for Service-Master in the spring of 1968, Ken and his wife Jean took their entire family on a special trip to Europe. It was at this time that he began painting as a strategic endeavor, which will be described later in the chapter.

Another good year of growth for the company followed in 1968, with annual revenue exceeding $26 million and net income exceeding $500,000. The next two years, 1969 and 1970, were more difficult. Figures 3.3 and 3.4 below show graphs of the revenue and profit growth after going public from 1963 to 1973. This paints a picture of a company on the move, with revenue growing from slightly more than $6 million in 1965, to almost $90 million by 1973.

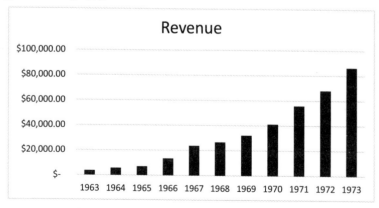

Figure 3.3. Revenue growth under Hansen after company
went public (dollars shown in thousands).[49]

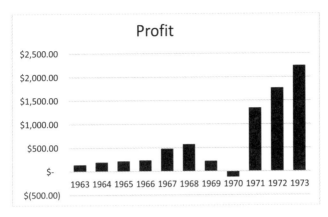

Figure 3.4. Profit under Hansen (dollars shown in thousands).[50]

The profit story, however, presents a different picture in Figure 3.4 above. Here we see the company recording a strong dip in profits in 1969 and a loss in 1970. In Ken Hansen's words, 1969 was "an awful year in redoing the business." Although the healthcare business and the franchise businesses continued to grow, one of the acquisitions they had made in 1965 was not performing well. In the words of Hansen and Wade from the 1969 annual report,

> ServiceMaster Communications Systems, Inc. was incurring a loss and constituted a drain upon both earning power and management time and talent which we believe could be more profitably invested in aspects of our business more closely related to the main thrust of our future growth. We sold ServiceMaster Communications Systems, Inc. to Cor-Plex International. Cor-Plex is in essentially the same business, and its corporate structure is better geared to it than ours.[51]

The sale was made in August 1969. In May 1970, they also sold the tool division that they had acquired in 1965.

This led to a renewed focus on supporting the healthcare business, with a decision to add other services they could provide to hospitals. The company started to provide plant maintenance and laundry services in addition to the housekeeping services. There was also a further expansion of the franchise businesses and a commitment to develop a stronger international business.

Near the end of the year, Burlington Mills put in an offer to buy ServiceMaster. The board agreed to reject the offer. Before Christmas, Ken Hansen went into the hospital for surgery for what initially appeared as lung cancer but turned out to be less serious. Recovery was still painful, but he made it home for Christmas.

Hansen's reflection on 1970 was that the business hit, in his words, "the bottom of the well." While the healthcare and franchise businesses continued to grow with a total revenue of $35 million, there were still some write-offs that had to be taken with the continued closing of the small businesses. In this same year, the company opened its second overseas venture: residential and commercial franchising in Japan.

In spite of some of these challenges, the ServiceMaster commitment to identifying and growing good people remained a constant. While there was a perception of some that only Christians could advance at ServiceMaster, especially if they had a connection to Wheaton College, Bisher Mufti provides a clear and different example.

Hiring and Developing Bisher Mufti

In 1969, Bisher Mufti, an immigrant from Jordan, was working at West Suburban Hospital in Oak Park, Illinois, as a housekeeper while going to business school. He was a hospital employee, but ServiceMaster was managing the hospital contract. The management team saw Mufti's good work, and his manager urged him to become a supervisor. To do this meant leaving the hospital staff to join ServiceMaster. He had planned to find a different kind of work after getting his degree but, since ServiceMaster offered more money, he accepted. Once inside ServiceMaster, however, he was given training and grew not only in his skills but also in his understanding of the business. Through his lens as a Muslim, he came to value the four objectives of the company.

He was a good worker and ServiceMaster was growing, so it wasn't long before he was promoted to assistant manager and then given an opportunity to manage a hospital in Milwaukee, Wisconsin. By 1972, he was back at West Suburban Hospital as the manager of the ServiceMaster work there. He was recognized for his quality work and invited to a ServiceMaster award trip with the company. He used that as the opportunity to honeymoon with his new wife Mary, whom he had met at the hospital. Mufti said, "We still joke about how tightly our lives were intertwined with the company."[52]

Another Transition Time

In 1971, the twenty-fifth year of the company's incorporated life marked a financial and organizational turning point. Revenue increased to over $48 million and net income was $1 million. This was the start of a continuous growth in revenue and profit that continued for the rest of the century—an unprecedented accomplishment for any business. While Hansen was fully engaged in his work, he applied to Wheaton College in April 1971 to take a literature class as a special student. In his application, he stated he wanted to do this "more to enjoy, use, and know for sharing life."[53]

The shareholders report for that year showed a picture of the board visiting a large hospital laundry in Philadelphia that was served by ServiceMaster. Although Marion Wade "looked good" in the picture, he later told Ken that his insides "didn't feel so good." The picture of the board taken in the spring of 1973 indicated to some extent Marion's deteriorating health condition.

In November 1973, Marion Wade died, marking the end of an era and forty-four years of leading the company. He had been serious about establishing a company that would last, serious about a strong moral foundation that would honor God through business, and serious about succession planning that left the company in a strong position.

This passage marked the beginning of a process of leadership transition. More responsibility fell on Ken Wessner, though he did not fully step into the role of president and CEO until January 1976, when Ken Hansen gave up his daily leadership role to become full-time chairman of the board.

During this transition period, the planning process that Ken Hansen had earlier introduced—focusing on the importance of developing businesses that would sustain a consistent rate of growth—was becoming a reality for the ServiceMaster team and for the shareholders of the company. In 1973, the company achieved $86 million in revenue and $2.2 million in profit.

At this transition point, Hansen was interviewed by Howard Gelfand of the *Wall Street Journal*.[54] The journal was still trying to make sense of this growing company with its Christian roots. When asked about hiring Christians, Ken said, "I've never hired a gentleman because he was a Christian, and I've never not hired one because he wasn't. But we do insist that a man be of high moral caliber." The reporter noted, however, that "the company's 2000 employees bring with them a missionary zeal," and that "company officials like to draw upon contacts made in church groups and Sunday schools for talent." The reporter then quoted an unnamed hospital supervisor in Chicago who said, "When I got out of school, I had to choose between becoming a pastor and working for ServiceMaster. I chose ServiceMaster because I felt I could do more for the Lord with the company than in a congregation." But before being too critical, the reporter quoted the notice to shareholders, "We have asked the Lord for a bright and sunny May 13." And then he noted, "It rained for several days before the meeting. An hour before it started, the skies cleared."

In 1974, the numbers continued to increase ($110 million revenue, $2.9 million profit) and again in 1975 ($145 million, $3.7 million). Ken Wessner's new leadership was not only accepted by the people of the company but also by the investment community. As was the case when Marion Wade was promoted to chairman and Ken Hansen became CEO, the two Kens continued to work together for the good of the company, using their individual gifts. The transition, in many ways, was hardly noticed. The picture in the annual report for 1974 shows the two Kens standing in front of a painting of Marion Wade.

Doing What Is Right

In 1974, Doug Pound went into the ServiceMaster headquarters for a job interview, hoping to get a middle-management position. He had heard about the position from a recruiter, had seen the four objectives, and believed this was a place he would like to work. His interview was interrupted with a knock on the door. Doug was asked to go to Chairman Ken Hansen's office when he was done. "I was just a kid with a sociology degree looking for a job. I didn't even know who Ken Hansen was. The person interviewing me, about three levels down from the top, wondered what was going on."[55]

When Doug arrived in Hansen's office, Hansen said he had been looking out of the window of his office and "noticed Doug's car had been dented by a rock thrown out of the gardener's lawn mower."[56] Hansen wanted to pay for the repair. It had nothing to do with the job interview, but everything to do with Pound's understanding of the company. The objectives were more than something on paper; they were lived out—all the way to the top. Doug took a job working with the ServiceMaster Corporate office, first in Chicago and then in Greensboro, North Carolina, and then in Dallas. Today, he is a partner with two other ServiceMaster friends, owning multiple franchises within the company. We will hear more later from Doug Pound and his unique insights about ServiceMaster that he observed over decades.

Hansen Leaves the Area

The year 1975 involved a significant transition for Ken Hansen and for his wife Jean. They sold their home in Wheaton to Chuck Stair, another long-term executive with ServiceMaster, and they moved into a large apartment in the Wheaton area with plenty of room for Kenny and their youngest child, Linnea. In addition to his responsibility to ServiceMaster, Hansen was also active with Wheaton College. He began working more closely with Billy Graham and was involved in the establishment of the Billy Graham Center there. He also served as vice chairman of the Wheaton College Board of Trustees. Through his involvement with the board, he began working with a young Bill Pollard, who was considering leaving the practice of law to join the leadership team at Wheaton College. Part of Bill's responsibilities would involve working closely with Hansen in the college's investments, finances, and general operations.

Pollard knew Hansen mainly by reputation and, when considering the offer from Wheaton, he said he was not sure he could work with Ken. He expressed this directly to Hudson Taylor Armerding, the president of Wheaton College from 1965 to 1982. The way Hansen worked this out said a great deal about him and his leadership.

When Bill returned to his office from his discussion with Armerding, he received a phone call from Hansen. In his typically abrupt manner, Ken said, "This is Ken Hansen. When do you go home from work today?" When Pollard replied between 5:30 and 6:00, Hansen said, "Can you meet me in the president's office at 6:15?"[57] When Pollard agreed, Hansen hung up the phone. After introductions in the president's office, Hansen handed Pollard an envelope that contained his letter of resignation from the Board of Trustees at Wheaton. Hansen then asked, "Will this satisfy you?"[58]

This striking gesture made it clear that Ken Hansen wanted Bill Pollard at Wheaton more than he wanted to be on the board, and it led to a discussion on how they might possibly work together. After coming to an agreement, Ken said, "Bill, I can't change the way I am, but if I ever get in your way, you have to kick me in the shins." Pollard later said, "Although there were times I felt like kicking him, they always turned out to be important times of learning."[59] Needless to say, he took the position at Wheaton.

About twenty years later in 1994, Pollard would speak at Hansen's memorial service:

> Ken Hansen and I had a very special relationship. We had grown to understand each other so that we could anticipate our thoughts and reactions, and we sensed from time to time a communication between us that did not require words. It was a communication of mind and spirit.[60]

At the end of 1976, Ken Hansen had a serious heart attack and, based on the doctor's advice, Ken and Jean decided to move to a warmer climate. In March 1977, they relocated to the Santa Barbara area.

Ken Hansen's Book

In the late 1970s or early 1980s, Ken Hansen wrote a short booklet (sixteen pages) titled *Reality: That Which Gives Purpose, Zest and Motive Power to Life*.[61] Ken had created a painting where he depicted his view of reality, and the book is an explanation of the painting. He had found that painting was a way he could express himself, and so he began sketching and experimenting through much of the 1960s. But in 1968, on a family vacation in Austria, he was inspired to create the painting that had been in his mind for a long time (an image of the painting appears in the photo section).

Several key observations from this booklet offer insight into Hansen and ServiceMaster. In the painting are the numbers "1 & 2." These refer to the first two statements of the Westminster Confession of Faith (a "widely used catechism"): "The Chief end of man is to glorify God and enjoy Him forever, and The Bible is the primary means of knowing God." From these, he concluded, "When a man enjoys God, the right and good ideas and experiences are richer; the wrong and destructive are antithetical to this enjoyment." He used green in his painting to describe his growth as a manager:

> When I moved from selling and accounting into managing, I was primarily task oriented as I worked with others. But as I grew in a vital union with Jesus, I came to see that I was viewing people as a means to get work done. I viewed work as the end accomplished. I realized that I was reversing the positions of means and ends which the Bible teaches. . . . Such changing is not easy. I am committed to using work to help people develop rather than to use people to accomplish the work as the end.

He also had the Greek letters "ΔΛK" in his painting, meaning "changers of ServiceMaster." When Hansen finished his MBA, he developed a formal training and development program for the company, creating a leadership organization that included designated leader-managers who were responsible for the strategic direction of the company.

Hansen also added a great deal of red in his painting, representing stress:

> I have learned many important lessons through stress. Trouble and problems bring pain. I listen more attentively to God and to others when in such pain. This listening helps me to face the realities of life rather than to yield to dreaming about make believe situations, or covering up mistakes and wrongs, or blaming others.

He also used the color black to represent failure. Failures of judgment, he wrote, "should be faced openly (not covered up) and then put out of one's memory bank." Playing off a famous quote by G. K. Chesterton, Hansen often said, "Anything worth doing is worth doing poorly—to get started. You have to get started, and some people spend forever studying something than simply getting started."[62]

To Ken Hansen, a second kind of failure is one of motive—that is, doing something with bad intent. This kind requires forgiveness by God and others. In the foreword to *Reality*, Ken Wessner wrote of Hansen:

Twenty-five years ago, he recruited me to join this unique company, and since that time we have developed a close friendship. Through the years I have witnessed his love and concern for others. . . . Ken is a perceptive and able thinker with the ability to teach with excitement and vitality. He communicates whether he is in a university classroom, a ServiceMaster seminar, or a mission class in South America or Africa. . . . The driving force in ServiceMaster for many years was Ken Hansen. His vision, aspiration, values, and commitment have their mark upon what ServiceMaster is today and what it will be tomorrow. The catalyst and motivating force in Ken Hansen's life is his vital relationship to God through a personal faith in Jesus Christ. Ken reflects God's love through his daily life. He is a servant-leader and a career builder for many in ServiceMaster. This is my friend, Ken Hansen.

Continued Involvement

Because of their involvement with ServiceMaster and Wheaton College back in Illinois, the Hansens kept an apartment in Wheaton for a time. Hansen described their years in Santa Barbara as happy ones, even though in 1980 he had surgery for the replacement of his aorta valve. He remained an active influence in the company for many more years as a board member, continuing to play a strong role in the growth and development of the company.

One example of this involves Doug Pound, who had met Hansen at his company interview in 1974. Doug had moved from Chicago to Greensboro to Dallas, and in 1979 was given the opportunity to own half the distributorship for ServiceMaster in Santa Barbara, California. The only problem was that he didn't have any money. Since Hansen was in Santa Barbara, Pound set up a meeting to explore the possibilities with him in person. Over the first five years of his time with ServiceMaster, Doug had proven himself by successfully carrying out some difficult assignments. Pound described how Hansen helped him:

> Ken got very creative in structuring a deal, fully legal but complicated, allowing me to buy the franchise. I had the opportunity to engage Ken Hansen in meeting with new franchise owners over the years as we grew the number of franchises from twenty to one hundred and twenty-five. It was a unique opportunity for me in Southern California, and a unique opportunity for our franchise owners to engage in this way, and it continued into the 1990s.[63]

Ken also continued to serve in other ways. Wes and Barb Mitchell themselves longtime ServiceMaster leaders, recall one incident at a dinner meeting at a restaurant with the Hansens:

A waitress spilled a whole tray of food by their table. By the time I realized what was happening, Ken Hansen was already down on the floor picking up all this stuff. . . . Needless to say all the employees in the restaurant were very impressed. Later, the waiters came to the table and one of us said, "You probably don't know this, but the man who cleaned the carpet for you is chairman of the board of a Fortune 500 company."[64]

Hansen Later Years

Ken Hansen had truly come to see his work in business as Christian ministry. On March 21, 1986, Ken wrote to the Alumni Association at Wheaton College, "Our business has been one major outlet for our ministry."

By 1988, Ken and Jean had made the decision to sell their home in Montecito and move into a reconstructed apartment at Samarkand, a Christian retirement community close to their home. The reconstruction took many months, which meant that their new home would not be ready until the end of March 1989. As the day of the move finally approached, Jean became seriously ill and was rushed to the local hospital. Her heart was failing, and in the afternoon of April 1 she left this life and went to be with her Lord and Savior.

When Samarkand was finally completed, Ken and Kenny moved in without Jean. Hansen's conclusion to this sad departure of his wife was, "'Tis Jesus the first and the last whose spirit will guide us safely home, we will praise Him for all that is past and trust Him for all that is to come."

In the last years of his life, Hansen would enjoy multiple honors. In 1991, he was elected to the American Business Hall of Fame, along with colleagues Marion Wade and Ken Wessner. In 1993, he received the Distinguished Service to Society award from Wheaton College.

He was also a generous man with both his time and his resources. He was involved with teaching overseas and served on many boards, and he also taught Sunday school and ran book discussion groups in his home. He was a key donor and instigator for both the Billy Graham Center scholarship program and the Marion E. Wade Center at Wheaton College. In his generosity, he still remained focused and frugal. The archives at the Billy Graham Center contain correspondence from 1984 between Ken Hansen and Wheaton College, in which he ensured that the funding he provided would be directed exclusively toward programs that Hansen wanted to support.[65]

In his last years, Hansen continued to make a contribution to ServiceMaster through his counsel as chairman (1973–81), vice chairman (1981–87), and director emeritus and adviser (1987–94) of the board of directors. The transition in 1981 is worthy of special note. In 1981, when a new CEO was hired, Ken Hansen stepped aside as chairman of the board so that Ken Wessner could move into this position.

In 1993, both Ken Hansen and Ken Wessner experienced serious health issues and died in 1994. At Hansen's memorial service on May 14, 1994, Bill Pollard said, "He fanned into a flame the gift that God had given him and reminded us all that this gift was not a spirit of timidity, but a spirit of power of love and of self-discipline."[66]

4

THE KEN WESSNER YEARS

In the summer of 1954, I met two men of vision who shared with me their dreams for their business. Marion Wade and Ken Hansen were leading a business with about $1 million of revenue. I felt drawn to share this life ministry—using this business as a vehicle. However, there were negatives.[1]

Having worked since 1946 with the Club Aluminum Products Company, Ken Wessner had advanced beyond general sales to a point where he could pursue his marketing specialty. Now that he was married and was responsible for his young family, he wondered if he should step back and hope for a bigger opportunity with The ServiceMaster Company and its compelling vision.

Ken had built a strong foundation for ethical business working with Herbert Taylor, the president at Club Aluminum. Taylor had taken on a failing company and introduced both a strong attention to ethics and a process orientation to business that were instrumental in raising the company from the ashes. Taylor's strong commitment to ethical business was embodied in a Four-Way Test he developed and applied in the company as an ethics test:

1. Is it the truth?
2. Is it fair to all concerned?
3. Will it build goodwill and better friendships?
4. Will it be beneficial to all concerned?

This code was later adopted by Rotary International and is still used today. This work shaped Ken Wessner's view of ethics before he came to ServiceMaster.

Taylor also developed a process orientation to planning and execution, which focused on the use of data. His simple Four-Way Plan ("Get the Facts! Plan with the Facts! Sell the Plan! Follow Through!") represented a step-by-step process for planning and execution that became foundational for Wessner. It turned out that Ken Hansen also knew Herbert Taylor through youth group connections and had already adopted his Four-Way Plan as a strategy development tool in ServiceMaster.

This background prepared Wessner as a good fit for ServiceMaster, but should he take this step? "For me," he said, "this was a 'stretching' decision, but I accepted the challenge."[2] As in real life for all of us, there are good and bad choices. Although this one worked out well in the end, there were times when it looked like it might have been a mistake. As it turned out, Hansen was hiring his replacement, though neither of them realized this at the time. Wessner stepped into his leadership role, rather vaguely defined at first, in 1954.

Wessner Early Days

Kenneth T. Wessner was born on May 1, 1922, the first of two sons, to Thomas and Carrie (Whitmoyer) Wessner in Sinking Spring, Pennsylvania, about seventy miles northwest of Philadelphia and just outside of Reading.[3] His brother, Wayne, was born two years later. Ken grew up poor, but as he said, "so was everybody else in our neighborhood." During the hardest years until high school in 1936, "I had only one shirt to wear, but it was always clean. My mother would wash, dry, and iron it each night and have it ready for me to wear the next day."

He learned important lessons about integrity and high standards from his parents, who he characterized as people of their word. "My mother and father were one hundred percent honest in their dealings, and they paid all of their bills on time. Their example of this kind of discipline has had a lasting influence on my life." Through observation and practice, he also learned the importance and dignity of hard work. Reflecting on that time, he came to a thoughtful conclusion about work: "Work does not bring dignity to the individual, but the individual brings dignity to the work."

As a boy, he took care of a large yard and garden that provided both beauty and food for the family. The garden had enough vegetables for them to eat all year because of his mother's canning skills. He was not paid for the work, but he learned through it the principle of discipline and shared responsibility. "We were a true family unit, and everyone was important."

His father was a garment worker who sewed ladies corsets for a company in Reading. From his father, he learned about attitude. He recalled that when he was only five or six years old, he told his father that he couldn't do something because he was only a boy. His father sat him down at the table and said, "Yes, that's true, but you are an American." He then took a piece of paper and wrote on it: AMER-I-CAN. "When you are an American, you always say, 'I can.'" That simple lesson instilled a spirit and mind-set of "I can do it" that "has served me well throughout life." Later, when Ken graduated from high school, he identified one of his irks as "pessimists." He also learned about handling money from his father, playing games of making change with real dollars and coins. Then his father taught him, through games, to use these coins to buy and sell things, teaching him the difference between spending and investing. Perhaps this was the foundation for his high school ambition: to be a business executive.

It was his mother who always encouraged him to excel, planting in him a sense of pride. He described her this way:

> She believed in me, and her confidence generated my self-confidence. My mother always had a vision for the future, and she was always looking on the bright side. She could think, plan, and talk about the better things to come. At the same time, she was very practical and realized that only with work and commitment would a dream become reality. Her positive attitude was contagious and has influenced me throughout my entire life. I, too, have become a visionary and have dreamed dreams, but at the same time I've been aware of the work commitment necessary to accomplish the goals I set.[4]

During his teenage years, his mother made a confession of faith in Jesus Christ as her personal savior. "This good woman became a godly woman," he recalled, and she had a profound influence on her husband and sons through her lived example.

> Numerous times, for instance, she welcomed into our home a boy who was beaten by his drunken father. She also cared for her sick stepmother—who had greatly mistreated my mother in earlier years—during the last years of her stepmother's life. My mother did what she thought she ought to do, and that went beyond what she was expected to do because she had a special love for God and for people. My mother's life gave me a service attitude in my thoughts and actions.

Because of the example of his mother, his father, brother, and he all became followers of Christ.

> This new dimension of our family had a far greater influence than any other lesson my parents taught me. My decisions and actions became Christ-centered and gave every word and action greater value.[5]

By the time he entered high school in 1936, the family was a bit better off economically. He still worked hard, but he had room for a variety of activities, including his role as staff reporter for *The Spectator* (his high school newspaper), band, and Hi-Y Chaplain. The 1940 Wilson High School yearbook states that the "Hi-Y was a club whose primary purpose was to create, maintain, and extend throughout the school and community high standards of Christian character." He also was active in sports including soccer, track, basketball, and baseball.

In basketball, he played guard, forward, and center, and was the third highest scorer on the team, scoring eighty-two points his senior year. He also played baseball, leading to the thrill of his career when he pitched a no-hit, no-run game. Although the yearbook did not show evidence of this team, he reported this in his high school highlights. Karen Troutman, public relations director for Wilson High School, suggests that he may have played for a team outside of the school.[6] He was good enough to receive an offer from the St. Louis Cardinals professional baseball team, but he decided not to take that direction. He and Marion Wade, however, later teamed up to make a powerful battery *in business*—and, according to Wessner's son, David, they did have conversations about baseball once he started working at ServiceMaster.

The one-word description of him in the yearbook was "handsome." And one of the irks he described there was "chemistry tests." Apparently, he did all right in chemistry in spite of this because he went on to develop research at ServiceMaster, including hiring PhD chemists. Years later, reflecting on those high school years, Wessner said, "If I were to list the ten people who had the greatest influence on my life, one would be my high school coach, Walt Risley. He taught me to win. I am thankful for the opportunities that have been mine to win at team sports."[7]

In 1940, he went to Kings College in Belmar, New Jersey, about 125 miles from home. After the first year of college, he made the decision to transfer to Wheaton College in Wheaton, Illinois—more than 700 miles from home. His parents still had limited means, so they gave him $100 and he hitchhiked to Wheaton, arriving more than a week after classes had started in the fall of 1941. With special dispensation from President V. Raymond Edman, he was able to enroll and start classes.

At Wheaton College, he joined the class of 1944 and met a classmate, Norma Cook, his future wife. While at Wheaton he majored in economics, served as advertising manager for *The Tower* (the Wheaton College yearbook), lettered in baseball, and was a member of the "W" club. A prominent picture in the yearbook shows "Big Ken Wessner pouring a fastball through the middle." And he spent "many hours" working in the dining hall (he estimated thirty-two hours per week) to pay for his schooling.

World War II, however, interrupted his graduation plans. On February 7, 1943, he entered the United States Army Air Forces[8] as a captain, stationed at the Navy Yard in Charleston, South Carolina.[9] He was in the service for three years. His résumé shows time at the Boca Raton Radar School (Florida), the Charmite Field Electronics School (Illinois), the Truax Radio School (Wisconsin), and the Sioux Falls Radio School (South Dakota). On January 25, 1945, Ken and Norma were married while Ken was still in the army. Norma had graduated with her class in 1944.

In January 1946, Ken and Norma returned to Illinois so Ken could complete his schooling at Wheaton College. He needed to apply again, and he received a letter from the director of admissions with a challenge:

> This letter is to confirm your admission to Wheaton College for the second semester of 1945–46. If for any reason you have changed your plans and

do not wish to enter at this time, please let us know at once in order that some other worthy student may be offered this opportunity.

We trust that you will do your very best to vindicate this expression of our confidence in you at this time when many must be rejected, and trust that your work here may be a real credit both to yourself and to the College.

Albert S. Nichols
College Examiner and Director of Admissions

He graduated in January 1947 and included some course work through correspondence to complete graduation requirements.

After graduating, Ken went to work for the Club Aluminum Products Company. For three and a half years, he was a district manager and handled assignments in Chicago, Cincinnati, and Minneapolis. Then he moved into the home office as sales promotion manager of their Food Store Division, and the family moved to Arlington Heights, Illinois. During this time, Ken and Norma had two children, Barbara (born 1948) and David (born 1951). While at Club Aluminum, Ken also became involved in other service work as business manager of the *Wheaton College Alumni News* and as a member of the Gideons.

Early Days at ServiceMaster

When Wessner started working at ServiceMaster in the fall of 1954, his first assignment (of course) was to work in the cleaning services of the company. As a hard worker, he did the work willingly, and it helped him get a sense of the labor and the life of the average worker in the company. The experience shaped his leadership.

Then he was given responsibility to grow the franchise business for the company, with the western states as his territory. For two years, although he was successful by most measures, he never saw his family. He would travel for two weeks, be home for a weekend and then back on the road again. His daughter Barbara remembers that, on those rare weekends when her father was home, she and her brother would go over to their grandparents' home so her parents could get reacquainted. She hardly saw him.

Wessner made two adjustments in his approach to work. One decision related to his family.

My wife, Norma, was going through a crisis period of poor health. Our daughter, Barbara, was twelve years old, and our son, David, was nine. There was real strain and stress in our family. We decided to increase our commitment. Our relationship became one of complete commitment to each other. Through this experience, we were drawn closer to each other.

We communicated together better and waited on God together, praying daily for each other, my wife at home and me in a hotel on the road. The times we were together were times of quality, appreciation, and love. We understood each other's conditions better than we understood our own, and we found ways to help each other. Instead of this time being a period of drudgery, discouragement, and resentment, it was a growing experience—very meaningful to our family.[10]

While this effort to improve quality time with the family got them through for a short time, time with the family improved a few years later.

His second adjustment was to understand the nature of his work as ministry. He had taught a class of adults at his church for the previous five years. But he said that in his day job,

I felt that I was an "ambassador" of my Sunday school class and church into the business community, a person with the opportunity to reach out to many people in the business world. There was a great deal of stretch involved, and it was impossible for me to get fully involved in the "reaching out" process to people in both areas. A decision had to be made. It was a hard decision, but the right decision for me then was to resign my class responsibilities and do "missionary" work via my business contacts. This decision, I believe, led to greater Christian maturity than if I had given up my work, sought other employment, and kept the Sunday school class.[11]

One innovation that came from this time was the development of master franchise licenses. The company sold distributorships to individuals who then could, in turn, sell franchises in their regions. The distributorships made their money by earnings from the franchises, selling fees for new franchises, and selling fees for chemicals and equipment supplied to the franchises. The challenge was getting the money flow right.

Bob Groff, who came to the company in the 1970s, was one of the early owners of a distributorship, and researched the history:

The distributor would collect fees but only needed to send $800 per month for each franchise back to the corporate offices. Later, they improved this a bit with $800 plus 1% of revenue. But there was not enough coming into Corporate to support the updating of manuals, the training, and the research.[12]

Ultimately this improved, but it was part of the experimentation to "get it right."

Launching the Hospital Business

In 1957, Marion Wade had been giving a talk in Chicago when he was approached by Sister Mary Asumpta, who worked at a nearby hospital,

Ken Wessner recalled later.[13] She asked Wade, "Why aren't you cleaning hospitals?" When Marion came back from his talk, having written Sister Mary's name and contact information on a piece of paper, he gave the paper to Ken Wessner and said, "Call this sister. She has something to say to us!"[14] That remark launched a discussion between Wade and Ken Hansen on this potential business opportunity. Ken Wessner was initially reluctant, and when asked to join the hospital activity, he responded, "No, Ken, I don't even like hospitals." But once Wessner got engaged in the work, he became enthusiastic about its potential. Between 1957 and 1959, Hansen and Wessner studied the hospital market, trying to understand customer needs. They made numerous hospital visits doing what Hansen called "listening, trying to understand what the customer wanted through understanding and asking questions."[15]

"As we listened, we thought we heard administrators saying that their time could be better used if they could have professional help for some of the more nonpatient-related functions of their hospitals," Hansen said. They heard that the administrators were ready for the services of a specialist organization that would accommodate their needs. At the same time, other companies heard there was going to be a lot of money spent by hospitals for contract housekeeping. Hansen added, "This is not what we heard at all."[16] Others approached this job simply as more buildings to clean.

Initially, ServiceMaster looked into introducing the service in partnership with Crothall, a New Zealand company that was carrying out this service in England.[17] Wessner left for England on January 4, 1962, for three months to observe Crothall's hospital cleaning services. While he learned enough to develop a plan for a partnership, he also identified what he thought was a better way to do that kind of business. Norma joined Ken at the end of the three months, and they enjoyed some much-needed vacation in London, Paris, Germany, and Switzerland before returning home.[18]

Although the proposed joint venture with Crothall did not work out, Wessner had learned enough to recommend that ServiceMaster enter the business on its own. ServiceMaster paid Crothall with stock for what they had learned, though Crothall later entered the US market.[19] ServiceMaster decided to implement the business in its own way. Rather than move all of the housekeeping people to the ServiceMaster payroll, the workers would remain on the hospital payroll. ServiceMaster would develop training and processes and then provide oversight for their work. Hansen and Wade agreed with Wessner and put him in charge of making the sales and delivering the service.

In 1961, Wessner was named vice president of ServiceMaster Industries, Inc., and headed the newly organized hospital service division. The title must have seemed more aspirational than real, since the company didn't land the first customer for the hospital division until the following year.

In early 1962, the lead prospect for the hospital business was Lutheran General Hospital in Chicago. Wessner had made numerous presentations there, and he finally had the opportunity to present the case to the board of directors. While Ken was waiting outside the board room for a decision, one of the board members came out and asked him for a financial statement, and he knew he was in trouble. The company had debt on its books and was in the process of raising capital through its initial stock offering, but there was no explanation of that on the financials. Bill Pollard later reported, "Ken asked if he could go back into the meeting and explain the balance sheet, but the board would not allow a further presentation." Ken found out later that in the midst of the discussion, one of the board members had spoken up in favor of ServiceMaster by saying, "I don't care what is on the balance sheet. I know Ken Wessner, and when he gives his word, he will do the job!" Bill Pollard noted, "Without that meaningful relationship of trust, we would not have made the first sale of what turned out to be a $2 billion dollar business providing opportunity to more than 150,000 people."[20] That contract turned out to be a good deal for the hospital as well as for ServiceMaster. "During the first year of the contract, the hospital reported a 50% drop in bacteria prevalence, thanks to ServiceMaster's leadership."[21]

Ken Hansen told Wessner to develop more contracts in Chicago before taking the business to other areas. This was the key moment for Wessner to be back at home on a regular basis, and this provided the opportunity for him to be with his family, according to daughter Barbara.[22] She recalled that, shortly before this time, he had just about decided to leave ServiceMaster for the sake of the family, because of all the travel. Instead, this work launched his career, changed the course of the company, and improved life in the family.

Marion Wade also had a hand in growing the hospital business. He was a brilliant speaker, but for some reason he was reluctant to speak in front of hospital administrators. Yet Wessner was able to persuade him to lay out the plan and instill confidence in the prospect. Not only did Wade have the oratorical skills, but he also had the right appearance and business experience. As Hansen admiringly put it, "Nothing beats a gray head who has proved himself."[23] So, with plenty of prodding from Wessner, Wade made his appearance, impressed the audience, and let Wessner close the sale. The shingles on the roof continued as the three leaders used their combined strengths to grow the company.

Ken Wessner's stock as a key leader continued to grow, though it was not fully recognized by both Wade and Hansen at the same time. Responding to the question of likely candidates to succeed Hansen as late as the early 1960s, Hansen reflected, "You couldn't tell that Wes would be the next CEO at that point. But he did a towering job and simply outgrew everyone else in the business."[24] It was about this same time in 1963, however, when Hansen became quite ill and Wade turned to Wessner as the next leader of the company. When Hansen recovered, although Wade recognized Wessner as ready, the transition did not happen at this point.

Throughout the 1960s, Wessner expanded the hospital management services business through a hospital survey that identified potential customers, an organized sales effort, educational and training programs, a constant improvement of operating procedures, and a periodic addition of a new service. As the number of customers expanded, Wessner also introduced organizational changes. He divided the country into geographical divisions with a vice president in charge of each region, and he divided the work of the division into three categories: sales, operations, and control. He also began to grow the emphasis on research in order to continue winning hospital contracts based on the ability of ServiceMaster to deliver better results at a lower cost than the hospitals themselves. They looked at processes, tools, and chemicals as elements of achieving the results, and they also further developed their employee training programs. By 1971, revenue from the hospital business had grown to $35 million, which was a significant part of the total revenue of $44.7 million for the company that year.[25]

In the winter of 1971, Ken and Jean Hansen asked Norma and Ken Wessner to meet them on the island of Grenada in the Caribbean. Wessner recalled:

> We thought it was for a few days of vacation, but Ken soon told us he was asking me to leave the hospital business and become Executive Vice President and Chief Operating Officer for ServiceMaster. Frankly, I did not want to leave the hospital business, nor did Norma. I loved my work, found fulfillment and joy in it. Both Norma and I experienced pain as we talked and prayed together. I told Ken I would accept the responsibility on the basis that I would be serving others in our company. I set up my office in the back area next to the Board Room, and most of my work was done away from my office—in other managers' offices and in the field. There was a joy in serving and helping others.[26]

Two years later in 1973, Ken Hansen stepped into the role of chairman of the board when Marion Wade died. Wessner was put in charge of the company, first as president and later on January 1, 1976, as CEO.

Finalizing the Objectives

For many years, the leaders of the company had been tweaking and refining the objectives of the company. They went from one, "To Honor God in the Marketplace," to three in the Wade years:[27]

1. To Honor God in the Marketplace
2. To Provide a Good Living for Many People
3. To Help People to Grow

By 1967, they had six objectives:

1. Honor God
2. Good Corporate Citizen
3. Market Oriented
4. Results Oriented
5. People Oriented
6. Growth Oriented

In addition, there were numerous subpoints under each one. While they captured what the company wanted to do, they were not sharp enough or memorable enough.[28]

In 1973, Ken Wessner gave a talk to a group of hospital executives, with Hansen present, in which he listed four goals. Afterward, Hansen excitedly pulled Wessner aside and said, "That's it! But we'll have to change the order." In his presentation, Wessner had stated the objectives with the first one at the end. Later they referred to the first two as end goals and the last two (excellence and profitability) as the means to achieve the end goals. Those four goals, in Hansen's revised order, remained the objectives of the company for the rest of the century. This doesn't mean that they remained static. As these were lived out in the company in a changing culture and business environment, they continually took on new focus and meaning, and they still continue as the objectives for many current ServiceMaster franchises:

1. To Honor God in All We Do
2. To Help People Develop
3. To Pursue Excellence
4. To Grow Profitably

Holding the Objectives in Tension

There was no simple resolution of the tension between the four objectives, but there was a requirement to weigh people, growth, excellence, and profit while being grounded in honoring God. Financial pressures might push the leader to set aside the ideals of valuing the worker. Excellence might be challenged by cost. The high standard of honoring God in all you do might create tension in the nitty-gritty reality of the business. But because there is tension, there is the need to hold the objectives together, ignoring the easy path of picking one over the other. An emphasis in one area doesn't mean ignoring another. Malcom Guite talked about this kind of tension related to virtues: "Virtues are not a rulebook, but more like a country dance. First one virtue takes the lead, and then another."[29] This is the way the leaders sought to carry out the objectives.

Ken Wessner and the other leaders would quickly tell you that the leaders, and others in the company, didn't always find the right balance. But they did seek it. And when they found themselves out of balance, they tried to regain that balance.

Challenging Times

Though ServiceMaster was a thriving, publicly traded company in 1973, this was a difficult period of time in the United States. The Vietnam War was raging, and the country was in one of the two worst recession of the last half of the twentieth century. Technically, the recession was between November 1973 and March 1975, though unemployment hit its peak of 9 percent in May 1975. In addition to the war, three key external events seemed to drive this recession: the price of oil quadrupled; wage and price controls led to high prices, which reduced demand; and the country went off the gold standard, which drove inflation.[30]

Although this period could have been a time of great uncertainty for the company as well, it was not. As Wessner and Hansen adjusted to new roles and this external turmoil played out, the company continued to grow. Just as in the previous transition, Ken Wessner stepped strongly into his new leadership role, providing new ideas at just the right time. Ken Hansen continued to play a significant part from his chairman role, creating strength, not competition. Similar to when Ken Hansen took the lead, Wessner did not simply "carry on" but rather "built on."

He started with a strategy for growth and then focused on ways to achieve it. He uniquely brought a strong process orientation to the company long before most companies recognized this need.[31] He invested in research to establish these processes, and then added an emphasis on training that allowed people to flourish in their work and customers to benefit from better work at lower cost. His execution of these activities proved themselves in results.

Figures 4.1 and 4.2 below capture the revenue and profit growth over Wessner's tenure when revenue grew from $86 million to $700 million and profit grew from $2.2 million to $25.6 million.

Strategy for Growth

Ken Wessner believed in the mission of the company and its foundation in the four objectives. While giving a commencement address at Trinity

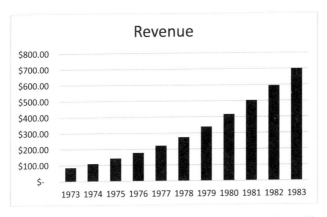

Figure 4.1. Revenue under Wessner (dollars shown in millions).[32]

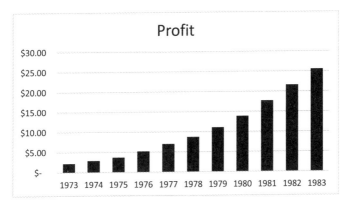

4.2. Profit under Wessner (dollars shown in millions).[33]

Western University some years later, he stated, "We must be prepared and willing to change anything in our business except our values."[34] In keeping with the four objectives, like his predecessors, he saw the need for growth rooted in creating opportunity for the people of the organization. He also continued to build on the strong business foundation that Ken Hansen had laid. In each of these areas, he lived the foundations of the company and talked about them at every opportunity. In the spirit of Marion Wade, "If you don't live it, you don't believe it."

ServiceMaster needed to grow profitably, so Ken Wessner followed a structured process to figure out the best approach, much as he had in developing the hospital business. He laid out four choices in a two-by-two matrix following an approach from Ansoff.[35] The two axes were "expertise" (current and new) and "markets" (current and new) as shown below in Figure 4.3.

Figure 4.3. Ansoff expansion opportunities from current market and expertise to three other options.

Wessner decided to apply company expertise to new markets rather than try to develop new expertise. With the great success of the hospital market for cleaning and support services, the leadership team chose to stay with cleaning and support services and apply this to expanded hospital services, educational institutions, and ultimately businesses. As a result, several large contracts followed, including one with Duke University. Wessner was positive about the potential for growth, but he "felt a strong sense of limits about what the company could do." There is little doubt that this was based, in large part, on the difficult period the company had gone through with the losses associated with acquisitions outside the expertise of management. According to researcher Laura Nash, "It also is consistent with the evangelical emphasis on fiscal conservatism and the tangible creation of value."[36]

Wessner did not achieve this growth by accident (considering the times the country was in at the start of his tenure) or simply by hard work. He developed and nurtured the processes and discipline of the company through succession planning and recruitment, research, training, and management processes.

Growth of the Business

For much of Wessner's tenure, ServiceMaster achieved its growth through the hospital business. The company not only grew the number of hospitals it served, but it also added new kinds of services to its hospital offerings. "We began in housekeeping in 1962," Wessner recalled. "We added laundry management in 1967, and then followed with plant operations and maintenance in 1971. Clinical equipment or biomedical equipment came in '75, and material management in 1978."[37]

In the fall of 1981, the company added food services when it acquired Service Direction, a company with $4.6 million in revenues. Although food service had been part of the plan for the company's initial hospital offering, it had a few failed attempts to add this service through acquisition in the past. Service Direction was the first successful acquisition for the company. "Bill Pollard was the lead executive on this acquisition," according to Patricia Asp, who came to be a part of The ServiceMaster Company through this door. That spurred a growth for women in leadership. "I was the only female executive as a member of the Delta Group (an internal executive group)[38] for what I thought at the time was longer than I should have been. And my husband was the only male spouse. So, it was an interesting contrast to being in the very diverse environment of Service Direction."[39]

By 1983, ServiceMaster's healthcare management offerings included laundry and linen services, physical plant operations and maintenance, clinical equipment maintenance, materials maintenance, and the fledgling food services sector, in addition to its traditional housekeeping services. Of the six divisions, housekeeping, laundry, and plant operations provided the bulk of the company's revenues. While the company sought to sell multiple services to each hospital, most of its clients contracted for one or two of the services offered. Initial contracts were set for two years to make the company's initial investment in a project worthwhile. It then began a process of cross-training workers across these services, which allowed for increased efficiency.

In May 1983, ServiceMaster signed its first contract to supervise home healthcare, in which hospital patients were discharged before their care was entirely complete as a cost-reducing measure. Also in that month, the company signed up a large hospital chain, Voluntary Hospitals of America, for its standard management and housekeeping services, adding 135 new locations to its tally. Fees from contracted services, primarily to hospitals, made up about 97 percent of the company's revenues, with the remainder derived from franchisees that paid the company a monthly fee and purchased equipment and supplies from it.[40]

As its service package to hospitals had grown to include most of the support services performed in hospitals, the company's managers increasingly sought to become regarded as members of their respective customer's management team. Through this process, ServiceMaster was able to influence customers' decisions in ways that made their hospitals cleaner, safer, and more congenial places for them to carry out their primary objective of effective healthcare.[41]

In 1981, ServiceMaster also began offering its services to industrial customers with more than one thousand employees and factories larger than one million square feet. Back in the early 1960s, when the company started the hospital business, it had tried to offer services to businesses as well. But that strategy had failed. Now it focused on larger businesses and gained traction. The first customers in this division were Appleton Electric in Chicago and Motorola in Franklin Park, Illinois. Both of these moves helped to broaden the company's potential customer base and insulate it somewhat from factors that might affect the healthcare industry.

In 1981, ServiceMaster expanded into educational business in a way that demonstrates the limits of corporate planning and another value of empowering workers. One of the ServiceMaster managers in Pennsylvania, Rich Williams, was also on the local school board with one of his healthcare customers. This customer "requested for Rich to make a proposal to the school district for ServiceMaster to provide the same quality and results that were being provided to his hospital." Rich developed the idea with his boss, Stew Stambaugh, "to expand our plant operations and cleaning services to colleges, universities, and school districts." Bill Pollard didn't offer them much encouragement. "We were too busy with our own planning, listening to ourselves and not the customer," Bill recalled. They sent them back to "stick to their knitting, to continue to develop the healthcare market before us, and to let us at corporate get on with the strategic planning process."[42]

But Rich and Stew did not take no for the final answer. Although they did go back to their work, according to Bill Pollard, "they had grown up in an environment that encouraged them to continue to press their ideas and not give up on the process of selling their bosses on something their customer needed." Then Rich came back with a proposal where "he offered to put his entire annual compensation at risk if, at the end of one year, he could not sell at least four school districts with all of them running on a profitable basis."[43]

Stew and Rich not only accomplished their objectives, Pollard wrote, but they also "opened a market that has become one of our major sources of growth, now serving over 350 colleges, universities, and school districts with an annualized revenue in excess of $400 million."[44]

The additions of both industrial and academic customers represented an expansion of the original plan Wessner had laid out. They were now operating in the fourth quadrant of Figure 4.3: a new market with current expertise.

International Growth

ServiceMaster continued to develop internationally as well, and it began serving hospitals in Japan in 1981 and Canada in 1982.

Chapter 3 introduced Bisher Mufti when he was hired from his position as a housekeeper at West Suburban Hospital in Oak Park, Illinois, and he was given the opportunity to grow, which included managing hospitals for ServiceMaster in the early 1970s. In 1983, Mufti was given the responsibility to launch ServiceMaster Jordan. Before going to Jordan, he was called into Ken Wessner's office for a discussion. "How will you handle this assignment representing ServiceMaster there, since you will be a long way away?" Wessner asked him. As a Muslim, Mufti had a different religious view from Wessner that affected the first objective. Mufti's response was straightforward: "The company is built on the four objectives. These shape every decision. I know and believe in the objectives, knowing they are the soul of the company. I will make decisions based on these." Wessner smiled and replied, "That is exactly what we have done to build the company."[45]

After six years in Jordan, Bisher became an international vice president, working closely with Brian Oxley, who had worked in ServiceMaster Japan and was vice president in Asia. By the time Bisher retired from ServiceMaster in 2015, completing a forty-six-year career, he was president of International Operations.[46]

Growing ServiceMaster Japan

Meanwhile, Phil Foxwell, a young man just two months from college graduation, was called in for a meeting with Ken Wessner. This sparked a conversation that led Phil to his first full-time job after college with ServiceMaster. He had some early ties to the company, since his father had been a roommate of Ken Hansen at Wheaton College. "I used to call him Uncle Ken," Foxwell said.[47] Over the next decade (though Foxwell said, "I actually spent two decades working for ServiceMaster, since I worked two shifts every day"), he spent most of his time developing relationships, growing ServiceMaster offerings, and developing the ServiceMaster business in Japan. His growing young family was another part of his responsibility there in Japan.

When Foxwell first left for Japan, his manager, Dick Armstrong, had told him he would be there for two to three years. "There will be no financial support for home visits during that time," Armstrong warned him. ServiceMaster was continuing its frugal ways. Foxwell would have to buy his own plane ticket to visit his extended family in the States during his vacations, which he did.

Most of the business was developing agreements with other Japanese companies, and these companies paid a fee to deliver the products of the company, starting with hospital services. Developing the hospital market was different in Japan at that time. There were no standards for cleanliness in the early 1980s, and there were some strong cultural differences between Japan and the United States. "We made some of the traditional mistakes in developing the business," Foxwell said. "Starting to work with one company and then moving to another is a problem for a face-saving culture, and we had to learn the hard way. But I got an education in doing business cross-culturally that has created a business opportunity for me ever since." Throughout Foxwell's time at ServiceMaster, "Ken Hansen, even in retirement, continued to send wise words of encouragement and challenge while I was launching a wide array of business in Asia."[48]

Research

ServiceMaster already had a long history with research, going back to Marion Wade's work in developing both moth-proofing and carpet-cleaning solutions. Although Ken Hansen carried on this work with limited resources during the dramatic growth under Ken Wessner, the company wanted to focus more in this area as it was a key to the growth of the hospital business.

In 1977, Wessner made another key hire, bringing in Bill Bond as the new director of research. Bond's job was to create new ways to achieve both greater efficiency and higher quality in housekeeping work. His team included chemists and process engineers, about ten to twelve people in all.

Bond focused the research in three key areas, with emphasis on relevance to the mission of ServiceMaster. One of the housekeeping tasks was polishing floors in the operating rooms and hallways of hospitals. The process involved stripping the old finish, cleaning the floor, and then polishing. One innovation from the lab was a new polish that would last twice as long, thus reducing the time needed to do the process. This idea depended on the work of the chemists, in the spirit of Marion Wade's research.[49] Other chemical research was grounded in the company's deep understanding of its hospital customers. For example, Alex Balc, vice president for Corporate Development, pointed to the specific development of chemicals for the hospital business:

> There is no one else, to my knowledge, who designs products just to fit a work process to serve healthcare institutions. Others develop product for the broad market, but we differentiated ourselves and concentrated our technical and chemical specialists as part of a management process, not as part of a product promotion business.[50]

A second development started with the mop itself. One problem with the old mop was that it required workers to bend over, which was hard on their backs and didn't allow them to look other people in the eye. This was important to ServiceMaster both for workplace safety and for the dignity of the worker. The mop was also heavy, which added to these back problems.

So, the research department experimented with synthetic fibers to replace the wood handle, creating a mop that was taller, lighter, and easier to use. They also put a clip on the mop that enabled workers to detach the mop from the handle without bending over or getting their hands dirty on the wet mop. The motivation here was treating those who did the work with respect. As in the case of chemicals, the products were developed to support the company's services and were not for general sale. "It is our ultimate objective not to sell products," said Wessner, "but to provide service."[51]

Third, the process engineers looked carefully at the way traditional mopping was done and determined it was inefficient. They developed an S-pattern of mopping that did a better job with less effort. They also determined how big the mopping region should be. They were concerned with more than appearance. In the laboratory, they determined that "most germs are carried by dust," Wessner said. For the hospitals, they developed a dry-mopping system that "first helps remove dust and bacteria from the floor of a hospital room. Then a ServiceMaster buffing machine, working with a sanitizing floor finish, produces a polished, long-lasting surface. With our system, the heat from the buffing actually kills germs."[52]

According to Bond, all of these innovations were motivated by the company's four objectives.[53] The leaders of the company genuinely believed and lived the objectives, he said, and these things were done not just for the bottom line (the fourth objective of profit), but out of respect for the workers and a desire to do a superior job for their customers.

By 1985, the research staff had grown to eighteen employees including two people with PhDs.[54] The company not only made this investment in research, but it also touted it to analysts and customers. In a 1978 presentation to the New York Society of Security Analysts, Bill Pollard stated,

> Quality cannot be maintained; it must be constantly improved. And this is the reason we are making investments in research and development of work processes, products, and new equipment. One of our recent introductions is an item we refer to as a Sani-rinse dispenser. If you saw it today, you might say that it is a rather simple device. It dispenses cleaning solution on a measured basis directly to the mop head. Although it may look simple, it will make a significant difference in our business because it resolves the problems which were created by new environmental standards and avoids the costly double-bucket solution. It also reduces waste in the use of cleaning products. As a result, we have a cleaner floor, with less labor and less product used.[55]

The authors of *Service Breakthroughs* interviewed customers of ServiceMaster, and this is what they concluded:

> Through the years, this company has built competitive advantage, not only by assembling information about cleaning tasks and developing in-

formation systems for staffing and work allocation on individual jobs, but also by developing superior methods and materials in its laboratories. For washing windows, the company replaces ladders with specially designed, light-weight, long-handled squeegees using easy-to-remove Velcro-backed washable cleaning cloths soaked between uses in fluids developed in ServiceMaster laboratories. This probably explains why ServiceMaster's chairman, Kenneth Wessner, is so enthusiastic about giving a short lecture on the ServiceMaster method for washing a window or mopping a floor. The enthusiasm suggests the source of continuing support for the laboratory's budget.[56]

Eating Their Own Cooking

ServiceMaster developed a series of leadership principles to codify the practices they had been following over the years (see Appendix 1). The third one was, "We eat our own cooking. We bet the egg money on our own performance." They did at the company what they did for their customers, from tools and products to practices. So, ServiceMaster used its own products for cleaning and for support of its own buildings.

Beyond this, the company tried to make its beliefs visible to employees and customers when they visited the company. In her book *Believers in Business*, Laura Nash cited two examples of what was visible in the company:

When Ken Wessner showed me around ServiceMaster headquarters, for example, he stopped to point out a window between the cafeteria and the kitchen. He said, "We put that in because we think it's a good idea in food service. A window helps remind everyone about the importance of cleanliness to customers."

Then she observed that "even the pictures on the office wall demand attention. An oil portrait of the three successive chairmen of the firm at the headquarters building includes their spouses—a decision made with great deliberation, according to Wessner."[57] Throughout its history, ServiceMaster was more than a job; it was a family affair. The pictures echoed that.

Training

ServiceMaster impacted the lives of employees and customers, as well as the bottom line, by delivering efficient service with motivated, well-trained workers. Executing this mission for a growing, more diverse customer set required careful attention to providing training and development for its people. As new services were added and as new techniques were developed in research, the company needed to make sure that the people of the organization were able to deliver this value to the customers. In this, training was key.

Ken Wessner quoted Marion Wade when he said, "Don't expect to build a super company with super people. You must build a great company with ordinary people." Then Wessner added, "That's our job; that's our responsibility: to build winning teams with ordinary people. Our great need for the future in ServiceMaster is the building of winning teams—teams that will perform and produce increased results quarter after quarter, year after year."[58]

Ken Wessner had a passion for training. As he described it:

Every person that comes under our influence is in a training program. . . . First there is one-on-one training and then small groups. There are filmstrips, cassettes, and manuals. For the workers in hospitals, it is done, not only in English, but also in Spanish and in Polish. The level of training continues throughout the whole organization until you get to the most advanced training program, which is our own in-house MBA. It is a complete course in management leadership. We avail ourselves of the best professors in their disciplines throughout the Chicago area. We have professors from the leading universities who teach the subjects. They are the same subjects one would study in an MBA program, with strong emphasis on human relations and labor relations.

Our divisional officers and others in top management have completed this course. We've had 37 people complete it, and we have a current class of another 18. This program runs for about four years. We intend to continue it in order to train our managers and be able to handle the expanded business that we are experiencing. It's important, and we believe in it.[59]

While professors were brought in to ServiceMaster to deliver some of the training, the top leaders participated as well. Ken Wessner described his own role in training:

In the management skills seminar we hold twice each year, I have a session on Effective Management. I give the class choices in a case study, and every time some will say, "You have not given us enough choices" or "you have not given us good choices." My response is, "That is right. In life we do not always get perfect choices or good situations. We must go with the best we've got."

As chairman of the board, Ken Hansen got into the act as well. One of the development opportunities for younger leaders was something called the Delta Lambda Kappa group, usually shortened to the Delta group. They gathered for strategy and development sessions on a regular basis for the purpose of bringing fresh ideas into the growth of the company and growing young leaders. The name comes from the meaning of the three Greek letters: Delta, representing change; Lambda, the first letter of the Greek word for "service"; and Kappa, the first letter of the Greek word for "master." It comes together as "Changers of ServiceMaster."[60] In 1978, Ken Wessner said the following to this group,

When I became chief executive officer of ServiceMaster, Ken Hansen asked me, "Wes, what do you want me to do?" One of the responsibilities I asked Ken to carry was the planning and guiding of the Delta group meetings. This he did last year and this year. These two years have been a series, laying the foundation upon which we will do our long-range planning for the 1980s and 1990s, beginning next year. Each of us who has worked with Ken knows the stretch he requires, and we grow both qualitatively and quantitatively, performing more and better. I hope each of you has the joy in working together that Ken and I have experienced through the years. I could not have a better teacher or partner in my work than Ken.[61]

Sometimes the training had to be "on the job." In the 1970s, Bob Knapp graduated with a degree in physics from Wheaton College. Although he was smart enough, he was not sure what to do. He spent two years in the Signal Corps in the US Army, worked at Teletype Corporation, and then in his father's business. He heard about ServiceMaster from his friends Ken Hansen, Dick Armstrong, and Alan Moore through their church, which was adjacent to the college. Ed Morgan interviewed and hired Bob, and he told him that he would be in training for six to ten months while they decided where to assign him. One week into the training, he was called into Ed's office. Ed told Bob, "We are going to accelerate your training a bit." Two or three weeks after that, the company sent Bob and his wife to Denver, where Dick Armstrong gave him a week of training before he became the manager of the branch office there. "Honestly, at that time, I hardly knew what a 'roto' was."[62]

Training did not stop at the door of the classroom. Wessner urged his management team to be involved in people development and formation as a part of their work every day. In one of their retreats, he urged the leaders,

> Do not think of one large ServiceMaster team of which you are a member. But rather think of your team. Those for whom you have a direct responsibility. Then commit to yourself to building the best ServiceMaster team in the entire company. You will be a stronger leader, leading a stronger team. We will be a strong ServiceMaster if you have built a stronger team.

He likened this to Jesus building a strong team from the apostles, themselves ordinary people.

> Jesus taught those on his team. Do you teach those on your team, both individually and as a group? Are your team members like you? The fellows I trained had some of me in them, and did the job better than me.

Then he linked the importance of training to the second objective, helping people develop. And it wasn't just the people in the company.

> ServiceMaster has put before its managers the high and satisfying goal of helping people to develop. This includes those whom we manage in hospitals in the departments of housekeeping, laundry, plant operations and maintenance, clinical equipment, and materials management. It also

includes each of our licensees and their employees. The leader's job is to stir up the gift that is within people and to fan into flame the gift of God which is in each individual. Our responsibility in ServiceMaster is to stir up the gift, the abilities, of each individual so each person becomes fully developed and mature for making his or her contribution to the winning team and then goes on to being a leader on his own team.[63]

To do these things, the leader must be a certain kind of person.

Our chairman, Dr. Hansen, has given the challenge that ServiceMaster managers must have the heart of a shepherd and the heart of a teacher in order to lead and develop men and women. For the shepherd, there is no greater reward than that of seeing others develop. To have the heart of a shepherd is to be totally committed to the personal welfare of those he is leading.

For the teacher, there is no accomplishment to compare with that of successfully guiding a person to wisdom through acquiring knowledge and skill. He is motivated to keep abreast of the latest methods and constantly seeks to improve his abilities. His reward is in seeing his students learn and develop. To have the heart of a teacher is to be totally committed to the growth and advancement of those he is leading. It is also one of the most important ways any of us can grow in our own ServiceMaster careers. Each ServiceMaster manager with the teacher heart is enriched personally. He will be a better husband, wife, father, mother, neighbor, and employee as well as a better manager. The result will be fulfillment and satisfaction.

To illustrate his point, Wessner offered an example at the annual shareholders meeting in 1978.

Fourteen years ago, we began serving a hospital. In the housekeeping department was a well-motivated young man seeking opportunity. He entered our management training program and was in that program for over a year before being assigned to his first hospital as our manager for two years. He was then assigned to a second hospital where he served over a year before being promoted to the position of regional operations manager. On January 1 of this year he was promoted to a divisional vice president. These promotions were not given; they were earned. During this 14-year period, he attended many ServiceMaster seminars and training sessions, including the completion of the ServiceMaster graduate school program.[64]

The purpose of all of the training and development was way beyond efficiency and effectiveness. The company had other goals as well, including preparing people for their next step of growth and helping them develop. In a 1980 interview with *Health Care Management Review*, Pollard stated, "One of our objectives is to try to promote 20 percent of the people coming into our management training program from the worker ranks within the hospital." They measured themselves on this goal.[65] It was not just about title and rank, but who that person was. Wessner commented, "Training, indeed any management directive, is not so much about what we want people to do, but rather what we want people to be." At ServiceMaster, the focus on the dignity of every person through training came in many forms. The company offered counseling on hygiene and extensive teaching in reading and language skills (there was even a training program in Polish). In addition, there was the training program for the managers that required them to participate in front-line jobs, such as cleaning floors. The floor cleaning requirement was a good example of how the Christian emphasis on equality and humility also encouraged financial productivity. Wessner said that a manager who hasn't personally experienced what it's like to wear a green uniform and be treated like a nonperson can never fully understand the importance of his or her responsibility to see that all employees are treated with dignity and to make sure that the job itself is dignifying.

Of course, there was a bottom-line benefit to this focus on training, which was also noted by customers, as described the authors of *Service Breakthroughs*:

> ServiceMaster customers that we have interviewed, hospital administrators and school superintendents, repeatedly told us that one of the major influences in their decisions to contract with the company for housekeeping and other services was the positive impression they received in visiting Service-Master's laboratory and education facilities in Downers Grove, Illinois.[66]

Marketing

Many franchises got their start through hearing about ServiceMaster from Paul Harvey. Harvey was a popular news commentator on the radio between 1952 and 2008, during which time his news and commentaries were carried on more than one thousand stations across America, reaching at their peak 24 million listeners. For the 1983 ServiceMaster annual report, Harvey wrote an essay titled "The Freedom to Achieve." In the introduction, Ken Wessner said,

> Paul Harvey is a friend of ServiceMaster. We have been a sponsor of the broadcast for many years in which Paul shares the ServiceMaster story and the services we provide. In addition, I am privileged to know Paul as a close personal friend. You will enjoy reading this essay.[67]

Succession Planning and Delegation

Both Marion Wade and Ken Hansen had prepared for the day when they would step aside and give opportunity and responsibility to the next person. Ken Wessner was no exception to this commitment as this was taught throughout the organization and encouraged at every management level.

In a 1977 address to the Delta group, Wessner described his personal commitment to this practice.[68] In his talk, he described the 1980 strategic plan they were just launching (which will be discussed later in this chapter):

> The first phase [of the plan] will be taking us through the 1980s and the second through the 1990s, to the year 2000. I will be 78 years old then, if the Lord gives me life. By then I will be retired from the Board of Directors for eight years, and from my present position for eighteen years.

In 1977, he announced that he would be stepping down as CEO in 1983 and that he would retire from the board in 1992. He did both, though sadly he did not live long enough to reach 2000.

Thirty days before his announcement, he and Ken Hansen had hired Bill Pollard with the plan to promote him to CEO. Apparently, in spite of the careful development and training programs, Hansen and Wessner didn't believe there was an internal candidate ready to step into that position. But the hiring of Bill Pollard tells a great deal about succession, as it does about the company's commitment to its four objectives.

Bill had been offered a position in ServiceMaster with the suggestion that one day he might be in line to be CEO. He told the story:

> I was sitting in Ken Hansen's office waiting to sign the final documents of employment. I decided I need to know more about exactly what I would have to do to be CEO of this company. I started pressing the two Kens on their expectations and how long it would take for me to be considered for President and CEO. After about five minutes of listening, Ken Hansen stood up, looked me in the eye, and said, "Bill, the interview is over."[69]

Bill was ushered from the door and left the building, believing he had blown the opportunity.

> Two days later, Ken Hansen called and asked me if I wanted to know what had happened in his office that day. I said that I did, and we met for breakfast the next morning. Ken's words to me were simply put: "Bill, if you want to come to ServiceMaster and contribute, you will have a great career. But if you are coming to the company for a title or a position or to promote yourself, you'd better forget it."

Bill ended up taking a position at ServiceMaster, but in that interview he learned a great deal about his future bosses, as well as the company.

About a year after Bill was hired, Ken Wessner gave a major presentation to the New York Society of Analysts on October 16, 1978. Wessner took two people with him: the treasurer of the company, C. Daniel Claud, and Bill Pollard. He had Bill explain to the analysts the purpose and meaning of the four objectives and what they did for the company. Wessner had spoken on these for years and was eloquent in doing so, but he used this as an opportunity to delegate responsibility. Like Ken Hansen before him, Wessner was a strong believer in delegation.

Wessner applied the practice of succession planning at all levels of the company. The twenty-first of the leadership principles (see Appendix 1) was, "We pay based on performance and promote based on potential, not belief, tenure, gender, race, or friendships." Several years after the acquisition of Service Direction, Patricia Asp was informed that she was being promoted to head a major part of healthcare in the Midwest operations of the company. She said to Ken,

> Wes, if you are going to put operations in my title, and you are going to put me over housekeeping, plant operations, maintenance, materials management, clinical equipment, laundry—all those things—I don't think that is fair to the people I will be leading. I need to know the business model of each of these services. My background is in clinical dietetics, and I have been running food service.

> His response was interesting, and it says a lot about him. He said, "I understand, but you are being promoted because of your leadership ability, not your clinical skills. This is what we're going to do. I will get you an internal expert of every line of service. They will personally be responsible for your training. If you're going to be in there two weeks, three weeks, four weeks, however long it's going to take for every single line of service, and then you tell me when it's time to assume your new role."[70]

She went around to the hospitals in different places with Ken Wessner during the time she was in training. "Wes always pushed me," she said. "He would ask me questions. 'How are you doing professionally? Do we have a customer? How is your family? How are you doing spiritually?' I learned fast under a great leader."[71]

Evaluation and Performance Review

Although Wessner's attention to research, training, and succession planning were important, he wanted to extend rigor and process care to management processes as well. He looked carefully at evaluation systems and soon launched the next long-range planning process.

As Nash wrote, "He felt that it was crucial to build accountability into every position in the organization and to create evaluation systems that accurately reflect the contribution that each person makes."[72]

One innovation he created for management accountability was called "Rolling Quarters." Every month, the major programs and divisions would be reviewed in three parts, with the meeting scheduled in the middle of the month. The leaders responsible would look back at the previous month and assess how they had done against their goals. They would then talk about the current month: what to expect, and what they thought would be the outcome. Then they turned their attention to the next month: what is on the horizon, what are the expectations, what issues are possible, and what are we doing about them?

Each person presenting was responsible to provide numbers and identify key issues within a short period of time. There were no excuses. They had to let the data and circumstances speak. The agenda for the May 27, 1983, meeting shows a start time at 7:00 a.m. and detailed time segments for the three-hour-and-forty-minute meeting, which included twenty-five presentations.[73]

These were not only instituted at the corporate level but also in subgroups. Wes Mitchell described how his meetings went, which echoed the corporate meeting. When it was a matter of reporting numbers for the previous quarter, Wes explained,

> Every division head gets their own financial statements, and they talk about their numbers for the previous month. I made a commitment to never embarrass anyone in these meetings, but if the numbers embarrass them, that is not my problem. Without the Rolling Quarters meetings, managers could have said, "It wasn't my fault." Now they have the control they needed. They go from being a victim to "What are we going to do and how are we going to do it?"[74]

In a talk to the Delta group, Wessner said, "It is increasingly important that we have a sound assessment of the realities. How big is the opportunity? How soon can that opportunity be realized? With common sense let us make sound assessments of our business."[75]

Another Strategic Plan

On September 29, 1977, at a gathering of the Delta group at Lake of the Ozarks in Missouri, Ken Wessner shared with key leaders the development of a long-range plan that looked forward twenty years.[76] He called the plan "ServiceMaster Industries 20," which was abbreviated and pronounced "SMIXX." The company set up more than fifty committees of three to seven employees each to set goals for the next two decades. As one part of this process, the company vowed to reach $2 billion in revenues by 1990, from just $400 million in 1980.

This plan identified a slowing of growth in the hospital market as a major environmental threat to the company's continued rapid growth; it reiterated the goal of growing rapidly in order to provide personal growth opportunities for employees; and it consequently called for the development of new service markets as the means of maintaining momentum.[77]

SMIXX was the next step in the planning process which had begun in 1958 when Ken Hansen announced that the company had to clarify its goals. And just as Hansen had made his search a team effort, so Wessner made planning a group affair:

> Our current planning process in ServiceMaster looks forward over the next 20 years. There are hundreds of people participating in the process. They represent every segment of the company and every level of management. The effect of this enlarged planning process is a sense of teamwork, a shared interest pervading our plans for the future.[78]

The suggestion of the slowing of the hospital business became real very quickly, and this challenge became central to the work of the next CEO.

Making Hard Choices

During his tenure as CEO, Ken Wessner demonstrated his commitment to the foundational principles of the company in his speaking and his actions. He deeply owned the foundational work of the previous two leaders, and he believed in the mission of the company and its foundation on the four objectives that he had played a strong role in shaping. His passion for the four objectives led him to speak and write about them at almost every opportunity. In keeping with these four objectives, like his predecessors, he saw the need for growth rooted in creating opportunity for the people of the organization. He also continued to build on the strong business foundation that Ken Hansen had laid. In each of these areas, Wessner lived the foundations of the company. Again, in the spirit of Marion Wade, "If you don't live it, you don't believe it."

One way Wessner lived out the objectives involved making some difficult choices. As one example, he had to make a decision about an important business opportunity that fundamentally opposed his sense of Christian values. ServiceMaster had taken over a substantial hospital cleaning contract in the Northeast. The hospital's chief administrator turned out to be an abusive person. He had a drinking problem and a bad temper, and he used language that, in Wessner's terms, was simply unacceptable. This man especially abused his own staff. One day, he threw a wet tray at one of the ServiceMaster cleaners (trays were supposed to be dry). When the ServiceMaster manager in charge went to Wessner and expressed his concern for their staff, Wessner withdrew from the contract.[79] Commenting on this, Nash concluded,

> The decision to withdraw, was based on the *long-term success* of the company, *not the short-term threat to profit.* Continuous sound business judgment, a good plan for the future, a very consistent philosophy of employee development, and the fact that there were many contracts in place, all built a financial slack into the system that allowed Wessner to cut bait without forcing the company into a survival scenario. Having that slack did not make his decision any less ethical, for the slack itself was a product of the same set of values that had caused him to withdraw on that particular contract.[80]

Honors for Ken Wessner

In 1980, *Financial World* named Ken Wessner outstanding executive, and in 1981, *The Wall Street Transcript* selected him as the top CEO in the industrial services industry for the previous year. In arguing their case, the article said,

> He has produced substantial and consistent earnings gains in a seemingly unexciting business—cleaning and maintaining healthcare facilities and providing laundry and other support services for these facilities. Wessner's success appears to be the company's ability to recruit, train, and motivate employees.[81]

"Any amount of just throwing dollars against the wall doesn't work when you try to compete with ServiceMaster," said one analyst. Another said, "I would choose Wessner as the best. I don't have any second. He's put together a very fine company in the health services area. He is a man of extreme integrity."

He was selected for other significant honors as well: Illinois Business Hall of Fame, American Business Hall of Fame, Healthcare Hall of Fame (1992). The Healthcare recognition was particularly noteworthy, since it is rare for the healthcare industry to recognize people who did work in janitorial services and plant maintenance. His award cited reduction in infections attributable to the cleaning work.[82]

In 1988, Wessner returned to King's College, the school he had attended as a freshman back in 1940, to give the commencement address. The college awarded him with an honorary doctorate. In 1990, he gave the commencement address at Wheaton College and received an honorary doctor of law degree from there. In 1991, he was selected as the Business and Profession Leader of the year by Religious Heritage of America.

In 1988, while a member of the board of Prison Fellowship, Ken Wessner found himself seated next to a convict, Manny Mill. Manny had special permission to attend a weekend event the organization was putting on in Washington, DC. After a conversation over dinner, Ken promised to write to Manny. "And amazingly, he did," Manny said.[83] Not only that, but Ken supported him when he was released from prison and helped him attend Wheaton College for two different degrees. He also helped some other people coming out of prison find employment at ServiceMaster.

Manny has gone on to a successful career with Koinonia House National Ministries. Since leaving prison, Manny has had two sons: one has a first name of Kenneth and the other has his middle name as Kenneth. "He changed my life," Manny said. When Manny wrote his autobiography, he dedicated it to Ken Wessner: "To the living memory of the late Dr. Kenneth T. Wessner, my friend, mentor, and spiritual daddy, whose righteous legacy laid the foundation for the writing of this story."[84]

Final Days

In 1983, Ken Wessner stepped down from his CEO role as he had said he would back in 1977. He continued as chairman of the board through 1990, retiring in 1992, also as he had said. On March 29, 1994, he died of cancer at the age of seventy-one, just a few months before Ken Hansen's death.

In 1979, Norma Wessner wrote to the Wheaton College Alumni Association with an update on Ken. She included the comment, "Ken has taken all of the honors. I guess I can take partial credit in raising our wonderful children, Barbara and David."[85] Indeed, the wives of each of the leaders remained an important part of the company. This is recognized by their countless hours of entertaining and participating in the work of the company, as well as with the families. Norma lived long after Ken had passed, dying on February 6, 2011.

At Wessner's memorial service, Bill Pollard said,

From a human standpoint, Ken achieved much in his life. The result was not always clear at the beginning. A professional baseball career with the St. Louis Cardinals was a long way from leading the number one Fortune 500 service company. A teenager unsure about whether he was able to afford an education beyond high school was a long way from receiving two doctorate degrees. But as all these things came across Ken's path, they were not for him an end, because Ken's beginning point was with God. . . . [A]ll these things fall into place and life falls into place only with God.[86]

5

THE BILL POLLARD YEARS

Bill Pollard's tenure as CEO started well, or so it seemed. Even though 1983 marked the second largest recession of the second half of the twentieth century, revenue and profit continued to climb under his leadership. In 1984, *Fortune* magazine recognized ServiceMaster as the "shiningest star" of the Service 500 companies for its growth and performance between 1973 and 1983.[1] ServiceMaster had emerged onto the national and international stage in very heady company.

In 1983, however, the market pounded the company as its stock plunged from $37 to $17 per share.[2] Although this was no indictment of past performance, it was rooted strictly in expectations for future performance. Congress had passed a major change to the way Medicare costs were reimbursed to hospitals, leading to potentially significantly reduced hospital revenue. Analysts forecasted that cost pressures on hospitals would curtail their ability to purchase services, and hospitals were the primary source of revenue for ServiceMaster. Wall Street was predicting a difficult path ahead for the company and its new forty-five-year-old leader.

Shortly after becoming CEO, Bill went in for a review with his chairman, Ken Wessner. After Bill had shared his concern over whether one of the operating units would be able to meet its performance objectives for the quarter, Wessner reminded him,

> That is not your job. It's the job of the person leading the business unit. You are the CEO of the entire company. You have to start thinking about where this company is going to be three years from now, five years from now, not just next quarter. It is wrong to steal a person's right or ability to make a decision. See to it that he feels the responsibility to make them. If he doesn't, then you have to make the decision about whether he should be removed.[3]

If not focusing on the quarter and giving room for people to make decisions, Pollard wondered, then what is the focus? In this case, Wessner said, "We are going to need another growth curve. What that will be is your decision and it is your responsibility to make that happen."[4] Wessner delegated this task to Bill while challenging him to delegate.

In fact, the forecasted cost-pressures on hospitals were realized. In 1985, H. Lee Murphy reported that "many of ServiceMaster's 1000 client hospitals closed wings and pared spending."[5] In a July 1985 interview with

Pollard, *Forbes* magazine raised questions about the future of ServiceMaster. When asked about growth based on what was happening to hospitals, Pollard pointed to growth in the schools and factory business and said, "We are running and selling in both markets. I don't know where our mix will end up. There [are] lots of changes in our markets, but where there is change, there is opportunity."[6]

The reporter in Pollard's office observed a large number "2" sitting on his desk. This signified that ServiceMaster had a goal to be a $2 billion company by 1990. When the reporter reminded Pollard that they had not yet reached $1 billion in revenue and their largest market had just gotten a lot tougher, "Pollard replied with a grin, 'Well, I like to make tough targets and beat 'em.'"[7] Probing further, the reporter noted that ServiceMaster had no debt and they could afford a sizable acquisition. Pollard responded by saying that he didn't plan to buy a new business soon.

Though the company did achieve its $1 billion revenue goal in 1985, the questions continued into 1986. H. Lee Murphy, reporter for *Crain's Chicago Business*, was pessimistic about the company's future. In his article, he wrote:

> It took ServiceMaster Industries, Inc. nearly four decades to grow to $1 billion in sales. Never lacking for ambitious goals, the company figures the next billion will come in just five years. That objective seems incredible, considering that nearly three fourths of ServiceMaster's business is in providing managed services to the healthcare industry, which has been under severe cost pressures for more than a year.[8]

But Pollard took the company to uncharted waters. He found that new growth curve and made the $2 billion goal, while preserving the values of the company (or rather, this happened *because* he preserved and deepened the values of the company). Harvard professor James Heskett, in observing financial success at ServiceMaster, noted that for Pollard "the starting point for financial success was adherence to shared values."[9]

Bill's challenge was greater than that of the two Kens in one way: the company he took over had revenues of $700 million, unlike the revenues of $70 million for Wessner or just over a million for Hansen. The stakes—measured by revenue, the number of jobs impacted, and the number of investors who depended on ServiceMaster dividends—were quite high.

Bill, however, had faced adversity before. Being told he could not do something was not the final answer. He had tools at his disposal based on his work as a lawyer, and he had a deeply rooted faith that made it natural for him to value people. Further, based on the company's policy of "shingles on a roof," he had an ongoing relationship with both Ken Hansen and Ken Wessner, who would be excellent partners, bringing their own skills and experience to bear on the work. During his tenure, Pollard broadened this collaboration to bring in other trusted partners as well, particularly a lengthy relationship with Peter Drucker, noted business professor and consultant.

Pollard Early Years

C. William Pollard was born in Chicago on June 1, 1938, and lived there until his parents, Charles and Ruth Pollard, moved to Wheaton when he was thirteen. He had two older sisters, Virginia and JoAnn. The family also had roots in Lake Geneva, Wisconsin, which also played a part in Bill's formative years and continues to the present time as another place for family gatherings.

Bill's grandparents, Thomas and Elizabeth Pollard, had emigrated from the British Isles to Lake Geneva, where Thomas first worked and lived with his family on a farm near the lake. In 1897, Bill's father Charles was born. The grandparents later moved to the Chicago area, where Thomas started the Pollard Tea and Coffee Company, drawing on an art he had learned in London.

After time in the service in World War I, Charles married Ruth and they initially made their home in Chicago. Charles started his own sales and marketing company, representing a variety of manufacturers in selling their products. The company grew to have offices in Chicago, New York, St. Louis, and Los Angeles.

When Bill was about ten years old, the old farm where his grandfather had worked came up for sale, and his father Charles saw this as an opportunity to purchase it with four other friends for the development of a Christian youth and family camp. Bill remembers walking that land with his father, sharing the vision for the future camp, even though in its early state it included some run-down chicken coops and other farm buildings.

Bill also learned to sail on Lake Geneva, under the guiding hand of his father. Sailing, including learning to read the tides, became a metaphor for life and business from this experience: "I have found that there are tides and winds in life resulting in forces and currents that we cannot always see or control. Yet at times these forces create opportunities to make choices about a direction."[10]

Bill also recalled time with his mother when he was still in grade school. She led him to explore what it meant to be a Christian, which led to his commitment of faith: "It was the beginning of my learning what it would mean to be a follower of Jesus Christ."[11]

As with most of us, Bill's life lessons were often punctuated with learning the hard way. About a year after his Christian commitment, Bill's parents decided to send him to a Christian high school, where he signed a pledge not to participate in activities such as smoking or drinking. But as a freshman in high school, he and some friends decided to try out some of those "forbidden pleasures." Though he worked hard to keep this from the school and his parents, the truth ultimately came out. He was put on probation and labeled as one of those difficult kids. And though he kept his word not to do such things from that time forward, "I developed a contempt for how the school was imposing its authority."[12]

About a year later, he had another experience with authority—this time at the camp at Lake Geneva his father had founded. He had been going to this camp from the time it first opened and he knew the rules, included attending chapel twice a day. One hot morning, he and several other kids skipped chapel to go swimming in the lake. When they arrived, they saw another boy who had jumped into the lake without knowing how to swim—and he was in trouble. They dove in and brought him to shore. The kids then snuck back into camp without detection. The next day, however, the water safety patrol came to the camp office to thank the boys for what they had done, which made it clear they had ducked out of chapel. The boys were told to wear armbands with the message "in disgrace" for the rest of the week. "We broke the rules and needed to be penalized," Bill said, "but it was done in a way that I felt was an unfair exercise in authority."[13] These two incidents had an impact on the way he saw the appropriate use of authority. For a time, they also negatively affected his spiritual growth.

While in high school, Bill loved football. He was an end for the Wheaton Academy football team and co-captain his senior year. He also fell in love with a classmate, Judy Wyngarden. They were sweethearts through high school, and both decided to go to Wheaton College. Bill's primary motivation was to play football there. Judy, however, was admitted in the spring, but Bill was put on a waiting list because of low test scores. His school advisor told him either to apply somewhere else or to not go to college. Bill decided that he would either go to Wheaton or get a job as a painter or work in construction.

Three weeks before classes started, he was admitted to Wheaton College on probation. He immediately joined the football team, determined to do well in both football and his studies. Again, the sailing was not smooth. After three days of football practice, he began fainting. After ruling out heat exhaustion, he was sent to the hospital where it was determined he had a bleeding ulcer. No more football. It also meant he needed a strictly regulated diet that he could not get on campus, so he had to take his meals at home. His dream of college life was starting to fade.

In March 1957, his freshman year, Bill was called out of class with the news that his father had suffered a heart attack while his parents were traveling home from Florida. His father was taken to a hospital in Nashville, Tennessee. It was serious enough that Bill and his brother-in-law flew to Nashville that afternoon to be with his father. His father asked him how school was going and whether he was still considering transferring to Northwestern University to study engineering. Then some nurses came in and asked them to step into the hall. A few minutes later, there was a rush of nurses and doctors to the room. Then a doctor walked out to tell them their father had suffered another massive heart attack and died. This was a devastating blow for the whole family.

After the funeral, Bill had difficulty reentering school life. He remembers seeing the president of Wheaton on campus that spring, Dr. V. Raymond Edman. Bill was surprised that the president recognized him and encouraged by what the president said: "Bill, don't doubt in the dark what you have seen in the light."[14] Bill's faith was strong at this point, and it was an important reminder that he would see his father again in heaven.

He was accepted to engineering school at Northwestern University for the fall quarter, so he got a job as a painter for the summer and saved money for the coming school term. But then came the next blow. Without his father's leadership, his father's business went into bankruptcy, which meant there was no extra money for college. It would take all his earnings from his summer job to cover tuition at Northwestern. His mother had to sell their home, and with only a small income from a life insurance policy, he and his mother moved in with his sister and brother-in-law.

At this point, life wasn't about to get any better. When he went to enroll at Northwestern, which started in late September, they informed him that they would not take any of his Wheaton credits toward an engineering degree; they didn't see the value of the liberal arts courses he had taken at Wheaton. Since he didn't want to waste his year at Wheaton, he withdrew from Northwestern. Then his brother-in-law encouraged him to apply elsewhere, and he found that the University of Illinois would take his Wheaton credits toward an engineering degree. The only problem was that their school had started three weeks earlier. While they let him in, he soon found himself hopelessly behind in courses in calculus, physics, and chemistry. After spending a month trying to catch up, he withdrew from that school as well.

He returned home and found two jobs for the rest of the year: selling industrial lift trucks during the day, and men's clothes at Marshall Field's in the evenings. Working in sales proved to be a valuable experience, Bill recognized later. He was able to earn enough to reenroll at Wheaton that January. From the jobs he had held, he realized more clearly the need for an education. Now a motivated student, he determined to quickly get back on track and make up for the lost semester. In the summer of 1959, Bill and Judy were married. Bill was then able to graduate with his class at Wheaton in June 1960, after majoring in business and economics.

As Bill reflected on the value of this painful part of his life, he first "had feelings of letting [my father] down because I was not pursuing an engineering degree. I had developed a fear of failure and seriously wondered whether I would measure up to his expectations."15 But later, he realized that pain and difficulty were a part of his life experiences, which allowed God to shape and mold him. He also recognized that difficulties are often a consequence of bad choices, and that life is not just about you, but about serving others. This powerful, painful part of his life created a strong foundation for future dealings with adversity.

Early Career

There remained the question of what to do after graduating from college. After some consideration, including advice from his father-in-law and Wheaton professor "Doc" Volkman, Pollard decided to pursue the practice of law. Volkman provided a recommendation to his alma mater, Northwestern University, which enabled Pollard to receive a full scholarship. Finally, his plan to attend Northwestern was a reality, though in a way that was different from his original plan. With Judy's support, a rent-free apartment from her father (above his doctor's office), and the growth of the house painting business that provided living expenses, Pollard made it through law school in three years. He finished in the top 10 percent of his class and took a position with a major Chicago law firm, Wilson & McIlvaine. Bill and Judy had their first child, Julie, during the law school period. They went on to have three more children: Charles William III (Chip), Brian, and Amy. Pollard later said, "When I had a heavy work and travel schedule, [Judy] kept the home fires burning for each of our children."16

Pollard soon found that he loved practicing law, especially in the area of business and tax. It was "stimulating, rewarding, and consuming. The one major negative was there seemed to be no letup on the time demands."17 One of his early clients was Marion Wade, whom he helped with estate planning and preparing a sizable charitable gift. Wade shared his philosophy of money by saying, "Remember, Bill, money is like manure; it doesn't smell any better the more you pile it up."18

During his five years with the Chicago firm, Pollard commuted into Chicago on the train with Otis Halleen, another lawyer friend who was also a graduate of Wheaton College. Pollard and Halleen came up with the idea to open their own firm in Wheaton, closer to where they lived. After launching the new firm, it would take several years to build up the practice, so they needed to borrow money to start. After nine months, they were able to begin paying back the loan. "Finally," Bill recalled, "I was able to cover the cost of groceries, and my family was no longer eating food bought with borrowed money."19 He continued to find the practice of law rewarding, and now his commute was significantly less than going into Chicago. Ultimately, they merged with another law firm in Wheaton to form Vescelus, Leetz, Perry and Pollard.

Pollard's clients included Wheaton College and the City of Wheaton. One of his projects was working with a builder in Wheaton and negotiating with the city to develop the tallest building in town, just south of the railroad station. With twenty floors, it remains the tallest building in Wheaton. In addition to the college and the city, he represented a number of growing businesses. As his practice continued to grow, he worked on a major merger project for a Texas oil company. Although he enjoyed the work, he said it was "very, very consuming. Somewhere in the process, the extra time with family had vanished."[20]

Two weeks after the Texas deal closed, Judy found Bill unconscious on the bathroom floor. The doctors determined that the old ulcer had reappeared. After surgery and a hospital stay of three weeks due to complications, Pollard began to wonder if God was telling him something about his career choice.

Dr. Armerding, the president of Wheaton College, visited Pollard frequently in the hospital. Near the end of that stay, Armerding suggested that perhaps this would be a good time for Pollard to leave the practice of law and come to work at the college. This was a challenging question for Bill and Judy and gets to the heart of career choices we all face. Bill knew the salary would be much less than what he was earning as a lawyer. As he and Judy prayed about the possible transition, he asked himself, "Was money the issue? I knew it would be enough to support my family, and if it was the right thing to do, God would provide."[21]

The job Armerding had in mind for Pollard was to head up leadership and management of the Wheaton College business and fundraising areas. He also was encouraged to continue to teach in the area of business and economics, which he had already been doing as an adjunct. "If I took the job," Bill said, "I would definitely be choosing a road less traveled."[22] There remained one sticky issue, however, before he would agree to take that job. He knew that his work in finance would involve working closely with the board member who dealt in finance, Ken Hansen. As we saw in chapter 3, the problem with that relationship was resolved and launched a long and supportive relationship between the two men.

Over the next four and a half years, Pollard addressed a major project at Wheaton that was directly in line with his background and training. The college had been one of the beneficiaries of two large operating coal companies in Pennsylvania and West Virginia, and Pollard had the responsibility of turning this gift into monetary value for the college. This was during the oil embargo, and the price of coal had risen dramatically from $11 per ton to over $100 per ton.[23] Wheaton College was not in the coal business, so his challenge was to find a good buyer for the companies. Further complications with the will and the donor's family made this more than a simple business transaction. Over the rest of his time at Wheaton, Pollard gave substantial time to this work, ultimately wrapping up a successful sale.

One other issue came up in his fund-raising responsibilities that connected Pollard with ServiceMaster. In August 1973, Sears Roebuck and Company made the decision to sell its holding in ServiceMaster stock for the purpose of diversification. Apparently, because of the large number of ServiceMaster stock donations to Wheaton College, signers on the SEC document related to the Sears sale of the stock were ServiceMaster treasurer Thomas H. Beadles, Pollard from Wheaton, and Robert P. Knight from Sears.[24]

After the coal mines were sold and most of the donation issues were resolved, Bill decided that his work at Wheaton was completed. He had hired two new leaders who reported to him, and believed the department was well postured for the future. "I had learned a lot about life and the way it should be lived from Hudson, and my other colleagues at the college," he concluded, "and felt I could return to the practice of law without it becoming a jealous mistress."[25]

Because of his work and interaction with Ken Hansen at Wheaton, Hansen reached out to him to see if he would be open to considering a position at ServiceMaster (we discussed his unusual hiring process in chapter 4). On September 1, 1977, at the age of thirty-nine, Bill Pollard stepped into the role of corporate vice president of The ServiceMaster Company. From his interview for the position, Bill had learned several vital lessons about himself and the company that would shape his own future leadership:

1. Never give a title or a position to someone who can't live without it.
2. Determine up front whether the leader's self-interest or interest of others would come first.
3. Know whether, as a leader, you are willing to do what you ask others to do.
4. Know whether you, as a leader, have the heart and commitment to develop people, not only in what they are doing but also in the people they are becoming.[26]

In his new role, he would quickly put into practice these key lessons.

Getting Started at ServiceMaster

Though Bill Pollard was hired into ServiceMaster as a corporate vice president with the thought that he would become CEO at some point, his first assignment was not surprising:

> Ken [Wessner] soon tested my commitment, and also took time to teach me what it was like to walk in the shoes of the people I would lead. During the first eight weeks, I spent my days with the service workers, doing the service tasks we performed for our customers. I learned the reality of my dependence on, and responsibility to, the people I would lead.[27]

Since he still had his obligations as a new vice president, he ended up working a number of evenings in order to fit it all in.

This practical lesson about the actual role of the worker in a service organization soon became very real and personal. One incident stands out for Bill from those days as "a vivid reminder of how others often treat and view those who serve in routine assignments."

> I was working in a busy corridor of the hospital. I had just set out my wet-floor signs and was about to mop the floor. People were streaming back and forth when suddenly a lady stopped and asked, "Aren't you Bill Pollard?" I responded that I was, and she identified herself as a distant relative of my wife. Then she looked at me, and my mop, and shook her head and asked, "Aren't you a lawyer?" as if to say, "Can't you get a better job?" I paused, looked down at my bucket, and said, "No, I have a new job."[28]

Early in his time at ServiceMaster, it was important for Bill Pollard to learn what Marion Wade, Ken Hansen, and Ken Wessner each had to learn: service work is important, dignified work, and those doing the work are human beings worthy of dignity and respect. People, however, tend to look at service workers as somehow inferior or they just ignore them, so experiencing this wrong perception firsthand was a vital step to understanding it. It required leadership to understand this and thus shape the work environment and culture to enable workers to feel the importance and dignity of their labor. To keep this experience "top of mind," the company had an annual "We Serve" day in which executives participated in the actual work of the company. "It wasn't just for show," Dave Baseler recalled. "We worked hard and often found we couldn't do the work very well. It was a humbling, important experience."[29]

Pollard quickly came to understand that learning and growth were needed for every aspect of the work. After submitting his first financial analysis to Ken Wessner, he remembers walking into the meeting and seeing his memorandum marked with red. Ken said, "I am *pleased* but not *satisfied*." At first Bill reacted, as many of us would, in a defensive manner. Later he would say, "I soon became aware that I was learning and saw the opportunity to improve and achieve an even better analysis. He helped both me and my work-product to improve."[30] The ServiceMaster second objective was in play again.

Though Pollard was not yet ready to lead the company, his influence was broadly felt at this early stage of his time there. Susan Baker had joined the company as a corporate attorney about the same time as Bill in 1977. As she recalled, "Bill Pollard was such a powerful force; he played a strong leadership role even without the title."[31] His leadership was also clearly recognized by those at the top. In January 1983, Pollard stepped into the CEO role after he had been with the company for just about five years.

Early in CEO Role

In 1983, one of the company's many innovations was in launching the home healthcare business, which it started in partnership with the Voluntary Hospitals of America. Susan Baker was the attorney on this project and worked closely with Pollard. She saw this as a great opportunity for ServiceMaster, with the new service creating future growth potential and a strong cultural match. She learned even more about Bill's leadership and the strength of the culture on this project:

> This really was a special company. There was great training and support, allowing people to do things they may not have thought possible. The company truly believed in the four objectives. That meant mission was important, not just profits. It meant you could make a mistake, live to tell about it, and learn from it. For women at that time, it was a great environment. If you thought you could do something, you were empowered to do it.[32]

Ed Catmull, a cofounder of Pixar Animation Studios, identifies one hallmark of an innovative environment as being allowed to make mistakes. "Mistakes aren't a necessary evil," he wrote. "They are an inevitable consequence of doing something new. . . . Failure is a manifestation of learning and exploration."[33] Of course, ServiceMaster, like Pixar and any other company, was not always as open to new ideas as it should have been. For example, we saw this in the previous chapter when Rich Williams tried to propose that the company enter the educational market with its cleaning and maintenance work and encountered initial resistance.

A continuous learning environment from the bottom of the organization to the top was a key to the continued growth the company wanted. In 1985, Bill Pollard led a process to establish a restated and focused vision statement that defined the role of the company going forward: "To be an ever-expanding and vital market vehicle for use by God to work in the lives of people as they serve and contribute to others."[34]

International Expansion

Included in this plan for growth was international expansion. In 1981, Hassan Moharrak was managing Al Majal, a company he owned with three others in Saudi Arabia, when he first learned about ServiceMaster through a friend in Jordan. The more he found out about ServiceMaster, the more intrigued he became: "I particularly loved the four objectives. I loved the idea of doing business to honor God."[35] So he inquired about representing ServiceMaster in Saudi Arabia. In 1985, he brought seventeen people from his company to Downers Grove, Illinois (the headquarters for the company), to begin training in ServiceMaster systems and to reach an agreement. He said,

> Our company [Al Majal] was doing about $1 million in business at the time. The training was amazing! When I was going through the training myself, I met Bill Pollard, the number one person at the company. He had been through the training himself! I was so impressed with the passion of the leadership in developing and applying the four objectives, refining the mission, and caring for the people.

That same year, Hassan signed an agreement and changed the name of his company to Al Majal ServiceMaster.

> When our people went there, we understood the company was very religious. But we found this passion for people, for helping them develop, for training to do great work, and recognizing the dignity of their work. It was a great match for our own Muslim faith. We had a great respect for the leadership at ServiceMaster.

> Let me tell you a story. When Bill Pollard came to visit us, we all saw how real he was. We were visiting our biggest customer, National Commercial Bank, and we met with Bill with the chairman of the board. Bill was pleased to hear the good report of our work. But as we walked through the building, Bill stopped to talk with someone doing the cleaning work. After introducing himself, Bill asked his name and asked him about his work. That young cleaner from India felt honored that day! We grew our own company across Saudi Arabia, and then to Egypt and Sudan. By 1998, we had grown to $250 million in revenue.[36]

Bill Pollard also believed that while it was important to raise the question of God in the minds of others, as a business leader, his role was not to preach at them:

> For me, the world of business has become a channel of distribution for fulfilling and living my faith—a channel that has reached from a janitor's closet in Saudi Arabia to the Great Hall of the People in Beijing. The marketplace has provided a wonderful opportunity for me to embrace and engage those who do not believe the way I do, but whom God loves and who should see by my words and actions the reality of his love.[37]

Early Acquisitions

Since trying and failing with acquisitions in the mid-1960s, ServiceMaster focused on growth from within. Wessner's strategic plan emphasized this type of growth. Bill's success with the acquisition of Service Direction in 1981, however, opened the door to that possibility. As recently as 1983, he had stated that he had no plans for acquisitions. But by the end of 1985, the company had made a small step toward the lawn care business with the purchase of Village Green, and they also acquired Seaboard Energy Systems to support plant and maintenance operations. Although both companies were relatively small, they represented a significant start of an acquisition process that would take the company in new directions.

The Big Shift in 1986

The year 1986 stands with 1929 (the year the company was started), 1947 (the year that company was incorporated and named), and 1962 (the year the company went public) as another major transition point. It was in 1986 that Bill Pollard led ServiceMaster in *two* different directions at the same time that changed the future for the company.

Limited Partnership Formation

One of Pollard's goals was to posture the company for future growth, and that required more cash for investment. He was looking for a way to get the company onto a new, higher growth curve in line with their stated goal. As a company with relatively low capital costs, where investors were paid with generous dividends, Pollard realized that profits were essentially taxed twice. The first tax was paid by the company on its profits. Then, after dividends were paid to the shareholders, those shareholders had to pay taxes on the dividends. He wrote,

> With the help of Goldman Sachs, we decided to choose a road less traveled and convert our public corporation to a public limited partnership. The process of liquidating a public corporation and simultaneously forming a public partnership was complicated and required approval of both our shareholders and the U.S. Securities and Exchange Commission.[38]

The process was further complicated by the fact that their "individual shareholders would have to pay a tax" for gains from the liquidation. A second complication was that "it had to be done before the year ended because a change in the tax law regarding corporate liquidations would become effective the next year."

The time pressure on the project was enormous. Susan Baker, working closely on this project with Pollard, recalled,

> This project required a very focused effort, with long nights. Bill Pollard was a very forceful leader, so there was no doubt the project was going to

get done, even when we didn't think it was possible. Getting the existing shareholders on board, explaining to them the value of the tax hit they were going to take from the liquidation, was a very hard part of the process. Some of these shareholders were "mom and pop" investors who had held stock from the beginning, and it was a difficult, stressful conversation. Though we did complete requirements by the end of the year, intense work continued dealing with the transition. In the end, it worked well for the company and its shareholders, but I always wondered if we didn't lose some of our focus on the daily business during that intense period.[39]

In December 1986, in the midst of the high pressure, Pollard took a phone call from Ken Hansen. Ken was having second thoughts about the conversion to limited partnership and wanted to talk with Bill about it. Dave Baseler remembers being in the room and deciding he needed to leave to let the two of them talk privately: "Bill was under great pressure, the clock was ticking, and he took the time to listen to Ken Hansen's concerns. I am not sure another leader would have done that."[40]

The leaders also had to assume a great deal of personal risk. The deal required that some of the leaders step up as general partners, putting all of their personal assets in jeopardy. This was the case for Bill Pollard, Bob Erickson, Chuck Stair, and Alex Balc. Pollard recalled,

Chuck, Bob, and Alex had been with the company since their college days. Each had played a significant role in the development and growth of ServiceMaster. Chuck was now serving as the group president for five separate divisions serving hospitals in the East. Bob had served as a division president in the West and was now serving as the CFO of the company. Alex was serving as the leader of a support group for all of the divisions of the company.[41]

He also commented about this event:

As a lawyer, I knew what I was asking them to do. It was a big risk. But their response was unanimous and immediate. They believed in what they were doing and in me. Not often does a leader have to ask this much. But their response gave me a renewed strength and vitality to accomplish the task.[42]

The change meant the company was able to substantially increase shareholder dividends, while at the same time "over the next ten years, they estimated the tax savings would provide over $750 million to invest in the future growth of the business."[43]

One other adjustment, however, was still required. Since shareholders would no longer have the right to vote for directors, Pollard noted, "We added the requirement in our partnership charter that a majority of our directors must be independent and that we would continue to hold our annual meetings and be responsive to the questions and comments of our shareholders." On the cautionary side, he also observed, "It is now more difficult for pension and retirement funds and some other types of institutional investors to own our shares."

Pollard did see a positive impact of the change on employees who owned stock. "I was walking briskly through the mailroom, when Rose Pacholski, one our employee shareholders, called out in a loud voice, 'Howdy, partner.'"44

Acquisition of Terminix

During the fall of 1986, an agent for E. W. (Ned) Cook, the owner of the Terminix Company, announced he was looking for a buyer for his company. In 1927, two years before Marion Wade began ServiceMaster, the E. L. Bruce Company in Memphis, Tennessee, had started Terminix. Bruce manufactured hardwood floors and wanted a solution for protecting their floors from termites. Just as Marion Wade had done, they developed their own chemicals for this process and began franchising in 1957. In 1962, Cook Industries bought the Bruce Company, including Terminix, and started international expansion. In 1972, the company became Terminix, International, which highlighted their work in eleven other countries. They were also in forty-seven states in the US. When Bill Pollard heard they were on the market, he "jumped at the opportunity" to pursue the acquisition, even though the company was large and he was in the middle of moving ServiceMaster to a public limited partnership.45

The CEO of Terminix at the time and key to these negotiations was Carlos Cantu, whom we will meet in the next chapter. As Cantu remembers the meeting, "After my pitch about how great an organization Terminix was and about its excellent potential for growth, Bill asked to meet privately with me. I expected to further discuss the financial and market projections I had presented, much as I had done with other interested parties."46 Cantu was surprised when their private talk took a different direction:

> We embarked on a conversation about people and our respective philosophies of management, leadership, and responsibility to our associates in the workplace. I found it unusual but refreshing to talk about value, the dignity and worth of the individual, the significance of God in the work and lives of people, and the essence of the four objectives. I could certainly relate to these expressions of value and responsibility, since they clearly reconcile with my personal perspective on people and ethical standards. But interjecting these thoughts into a discussion relating to a potential business acquisition was, to say the least, unexpected.47

How did Carlos respond to this conversation about God in the middle of a negotiation?

At no time during the course of our conversation did I sense Bill's tone or message to be threatening or confrontational. Quite to the contrary, it was unmistakably a message of inclusiveness and an invitation to share. It was a clear reflection of the philosophy of ServiceMaster: one of respect for the culture, dignity, and beliefs of all people.[48]

Although ServiceMaster was not the highest bidder for Terminix, it ended up with the deal. This was in part because the Terminix leadership team was convinced this was the type of company in which they could thrive. Charlie Hromada, who had joined Terminix in 1954, said, "We were a very sleepy company, tied to the hardwood floor business. As new opportunities to expand came up, we wanted to do more, but were not allowed to."[49] Through the arrangement with ServiceMaster, the leaders of Terminix saw the opportunity to reach greater potential.

In addition, the contract included "earn-out" incentives for growth for the key individuals of the company. To finally seal the deal, Pollard had to extend the earn-out opportunity to the seller as well. Pollard said he was reminded of a statement Ken Hansen had frequently made: "Bill, sometimes you have to move sideways like a crab."[50] That is, one needs to keep the end objective in mind during negotiations.

Terminix was not the only acquisition for ServiceMaster in this frantic three-month period at the end of 1986. The company also acquired American Food Management, headquartered in Missouri, to provide food service to the educational market.[51] To close these deals, the ServiceMaster team had to develop new banking relationships to secure funding for those acquisitions, including $165 million for the Terminix deal alone. This period of time is forever engraved in Bill Pollard's mind:

> Some of our institutional investors were not in favor of the move to partnership form, and began selling their stock, and the price of our shares began to drop just as we started sending proxies for shareholder approval. This added to the task of communicating confidence and calm in troubled waters. In addition to all of this, we still had a business to run and another year to close with growth in earnings. Once again, it was a time when I felt very ordinary, supported by people committed to accomplishing the extraordinary. Our plan of reorganization and the acquisitions were approved and completed by December 30, with one day to spare.[52]

The Challenge

The sense of relief is obvious, especially since major goals were accomplished within severe time constraints. But there was no rest ahead. It was one thing to transform the structure of the business and add two acquisitions, one of which was major. It was quite another to integrate the new acquisitions into a company with different cultures, backgrounds, and practices. As 1987 began, it was this huge challenge that Bill Pollard and The ServiceMaster Company faced.

How does a newly acquired company come to know, and believe in, the established four corporate objectives? The leadership of Terminix had been doing things in its own way for many years and, while they recognized the appeal of the objectives, it would not be easy for them to own and practice these objectives themselves. In addition, they were already invested in their own good practices. Integration is also about the small things. For example, when traveling for business, Terminix employees expected private hotel rooms, while the more frugal ServiceMaster Company generally had people sharing rooms. Terminix company events often had open bars, while ServiceMaster was dry for company functions. In order to maintain growth and profitability, however, the companies needed to come together.

International expansion represented a different dimension of these challenges. How do the four objectives continue to promote excellence in international settings with different traditions and laws? While ServiceMaster had expanded internationally before, this activity was also accelerating. This meant that the company could not take a long pause while these integration issues were worked out. The global market continued to change, and the need for growth likewise required that the company continue to develop. ServiceMaster needed to continue to grow its existing businesses and still provide excellence, provide value to the customer, and maintain its reputation, while at the same time continue the growth cycle.

Growth itself calls for continued diffusion of leadership, and it became no longer possible for a single strong leader to have the level of influence needed to ensure culture and practices throughout the growing company. There are several ways companies respond to developing and infusing the culture throughout the organization at times of acquisition, expansion, and growth. Some leaders will impose their established practices and culture, creating measurements of performance beyond financial and customer satisfaction for the newly acquired business or location; while others will move someone familiar with the practices of the acquiring company into a leadership position in the acquired company.

Relentlessly Teaching

Bill Pollard, however, took neither of these approaches. Rather, he became the relentless teacher, never losing an opportunity to talk about the meaning and purpose of the four objectives. He followed in the footsteps of his predecessors who had done the same. He ensured that the financial goals were achieved while talking about the culture, values, and objectives of the company. He did this in large groups, small gatherings, customer interactions, the boardroom, with the press, and in public gatherings. When he went to a new location, he met with the leadership but also with people on the floor doing the work.

He frequently talked about the nature of people and the path to their engagement in the business:

> You can buy a person's time, you can buy a person's physical presence at a given place, you can even buy a measured number of skilled muscular motions for eight hours a day; but you cannot buy enthusiasm, you cannot buy initiative, you cannot buy loyalty, nor can you buy the devotion of people's hearts, minds, and souls. It is when people are motivated to do what money can't buy that they contribute and respond with new and better ways to serve the customer.[53]

Pollard was also a relentless storyteller, putting names and faces on the practices in the company. He told the story of Shirley, a housekeeper for fifteen years at a 250-bed hospital, who personally understood the company's objectives:

> She came to us seeking a job. But she brought to us an unlocked potential seeking to accomplish something significant. She recently confirmed the importance of her cause when she told me, "If we don't clean with a quality effort, we can't keep the doctors and nurses in business; we can't accommodate the patients. This place would be closed if we didn't have housekeeping."[54]

His teaching, of course, went beyond motivation and purpose. ServiceMaster helped people develop by providing the training, cleaning agents, tools, and techniques to do the work efficiently and well. In addition to quality, low-cost work, leaders also supported the dignity of the person. When Pollard visited one of the hospitals ServiceMaster was managing in London, he told the leadership team there that he also wanted to meet with the workers.

> As I was introduced as the Chairman of ServiceMaster to one of the housekeepers, Nisha, she put her arms around me, gave me a big hug, and thanked me for the training and tools she had received to do her job. She then showed me all that she had accomplished in cleaning patients' rooms, providing a detailed before- and after-ServiceMaster description. She was proud of her work. You would have thought she owned the company.[55]

His teaching extended to the boardroom as well. During his years of leadership, in addition to a prayer, devotional, and business agenda for the board, he talked with them about the meaning and value of the four objectives. He later compiled these teachings in his book *Serving Two Masters?*

Reflections on God and Profit.[56] These presentations and stories were a part of any leadership team visit he made.

Beyond the usual leadership from the top, other leaders had specific teaching goals for their workers throughout the company to have ownership and be able to teach these leadership objectives:

> To encourage teaching, we must openly reward those who mentor and develop others. At the same time, we must be careful not to transfer the responsibility of learning from the student to the teacher. The student is the worker, not the work product, and the worker must have active participation and ownership in the result. If leaders in the company are too busy to teach, they are too busy to work for us.[57]

This was echoed by Chuck Stair, a leader of Management Services whom Pollard called "a leader who was a strong, experienced, and caring person":[58]

> We are not only teachers but also reproducers—reproducing in our people the motivation that has been born in us; reproducing the climate that has allowed us to grow; and reproducing the servant leaders who will be needed in the business.[59]

Bill also wanted to make sure the leaders stepped up to the responsibility and risk required by their leadership role. He speaks of challenging a person in his new leadership role to buy stock in the company to put himself on the line for growth.

> Several years ago I was visiting with one of our officers about his promotion and the opportunity that came with it to acquire shares of ServiceMaster stock. It would mean he would have to borrow some money to purchase the stock. He was delighted about the promotion, but he questioned the risk of going into debt to buy the stock. I asked him to make a simple T-account balance sheet so I could review with him his personal assets and liabilities.

> The only indebtedness he listed on [his personal account] balance sheet was the mortgage on his house. I then asked him about the indebtedness he had assumed when he took over the responsibility of leading this important unit of ServiceMaster which involved over 1,000 people. How were the opportunities [of these people] going to be affected by his leadership? Would there be more or fewer jobs and opportunities a year from now or two years from now, and would his leadership make the difference? How did he quantify this obligation to the people he would lead? It was a debt of duty as real as any bank debt he had ever incurred. It was much larger than what he would have to borrow to purchase the ServiceMaster stock. Was he willing to assume the obligation to those he would lead, or was he interested only in a job with a title?[60]

Visual Pictures

Teaching was also done visually in many different ways. In 1989, Dale Sheets was director for people in the Industrial Management Services Division of the company.[61] He wanted to help the employees to better relate to the four objectives, so he built a balance beam form that rested on a fulcrum labeled, "To Honor God in All We Do." Then he created three blocks labeled with the other objectives, placing them on the top of the beam. Holding the beam in balance meant it was not possible to simply focus only on the finances, the people, or excellence. They all had to work together.

One day he showed what he had done to his boss Jack Schultz, president of Industrial Management Services. A few months later, Schultz had a meeting with Bill Pollard, showing him what Sheets had created. The next morning, Pollard told Schultz that he wanted to have one hundred of these professionally made. They were then given to every executive across the divisions as a way to explain how the objectives of ServiceMaster actually work in the lives of people. On October 17, 1989, Bill wrote a letter to Dale,

> Thank you, Dale, for your creative efforts in developing the model for the tension/balance of our company objectives. In my closing remarks at the Fall Delta, I instructed each Delta member that this model is to be displayed in his or her office at all times. We have you to thank for this concept and the contribution it will make to the enhanced communication of our company objectives.[62]

Soon, whenever employees or visitors entered the ServiceMaster headquarters building, they were confronted with "a curving marble wall that stretches 90 feet, and stands 18 feet tall," and prominently carved into the wall were the four objectives.[63] In 1991, the company changed its headquarters address from 2300 Warrenville Road to One ServiceMaster Way. In 1992, a sculpture of Christ washing a disciple's feet was added outside the lobby to represent "a striking and practical example of servant leadership. It will be a reminder to all of us that our company has been built by those who have made career commitments as they have served and led with a mission and purpose."[64] The company also etched the names of employees with twenty-five years of service into the marble wall behind the statue (see the photo section for images of the balance beam and the wall).

They also chose to create a unique and shared environment with their office space. Pollard wrote, "Nobody works behind closed doors. Glass is everywhere, confirming our desire to have an open office and open minds. No executive office captures an outside window. The view to the outside is available to all working in the office."[65]

In 1984, Dave Baseler joined the company's marketing team and observed that the "yellow" ServiceMaster trucks and cars were what he called a "muddy" yellow color. The company originally bought their vans and trucks from General Motors, and GM modified the colors each year. So Dave worked with a DuPont paint engineer to create a brighter yellow color that would standardize the vehicles across the company. In 1986, this corporate identity program was approved, including the cheerful yellow color.[66] Dick Armstrong, an executive at the time, even led the way in having his company car repainted in ServiceMaster yellow.

In 1995, Bill used another visual teaching device at a large company gathering. He told the story of the company through a video series of interviews called "Lightposts of Our Heritage" with people who had served for a long time under various leaders and who had joined ServiceMaster through various acquisitions. Each interview was conducted under a different lightpost, and each acquisition added a piece to a large puzzle that came together spelling out "ServiceMaster."

Keeping This Real

Bill Pollard strongly believed that the company's four individual objectives lived in tension, but tied together they created the key to success for the company. When *Fortune* magazine suggested that company profits were derived from the way the company treated people, Pollard responded,

> Our ability to outperform others may have something to do with our objectives and the meaning of our name. This does not mean, however, that one should expect or promote financial success or gain from seeking to honor God. It does not translate. While financial returns are important, as our track record clearly reflects, they are a means goal, not an end goal.[67]

Yet profit was indeed important. Ernie Mrozek started with the company in 1987 and worked with Bill Pollard on many of the acquisitions. He recalled,

> Sometimes others thought we would be more relaxed about profits, pricing and things like that because of the way we articulated those values. But again, we recognized that as a public company, we also had a responsibility to provide a meaningful return to our shareholders that was part of balancing all of our values.[68]

Pollard also acknowledged that when this work was carried out by imperfect people, much forgiveness was required and there was always the need to face up to mistakes. The open environment helped. He wrote,

> At ServiceMaster, we have experienced our share of mistakes. We have our warts and moles. We can make both good and bad choices. But because

of our open and expressed starting point, we typically cannot hide our mistakes. They are flushed out into the open for correction and in some cases, forgiveness.[69]

Throughout his books, he provides illustrations of the times when he needed to go back and ask forgiveness:

> While participating in a unit review, I pressed the manager in charge as to why his performance and that of his unit was so poor. . . . My comments became more focused on the deficiencies of his personal performance. My comments were out of line. When I realized what was happening, I stopped the meeting, apologized, and asked forgiveness. Was this a perfect solution? No. But a leader's life is always on display, and when there is a mistake, it must be acknowledged and forgiveness sought.[70]

Other people have described situations where they needed to confront him over the way he responded to people when he didn't recognize it himself. He was a passionate leader who saw issues clearly and did not always express himself well, but he was also willing to seek forgiveness.

The success of the ServiceMaster yellow trucks and cars did advance the corporate identity. But when it was extended to the cars driven by executives, it backfired. Executives didn't necessarily want to drive yellow cars! Dan Kellow, a vice president in the franchise part of the company, told this story:

> I was meeting one of our franchise distributors at O'Hare Airport. When I stopped in front of the terminal, a man got in and started giving me directions. I told him this was not a cab. He looked at the car very clean and nice and at me, suit and tie, and realized this was not a Chicago cab and got out very quickly. These cars were so ugly that when I took my kids to school, they would duck down so their friends would not see them![71]

Yellow cars for executives were finally recognized as a bad idea.

In spite of the fits and starts, this relentless focus on the culture and identity of the company, which was established early in the acquisition and expansion process, bore significant fruit. It created an army of converts as the company grew and as leadership at all levels developed. But it did not, and could not, inspire everybody. Regarding the first objective of honoring God in all they did, one executive at Terminix said,

> My take on the first objective is that it was all well and good, especially if you are working with a homogenous group of people such as Service-Master was in its early years. Often, the consumer services group would wonder why we took so much time discussing the objectives. We would smile a lot and nod, then get on with the business of serving our customers, developing people, and making money.[72]

Continued Growth

Between 1987 and the end of Bill Pollard's time as CEO at the end of 1993, the company made a number of additional acquisitions and grew around the world. In 1999, Pollard returned as CEO, which will be described in chapter 7.

As ServiceMaster studied its competitors and further potential acquisitions, Pollard understood the fundamental importance of culture in a company. He shared,

> My former partner, Alex Balc, once gave a very thorough report on a competing company as part of our continued attempt to stay on top in our industry. He described some of the financial successes of this competitor (which were considerable) but also reviewed some of its problems with people, purpose, and direction. I will never forget his conclusion: "This is a company without a soul."[73]

Bill Pollard was uniquely gifted in acquisitions, and it was because of him that the company was able to achieve its continued growth while remaining rooted in its original values. This was due to his vision, his attention to detail, and his ability to learn things quickly. Doug Pound remembers being amazed at one of the acquisition discussions where he was present. The company under consideration had failed to send its paperwork in advance and instead brought along a seventy-five-page document with detailed financials, growth projections, and assumptions. When someone suggested to Bill that the meeting be deferred to have time to review all the material, he said, "Give me five minutes." The meeting then started, and Pollard proceeded to ask them questions for two hours covering financials, footnotes, and strategy. Pound said, "I was really impressed."[74] Lord Brian Griffiths, a ServiceMaster board member from Goldman Sachs, shared a comment from one of his colleagues who had worked with Pollard on acquisitions: "He told me he had never met anyone outside of the professional field of investment banking who understood finance and cutting a deal better than Bill. That is quite a tribute."[75]

Other Acquisitions

From 1987 to 1993, ServiceMaster made nine additional acquisitions, which are listed in the appendix. Here we will focus on four of these: Merry Maids (1988), American Home Shield (1989), TruGreen (1991), and Chem-Lawn (1992). Merry Maids represents a company that aligned with ServiceMaster's line of business as well as with the culture and values the company held. American Home Shield (AHS) took ServiceMaster in a new direction in services, however, and was a company with quite a different culture. TruGreen and ChemLawn, like AHS, had little in common with the original objectives or the services of ServiceMaster, adding complexity to bringing two competitors together.

Merry Maids

Merry Maids started as the dream of Dallen Peterson, a former executive at Fairmont Foods. After rejecting a transfer that required him to move, Peterson started and sold a company with a friend. Then he looked around for the next venture, with no interest in returning to corporate life. After some careful research, he and his wife, Glennis, decided to start a house-cleaning service and placed a three-line ad in the Omaha newspaper. Their first project began on December 27, 1979, which happened to be Glennis's birthday. The two of them took on, sight unseen, the job of cleaning out a small house for $66. After sixty-six hours of work, they weren't so sure about this new business.

But by 1985, they had grown to over 250 franchises coast to coast and future growth looked promising. Then a year later, Dallen had a heart attack. He recovered, but he began to look for a buyer for his franchise business. Ironically, he had chosen the same four objectives for Merry Maids that ServiceMaster had, which gave them a similar foundation for their business. Ken Wessner heard about this opportunity from a friend, Chuck Colson, who was also a friend of Peterson's. Wessner brought the idea to Bill Pollard, and Bill arranged to meet with Dallen in Omaha in June 1988. The opportunity looked good to Pollard, who offered a price of $25 million to purchase the company, wanting to close the deal by the end of the month.

There was some consternation within Merry Maids over this acquisition by a large company, with fears of added bureaucracy in spite of a promise that ServiceMaster would leave the company alone. Dallen came on the ServiceMaster board but did not want to get involved in working at the company. Dale, Dallen's twin brother, came in with the Merry Maids group as a manager. In an interview with Pollard in 1995, Dale stated,

> To begin with, there was a great deal of apprehension amongst our owners and the whole office staff. They had joined the Peterson family, not this big company. Bill told the staff that there was nothing to fix in Merry Maids. They could continue to be a family organization as a part of ServiceMaster. Then the officers flew to Downers Grove, and for the first time met Carlos Cantu, who had gone through the same thing a year and a half prior. I was so relieved. Today Merry Maids has over 1000 franchises in five countries, and we couldn't be happier.[76]

This deal worked financially and culturally.

American Home Shield

Founded in 1971, American Home Shield was a home warranty appliance and systems company. In 1989, ServiceMaster acquired it for $95 million, which filled a niche in the home services business. Unlike Merry Maids, this company was not a perfect fit either in culture or business discipline. Scott Cromie was CFO at the time of the acquisition. He said they were about $60 million in revenue and not very profitable when they were acquired. Culturally, "AHS had flowing alcohol, and not as much discipline on the business side."[77] David Crawford, who was on the sales side when the acquisition took place, echoed these comments:

> AHS was very entrepreneurial, but ran rather loosely. We were the very opposite of the culture of ServiceMaster that led to some clashes. There was a lot of anxiety that ServiceMaster would take over our culture. As we learned the objectives, we didn't understand at first. People who got fired would ask how that was honoring to God. But we learned it was about being accountable to do the right thing, and we grew.[78]

Cromie added, "ServiceMaster wasn't very good at consumer marketing, but brought some strategic things to the table. We grew dramatically after the acquisition."[79] Mark Lightfoot, AHS general counsel, recalled,

> We were a home warranty company, an industry that was just trying to survive. Our benchmark of success was very low at the time. We had thrown a lot of things against the wall, trying to hit home runs, hoping something would stick. ServiceMaster watched this process for a while and said let's get rid of all this clutter. Let's raise the bar so you are a top-quality national service company. Coming into the acquisition, it had taken five years to get a national realtor to endorse our product. It has taken less than a year to get the State of California to recommend our product exclusively to the realtors. At the same time the National Real Estate Association took less than a year after the acquisition to endorse the Errors and Omissions product to all the realtors in the nation. So being with ServiceMaster has made a huge difference.[80]

Lawn Care Expansion

In the early 1990s, the expansion of ServiceMaster into lawn care services was achieved with two more major acquisitions, moving the company into another niche of the services business. According to Don Hill of *Turf* magazine, it was not until about 1960 that professional lawn care became a big business.[81] The first of the emerging companies was ChemLawn, which was based near Columbus, Ohio. In the early 1960s, ChemLawn was "an offshoot of the original sod farm and Duke Garden Centers founded by Paul G. Duke and his son Richard Duke."[82] About a decade later in 1973, TruGreen was started near East Lansing, Michigan, with a science-based solution to lawn care, reminiscent of Marion Wade with his research into better moth-proofing and carpet-cleaning agents. TruGreen established a local business that quickly grew beyond Michigan, planting companies where ChemLawn also did business. Ron Anderegg remembers the early days of TruGreen, when he worked out of his garage:

> I did sales and Don Karnes went out to the customer. At first we had only one vehicle, and Don filled the 1200 gallon tanker truck using a garden hose—it took a long time!—and started spraying lawns for the customers. The first 60 he did, he streaked the lawns and we started getting calls. We went back out there and talked with every customer and made it right, and we didn't lose one of the customers. We learned customer service with that. By the end of the year we had five employees.[83]

TruGreen also added pest control to its business.

Rival ChemLawn fought off an acquisition from Waste Management and was acquired by EcoLabs in 1987 for $360 million, which was about the amount of their annual revenues from 241 branches across the United States. Meanwhile, Waste Management under Wayne Huizenga turned its attention to the smaller TruGreen, with fifty-five branches and $43 million in sales. In 1990, Waste Management took a 22 percent interest in the newly created ServiceMaster Consumer Services sector and acquired TruGreen. Shortly after joining ServiceMaster, Bill Pollard invited Don Karnes, Dave Slott, and Ron Anderegg to dinner at his country club in Glen Ellyn, the town next to Wheaton. Anderegg recalled,

> At the end of the dinner Bill made the effort to pull each of us aside and asked how we were doing personally and how our family was doing. It was the first time anyone we had been associated with had ever done that. It made a big difference for us, and it was what we talked about when we went out in the field to talk about the connection to ServiceMaster.[84]

By 1992, ChemLawn was languishing under the EcoLabs leadership and was sold to the ServiceMaster/Waste Management Consumer Services Group for the bargain price of $104 million, becoming TruGreen/Chem-Lawn. With this acquisition, lawn care went from being a small part of ServiceMaster to a big part of the company in just two years. The company was now in the business of lawn maintenance and landscaping for both residential and industrial customers.

Dave Slott, an early leader in TruGreen along with Don Karnes, found their entry into ServiceMaster to be a good fit in some ways:

> We were supportive of the theory behind the objectives. We liked the fact that the company that set the tone for ethics treated workers well, since that was very important to us also. But we struggled with having God so boldly stated in the corporate objectives for a public company.[85]

Organizational Alignment and Integration

The newly formed Consumer Services Division included the ServiceMaster franchises (including residential and commercial cleaning and disaster recovery) along with lawn care and Terminix. The other major parts of the developing organization were Management Services (the hospital business along with the growing industrial and educational services), a new developing People Services (consisting of child care and home healthcare services), and International (which included all business outside North America).

As could be expected, Bill Pollard faced a significant challenge in bringing these large pieces into a cohesive company. The plan to maintain ServiceMaster's original culture continued with teaching and discussion at every opportunity, to the point that some of the people in the acquired companies began to refer to Bill as "professor." As in the case of the Terminix executive, some understood and some did not.

Another task for Pollard was to find some ways to benefit both the company and the customers by bringing leverage for the customers from the various divisions. Paul Bert, an executive with the Consumer Services Division who had joined the company with the Terminix acquisition, created a single phone number, 1-800-WE SERVE, that allowed customers to find pest control, house cleaning, or lawn care through one phone call.

International expansion continued at the same time as these major acquisitions. Over the years of Bill Pollard's tenure as CEO, the company opened services in Saudi Arabia (1985); Oman (1986); Qatar (1987); Australia, Hong Kong, New Zealand, Singapore, Taiwan, and United Arab Emirates (1988); Portugal, Thailand, and Spain (1990); Canada, the Czech Republic, Italy, Korea, and the United Kingdom (1991); Brazil (1992); and Israel and Mexico (1993). In addition to opening in new countries, the number of franchises in existing countries grew, particularly in the UK and in Japan. By 1992, there were 300 franchises in the UK and 750 franchises in Japan.

The number of ServiceMaster offerings also grew internationally as new services were added across the world. In addition to Management Services and franchises in the United Kingdom, Terminix began offering service in that country in 1991.

International expansion required careful cultural adaptation. The UK office offered a unique problem in that they did not want to display and talk about the first objective. After some lengthy discussions, Bill Pollard ultimately had to find new leadership for that division of ServiceMaster. Although this UK leader was the only one who refused to post the first objective, there were some cultural challenges in other countries as well.

Japan provides a good example of how international growth required cultural adaptation for ServiceMaster. The growth was greatest in this country during this period, largely due to a strong leadership presence provided by Brian Oxley and Phil Foxwell. Brian had been raised in Japan and spoke fluent Japanese. Phil, whose missionary father was Ken Hansen's former roommate in college, went to Japan shortly after college to help ServiceMaster develop the area. He knew the culture and the language, and he quickly developed relationships there.

One of the key selling points for hospital services in the United States was that ServiceMaster met stringent cleanliness standards, but there were no hospital standards in Japan in 1982. This meant the sales plan required adaptation. Then there were the cultural norms, particularly around "saving face." Foxwell found that the ServiceMaster people from the US had a great deal to learn, sometimes causing problems related to cultural issues that could have been avoided.

Bill Pollard readily admits the errors that had to be overcome as Japan was developed. The first error they made was cultural. Bill had gone to Japan with Peter Drucker to conduct a management seminar there. The general business public was invited, but a special invitation had gone to the ServiceMaster Japan team, and they had agreed to come. But when the day came, none of ServiceMaster Japan team showed up. The next day, Pollard was scheduled to attend some management meetings at the ServiceMaster office in Osaka. He was so frustrated by their missing the seminar, however, that he decided to fly home and skip the meeting in Osaka. When he explained his reasoning to Peter Drucker, Peter urged him to reconsider. Later that evening, Drucker called Pollard and asked him to come to his room. Drucker looked Pollard in the eye and said, "Bill, you are suffering from hubris. It's time for you to eat some humble pie."[86] The Japanese team had not come out of protest to a delay in bringing one of the new services to Japan. Bill realized then that someone needed to break the conflict. Drucker then advised Pollard to meet the Japanese business partners and rebuild this relationship for continued growth.

After he met with the Japanese team, Pollard had learned his lesson: "My leadership responsibility was not about me or my feelings. It was about what should be done for our business and for our people."[87] About six months later, the president of the ServiceMaster Japanese business partner died suddenly, and Pollard was invited to speak at the funeral. There he could talk about forgiveness and his own source of forgiveness in Jesus Christ. His talk was well received.

Later, Pollard showed some great insight adapting to the Japanese culture. The Japanese partner had a long-standing custom to start meetings with a Buddhist chant. When Bill visited and talked with the team about the first objective, the Japanese partner told him his remarks had "caused him some problems."[88] Because of Pollard's emphasis on the first objective of honoring God, the Japanese Christians now refused to participate in the opening Buddhist ceremony. To avoid causing a rift among the employees, Bill asked to participate and found himself impressed by their enthusiasm as demonstrated by these chants.

He was given the opportunity to explain how serving customers with excellence could honor God, even though some of those employees might not believe in God. Then Pollard negotiated a compromise with the Japanese team. The Christians would attend the ceremony, participate in the chorus about serving the customer, and remain respectful during the Buddhist chants. Then they would be given a chance to respectfully share something about their faith. This is an example of the kind of adaptation ServiceMaster needed as they expanded to different cultures.

A Limited Partnership Challenge

In 1986, as already noted, ServiceMaster converted to a public limited partnership with the goal of reducing the double taxation burden, and they were careful to be transparent and accountable in public meetings and with outside board members. This is because they wanted to continue to attract outside investors to their stock. But as one of the few operating companies to become a limited partnership (others were oil and real estate partnerships), outside investors were more reticent. In December 1991, Bill Pollard told *Chicago Tribune* reporter David Young, "I think the partnership forms have been abused and have acquired a reputation that is not all that favorable."[89] In his subsequent article, Young wrote that "institutional investors, who account for about half of the stock market, have been staying away from the Downers Grove-based company because limited partnerships convey no tax benefit to them, and because of the controversy over oil and real estate partnerships." Based on legislation that was passed in January 1992 after ServiceMaster had made the conversion, there was a ten-year limit placed on the length of time for these special limited partnerships.

Given this issue, ServiceMaster took the decision to the board in January 1992 to convert back to a public company, with 1-for-1 stock swaps, effective the end of the ten-year period in December 1997. They also began discussing the possibility of converting the company into two separate publicly held companies: Consumer Services and Management Services.

Financial Growth

Through all of the changes, acquisitions, and international expansion, ServiceMaster continued its trend, started in 1970, of growing revenue and profit each year. Figures 5.1 and 5.2 below show this continued growth of revenue and profit between 1983 and 1993. Through recessions, changing management structure, and developing culture in new organizations, the growth continued. One time on a call with Wall Street analysts, because of their discussion of the first objective, an analyst who was new to the calls with ServiceMaster raised the question of why the company would talk about God on an analyst call. Before Bill could respond, one of the more senior analysts said, "With profit and growth numbers like this, they can talk about anything they want."[90] By 1993, the revenue from ServiceMaster Consumer Services had grown to $940 million and net income for this sector was $70.6 million. In 1993, Management Services revenue was $1.8 billion, with profit of $61 million.

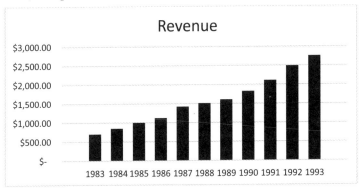

Figure 5.1. Revenue growth in the Pollard years (dollars shown in millions).

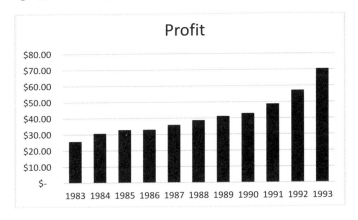

Figure 5.2. Profit growth in the Pollard years (dollars shown in millions).

Starting in 1992, the company began presenting a larger picture of net revenue, adding a line to the financial statement called "customer level revenue."[91] This number recognized that for the franchises the only revenue on the books was the franchise fees. The customer level revenue report included the revenue of the franchises and showed $3,543 million, compared with the operating revenue shown in Figure 5.1 of $2,500 million.

Of course, growth wasn't measured only with the revenue and profit numbers. Between 1983 and 1988, the number of franchises grew from 2,700 (2,200 in the US) to 4,100 (3,400 in the US). Then the company stopped listing the number of franchises in the annual report. The reason for the change was that it had become difficult to track the kinds of franchises (Merry Maids, Terminix, and ServiceMaster Clean) that provided different services and had different structures.

Another size measurement for ServiceMaster was the number of employees. In the 1993 report, the company showed 31,000 employees with an additional 180,000 people managed. The difference represented people who were workers on the payroll of the hospital, the educational facility, or the industrial facility while ServiceMaster Management Services managed them. By any of these measures, the company was large and complex—as well as growing and profitable.

External Recognition and Impact

In 1985, Harvard Business School began a detailed analysis of ServiceMaster, resulting in a case study that was completed in 1988. During this time, Bill Pollard had the opportunity to make numerous visits to the classrooms at Harvard to talk about the company and take questions from students and professors. Not surprisingly, the questions often centered on the need and importance of the first objective, "To Honor God in All We Do." He enjoyed the opportunity to talk about God with these students. When they suggested the company could accomplish the same objective by using honesty, he pushed back: Honesty based on what set of rules? Honesty does not include recognizing the value of another human being as made in the image of God—which is the reasoning that holds to the purpose and dignity of each worker. Pollard considered this time with the Harvard professors and students as an honor and a tremendous opportunity for the company and himself.

In 1989, *Fortune* magazine again recognized ServiceMaster as the number one "star" of the Service 500 companies:

> The shiningest star of the group [the same language that was used in 1984] is also somewhat unorthodox. ServiceMaster, of suburban Chicago, headed the 1984 list and leads the 1989 version as well with an average return on equity for the decade of—wow!—63.7%. Back-to-back championships may attest, in this case, to the power of religion. ServiceMaster experienced a stunning secular conversion between List 1 and List 2. Five

years ago the company was a garden-variety corporation that garnered 80% of its revenues from services, particularly cleaning, that it provided to hospitals. But as Medicare shrank what it would pay toward the bills of senior citizens, hospitals retrenched and ServiceMaster got squeezed. So the company sallied forth and transformed itself. For one thing, it borrowed $340 million, mostly to buy other service businesses that would fit its disciplined Midwestern ways. Brooding over ServiceMaster and a pack of other companies that decamped into partnerships, the government rose up to block this escape route from income taxes. By then, C. William Pollard, ServiceMaster's chief executive, hopes to have paid down debt, to have gained growth from his acquisitions, and to be making high returns on equity the old-fashioned way.[92]

In 1999, Harvard Business School returned with another case study that covered the period of growth through acquisitions under Bill Pollard's leadership. Pollard was delighted about another opportunity to talk about good business and invite others to wrestle honestly with the question of God.

In 1999, Pollard was selected as one of Corporate America's Outstanding Directors, which recognized his role on various corporate boards. The nomination letter stated, "Pollard has an unusual knack for holding management to tough standards while making its members feel valued."[93] One CEO added to this insight: "He does it in a unique fashion—one that occasionally causes sleepless nights. . . . Management can't just wiggle away with a finessed answer."

Bill Pollard the Leader

Between 1983 and 1993, Pollard led the transformation of a company, which had previously been driven primarily by internal growth, to become a star on Wall Street where the structure and offerings were quite different. Through it all, he sought to preserve their trademark culture with teaching and challenging, driven by a single purpose of maintaining adherence to the four corporate objectives.

David Miller, a professor who worked with Pollard in setting up a center for faith and work at Princeton University, came to know him quite well through the process. Miller reflected,

> Bill was relentless in his focus. I found him sometimes to be a great teacher, sometimes to be a prosecuting attorney as he argued the case for the right way of doing business. He could be very tough, and he could be very soft. He wasn't two different people, but one person with a deep passion.[94]

Many from within ServiceMaster echoed this sentiment. Scott Cromie, at the time the leader of American Home Shield, said,

Bill was the smartest man I ever met. He could at times be loud, pushy, and demanding. But I came to see that he was as committed to this business as any person could possibly be. He saw himself having a great responsibility to the people of the company, to the culture, and to making this work. This was not a job for him, but a life passion. He brought us all the traditions of the company, the insights of Ken Hansen and Ken Wessner. Though there were battles, this seemed to draw out the passion in others as well.[95]

Pollard did have a softer side as well. In 1983, he hired John, a man with special needs, right out of high school. The company crafted a job for John that allowed him to use his abilities so he could contribute. John's family also became an important part of his life at ServiceMaster, when day after day one of them would bring him to work and pick him up. John was a big basketball fan, and Pollard recalled taking him to a Chicago Bulls basketball game:

> It was an exciting experience for both of us. John gave ServiceMaster his best efforts and undeniable loyalty. He knew no other way to conduct himself. In return, he received a fair wage and, more importantly, a sense of belonging, of contributing, and of identity. He was treated as the subject of work, not just the object of work.[96]

Jane McGuffey, one of Pollard's longtime assistants, recalled times when he would be running out the door and she would call out to him, "Do you have a minute? May I ask you a question?" She said, "He would stop and give me his full attention. Mr. Pollard (I always called him that) walked the talk. He had the objectives etched in his heart."[97]

Patricia Asp, who had joined ServiceMaster through the acquisition of Service Direction and went on to many roles in the company, confirmed this: "Bill wasn't just a business leader. Bill was the spiritual leader of ServiceMaster as well."[98] He sought to serve as he led and to integrate his faith with his work. "While a business firm is only temporal," Pollard said, "it is the people who work there and the people it serves who are eternal."[99] As his predecessors did, Pollard sought to be an ambassador for Christ as he led. It was the ServiceMaster way—to become masters of service serving the Master.

Professor James Heskett, who studied ServiceMaster and other companies, acknowledges the strong role that ServiceMaster's unique culture had in its success. He also admits that the growth and acquisitions led to a "somewhat diminished culture."[100] But only a little. Throughout the 1980s and 1990s, Heskett attests that culture remained strong for ServiceMaster and its strongly motivated workforce. He notes that they were the only large service company that put its people at the center of its attention.

End of an Era

In many ways, 1993 was the end of an era. It was a year of transition for Bill Pollard. Both Ken Hansen and Ken Wessner died the following year.

In reflecting on his own leadership, Pollard said, "A leader must keep his promises to the people he leads, even if it is at his own personal risk and sacrifice. It is his obligation."[101] One of those obligations is to prepare for succession. At a speech in Windsor, England, he said,

> The servant leader should be of the mind that he or she will serve until a successor is identified and ready and not one moment longer. It is the availability and readiness of the right person for the future that should determine whether a leader steps aside and not any predetermined date, age, or other artificial criteria.[102]

At the end of 1993, Bill Pollard determined that Carlos Cantu was ready to lead and that it was time for him to step aside. On January 1, 1994, Carlos Cantu became the CEO and Bill Pollard the chairman of the board of directors.

6

THE CARLOS CANTU YEARS

Before this transition in 1994, Carlos Cantu had already been preparing for his leadership role as CEO of ServiceMaster. As early as September 1993, he had laid out his preliminary goals for what would be required to continue the growth of the company. He shared these goals with Bruce Hansen, a reporter for the *Memphis Business Journal*:[1]

> We have worked out our SMIXX ["ServiceMaster Industries 20"] long range plan, which will require some ongoing refinement. But these are the current goals:
>
> - Much of my time will be spent with assimilation of the acquisitions we have made, helping us gain efficiencies and integration between the various parts of the organization.
> - In particular, the integration of TruGreen and ChemLawn will require attention along with bringing the pest control pieces together, perhaps with selective acquisitions.
> - Two main engines drive the company: Consumer Services and Management Services. We have done research into customer needs, and believe there is a need for other services that are delivered quickly, reliably, with professionalism. The acquisition of VHA (long term healthcare) could combine with other acquisitions in this area to create a third leg for the company around home healthcare services.[2]

A story in the *Chicago Tribune* also reported:

> [Carlos Cantu] has no set agenda but plans to continue the growth. "We (also) want to explore international markets," he said. Those markets now account for less than 1 percent of the Firm's annual revenues, although ServiceMaster has a presence in Canada, Mexico, Great Britain and Japan—and other places.[3]

Personally, Cantu said he would be moving from Memphis to the Downers Grove headquarters. He anticipated he would continue to remain as CEO of the Consumer Services Division "for the foreseeable future." He said, "Rob Keith will assist and be responsible for Residential/Commercial, Merry Maids, and American Home Shield, while Terminix and TruGreen will continue to report to me."[4]

As with the past transitions, "shingles on a roof" would continue with collaboration between the CEO and the chairman. When Cantu began his role, Bill Pollard sent him a letter underscoring this relationship:

> Maximize your strength. Seek help and support in other areas. Be open and vulnerable to those you trust. As you initiate and make change, I have the hope and expectation that you will involve me for advice and counsel. Don't please me or try to keep things on an even keel with the way things were in the past. Do what is right for the future. My expectation is for you to be the most successful and accomplished CEO ServiceMaster has ever had. That expectation now becomes my single-minded goal.

Then Pollard added,

> There can be only one chief executive and you are the person for the job. I am looking forward to working with you and helping the Board of Directors to be a more effective approver and representative of our shareholders.[5]

In the letter, Pollard also reminded the new CEO of the foundations of the company, with the ongoing special challenge regarding the first objective:

> You have much to give the organization in understanding the scope of this objective. You will be tested from many directions. Draw few lines. Be patient with those who think they know all of the answers. Remember that we are not a church or a denomination. We accept God's mix of people as diverse as He has made or allowed it, yet we stand for what is right. You and I have a faith and trust in Jesus Christ that gives us an inner strength and discernment that not everyone will agree with, understand, or express in the same way. You will have your own way to carry out this objective through the organization. My expectation is that the meaning and purpose of this objective will have greater understanding and effectiveness among the people of ServiceMaster as a result of your leadership.[6]

This close working arrangement, confidence, and mutual respect was likely what led Pollard to recommend Carlos Cantu for the role of CEO in the first place, though in some ways he was an unlikely choice. Cantu was five years older than Pollard, while in the past, younger leaders had been chosen. No doubt, because of the growth of the company, it was harder to find someone younger who was ready to take on such a monumental task. Also, Cantu was a Catholic Christian, which ended the line of evangelical Protestant Christians with a Wheaton College connection. This was not a problem for Pollard, since throughout his tenure he had talked more and more about the importance of diversity.

Some aspects, however, remained the same as Bill and Carlos continued to emphasize the inclusive meaning of the first objective: "To Honor

God in All We Do." The 1993 ServiceMaster annual report features a cover focusing on diversity (brands, ages, race, gender, and occupation) represented by the company. It also featured an essay by Cantu titled "Unity in Diversity," in which he wrote, "Diversity, when managed properly, can unify the work force and provide a stimulus for social, intellectual, and economic growth."[7] In this essay, he also discussed the importance of maintaining the first objective:

> At ServiceMaster, our tradition has long extolled understanding of people who are different. The philosophy is based on the principle that, even though different, every individual is created in the image and likeness of God. As leaders, we do not rely simply on a philosophy of tolerance. Our charge is to actively pursue practices that pertain to recruiting, training, personal development and growth, and to ensure that these practices support and encourage a diverse work force to guarantee that opportunity for minorities and women is based on competence and character and not on circumstances of birth.[8]

The time was right for the first Hispanic Catholic leader at ServiceMaster. But as was the case with other leaders, he would encounter challenges both internally and externally.

Carlos Cantu's Early Years

Carlos Cantu was born in Brownsville, Texas, in 1934, the first son of his parents, Ambrosio and Natalia. Ambrosio came to the United States as a small child when his father, a sharecropper in Mexico, sought a life with more opportunity in the US. But when Ambrosio was in third grade, his father died of a heart attack. This ended formal education for Ambrosio, who was forced to drop out of school and work to help support the family. Ambrosio married Natalia and they had three sons: Carlos, Henry, and George. They later adopted a daughter, Margaret. At age ninety, Ambrosio was still working at the local Ford dealership in Brownsville.

Determined to provide a better life for their children, Ambrosio and Natalia emphasized education. Carlos remembers his father saying, "The opportunity comes to those who seek it and are prepared for it." And he remembers his mother pushing even harder. His parents sacrificed and saved to provide an education for him at a private Catholic school in Brownsville.

His parents constantly instilled respect for others, mostly by example. His father worked as an automotive parts salesman, but had a second job at the local Ford dealer, working evenings and weekends, which required him to have access to a telephone. In the 1940s, they were the first family in the neighborhood to have a phone in their home. His parents never said no to neighbors who needed to use it. Cantu recalled that "people would sit in the living room and on the porch, lined up to use the phone."[9] His parents demonstrated a service attitude and never asked for money to use the phone.

Through grade three, the school Carlos attended didn't emphasize English, and he spoke Spanish at home. But in the fourth grade, he transferred to St. Joseph's Academy where "he was forced to learn English as quickly as possible. An adept student, Carlos moved to the head of his class as soon as he was proficient in English, and he stayed at the top throughout his school years."[10]

Carlos worked hard through his early years. "His first job was selling pumpkins and squash when he was only ten. As soon as he got a bicycle, however, he got a paper route. After delivering papers for four years, he worked for Western Union as a delivery boy. He also worked at the Ford dealership each summer, sanding cars and doing janitorial work."[11] In high school, Carlos was vice president of his junior and senior classes. He also played football and was selected as co-captain of the team. Academically, he was interested in business and history. His sister, Margaret (Molina), recalled him as an intense and intelligent young man. "I always knew he would do well in life," she said. "He was at the top of his class and loved to read. He read about a book a day and seemed to retain much of what he read."[12] While in high school, he began dating Gloria Longoria, who attended the Catholic girls' school, Villa Maria Academy.[13]

As a first-generation Hispanic American, Carlos dealt with his share of discrimination: "But I don't like to dwell on it because nobody owes me anything."[14] He remembered talking with his mother about an ad that said, "Only Anglos need to apply." Carlos recalled, "My mother could have just passed this off as discrimination. But she didn't. She told me that ad meant I needed to have fluency in English."[15] But he didn't see himself as the only one in this situation. "This has probably happened to anyone who has immigrated. But the key is to seize the opportunity."[16] After interviewing him later in his career, a reporter observed, "Cantu has no hint of a Spanish accent or a Texas drawl. His is the elusive blended dialect of someone who has moved around a good deal."[17]

His parents also saved to make sure their children had the chance to attend college. Carlos decided he was not interested in law, so he began to focus instead on economics at Texas A&M University. His family helped him financially the first year, and then he was able to support himself with various jobs for the rest of his time in college. During the summers, he worked at cotton trading companies in the area and at the Texas Department of Agriculture. "The Rio Grande Valley is an agricultural area," he said, "and I became aware of commodities. I had summer jobs working for cotton brokers, and I became very interested in how markets worked and how goods moved." During the academic year, he worked at the school gymnasium. "They called it a gymnasium manager, but what I did was check out and put away the equipment and clean the place up. Sounds more like a custodian," Carlos said with a laugh.[18]

At that time, Texas A&M had only male students, with many students from the military, which meant that the university engaged in military-style discipline. "I enjoyed the discipline," he remembered, "and it helped me. I almost considered a military career, but there was not much happening at that time."[19] He also learned in college how to get "a better handle on diversity." In 1955, he graduated with a degree in agricultural economics and then began the search for his post-college career. In 1956, he married his high school sweetheart, Gloria.

Early Career

His interest in commodities and markets attracted him to a position with Cook & Company, a privately held business that dealt in commodities trading. Ned Cook offered Carlos a job as a cotton broker at the salary of one dollar per hour.[20] Cook would provide ample opportunity for Carlos's professional growth until the company was sold to ServiceMaster in 1986. Carlos would remain at ServiceMaster until he retired. Through this early time at Cook, Ned Cook also became a mentor for Cantu: "He supported me in learning, opportunities, and a great deal of encouragement."[21] His first assignment was grading cotton as a buyer.

Carlos and Gloria spent a short time in Memphis, where he learned to grade cotton, before returning to Brownsville where "he was based and traveled to northern Mexico for Cook managing all the cotton gins in that area."[22] During that period, sons Carlos Jr., Albert, and David were born. Between 1963 and 1968, the family moved to Tampico, Mexico, where two more children, Jorge and Gloria, were born. Then from 1968 to 1971, they lived in Mexico City, where their sixth child, Lorenzo, was born.

In the late 1960s, Cook acquired E. L. Bruce Company, which made hardwood floors. One of the Bruce divisions was Terminix. In 1969, Terminix considered going international and made a small acquisition of a pest control company in Mexico City.

> I was asked to assist in the acquisition by translating, etc. This was my first exposure to the pest control business. Then I was asked to participate in the management of that company in Mexico City. In 1970, my wife and I decided we wanted to move back to the U.S. to provide educational opportunities more readily available there.

He and Gloria discussed whether to look for a commodities position with another company in the US or to stay with Cook doing something else. "I

was offered a job with Terminix as regional manager in Indianapolis. I
went through training and moved in late 1970."

The transition from Mexico City to Indianapolis, Indiana, was challenging for the whole family. The children had been speaking Spanish in
school, and the weather, size of community, and culture were quite different between the two cities.

> Our kids developed a bonding in Indianapolis, since they spoke mainly
> Spanish, so they supported each other. They were a novelty to others, but
> that didn't last long. They were soon communicating well. All were inter-
> ested in athletics, and that helped the transition. But my wife was in tears
> from snowfall in November.[23]

Carlos remembered Gloria asking, "How can I get through the winter?" In
the end, the family thoroughly enjoyed Indianapolis, and it was the start
of a significant growth in his career.

Indianapolis represented a more diverse community than Brownsville
or Mexico City. From his time in Indianapolis, Carlos learned a key lesson:
"I developed a tremendous responsibility toward all people. In order to
be an effective leader, I had to be prepared to serve. That required being
constantly willing to listen and learn from every relationship." He said he
wanted to "convey to people that employment is an opportunity, not just
a job. I must ensure that there is respect for dignity of individuals regard-
less of race, religion, ethnic background. I need to keep this constantly
before me."[24]

While in Indianapolis, Cantu achieved "a good deal of success in the
process. And it was a team effort."[25] In 1975, he was promoted to vice
president for operations for Terminix and the family moved to Memphis.
In 1978, he was named president of Terminix and began to focus on growing the business. Former Terminix Vice President Charlie Hromada said,

> We decided in the early 80s to be No. 1 in the pest control business. Cantu
> took the lead in pointing us in that direction and we all jumped on the
> bandwagon and ran like heck to do it. He made people want to work for
> him because he was very knowledgeable, very astute and diplomatic in
> his demeanor. He was just a natural born leader. He was sharp in terms
> of looking at business operations and figuring out ways and means make
> them work better and more efficient.[26]

Paul Bert recalled the time when Terminix finally passed Orkin to
become the number one pest control company in the nation: "It was the
great 'Super Bowl' event that lasted over ten years and everyone knew we
were winning, including Orkin. People were truly excited where we were
going and would go to extraordinary lengths to help Terminix along on
the journey."[27]

During the ensuing period, Ned Cook made some changes in his privately held company. He got out of the commodities parts of the business and focused on Terminix, which was now the sole company. Due to a coming change in the tax laws and because all of his net worth was in one company, Cook decided it was time to sell Terminix before the end of 1986. Cantu, Ned Cook, and others began working with Goldman Sachs to find a buyer. Cantu recalled, "There were multiple bidders, including ServiceMaster, EcoLabs, Waste Management, and others."[28] This led to the discussions between Cantu and Bill Pollard found in chapter 5 regarding the Terminix acquisition by ServiceMaster. "Fortunately for all of us," Cantu said, "ServiceMaster was the successful bidder."

Carlos Cantu's Growing Role in ServiceMaster

After the Terminix acquisition, Cantu continued his role of leading that part of ServiceMaster for two years. Its rapid growth made this new part of the company an increasingly significant part of the overall revenue and the leader in growth. As Merry Maids and other smaller "consumer services" pieces were added to the ServiceMaster portfolio, ServiceMaster reorganized in 1988 and formed the Consumer Services and Products Group. Carlos Cantu was named executive vice president and chief operating officer of the group. He was also added to the board of directors of ServiceMaster. Chuck Stair, another director, had a similar responsibility for the Management Services Group.

Cantu's role in the Consumer Services area grew with the acquisitions. By 1993, he was president and CEO of the ServiceMaster Consumer Services Company, with responsibility for Terminix, TruGreen/ChemLawn, Residential/Commercial Services, Merry Maids, ServiceMaster Franchises, and American Home Shield, headquartered in Memphis, Tennessee. Revenues for the Consumer Services Company in 1993 were $940 million, with net income of $70.6 million. By comparison, Management Services, the more traditional part of the company, had revenues of $1.8 billion with net income of $61 million. These two new divisions of the company were making their presence felt.

Meanwhile, Cantu, along with the others at Terminix (and subsequent acquisitions) were learning about the culture of ServiceMaster and its four objectives. Paul Bert reports that when Cantu came back one day from an early meeting, he said, "I don't know why we are spending so much time on the philosophy."[29] But over the years, Carlos took ownership of the culture along with the four objectives.

The 1993 annual report documents the changing of the guard with a photograph of leadership: Ken Wessner (retired), Chuck Stair (CEO, Management Services), Ken Hansen (retired), Bill Pollard, and Carlos Cantu are shown, with the picture of Marion Wade in the background. Both Ken Wessner and Ken Hansen died the next year, severing the final working connection to Marion Wade at the top. Yet the "shingles on a roof" concept enabled Bill Pollard and Carlos Cantu to work closely together, and Carlos became committed to the objectives and culture, though he was less vocal than Bill. Patricia Asp recalled:

> Carlos was quieter than Bill. When Carlos became CEO, I was responsible for People Services, and he thought that he needed to get out there among the people because many in the organization just didn't know him. So, we traveled throughout the United States to major cities and met with all of the lines of service together in town meetings, where they could ask him any questions. We had presentations on our cultural values, but it was also, "Let's meet the new leader." I really got to know him through this process, and so did the organization. He listened and would take suggestions. He was a good, good guy, a real servant. I greatly respected him.[30]

Starting His CEO Role

When Carlos Cantu stepped in as president and CEO of ServiceMaster on January 1, 1994, he became the fifth CEO in the company's history. At that time, however, he was one of only six Hispanics to head a Fortune 500 company.[31] He was therefore celebrated by the Hispanic community, not just for his own work, but for creating a culture of diversity. He and ServiceMaster were featured on the list of "100 Best Companies for Latinos."[32] His first four years produced a strong performance, continued acquisitions, and a movement toward integration of the whole company.

Changing the Distributorship Model

As ServiceMaster grew, people at many levels took part in creating change. Bob Groff was an early owner of a distributorship in the Seattle area, served for a while in the corporate office, and then returned to his distributorship. His time at corporate helped him to realize that the distributor model set up early in the 1950s was no longer ideal. He recognized that some distributorships were doing well while others were not, yet they were the lifeblood of the individually owned franchises. Discussions began as to whether or not the company should own these distributorships or leave them in the hands of distributor franchise owners. They came to the conclusion that company-owned distributorships would be a better model. Between 1993 and 1994, Groff pitched this idea to Mike Isakson, who was then the president of Merry Maids in Omaha. Groff said:

We had some secret meetings there to try to strategize how to take this to Corporate, and in early 1995, I pitched it to Bob McDonell at Corporate. He agreed with the strategy, but said they would do this only if I would sell the distributorship first, and then come and lead the project of buying back the others. However, for family reasons, I couldn't move to Memphis where the Consumer Services Division was located. To do the job, I needed to travel a great deal anyway. So I offered my resignation (because I didn't want to move). They said I could take on this new role while working from Seattle, so I sold my distributorship back to the company, and proceeded to work the project until I retired in 2002. We bought back all but six of more than one hundred distributorships.[33]

Dealing with Culture

Size continued to be a challenging factor in promoting the established culture throughout the company, particularly with the acquisitions. In his 1996 book *The Soul of Firm*, Bill Pollard discussed his decision to capture the "soul" of the company. In this book, he carefully developed the key elements of the ServiceMaster culture and their objectives, and it was filled with illustrations of this "soul" in action in the work of the people of ServiceMaster. It showed the careful, delicate, and challenging balance between the four objectives, and it made it clear that this soul must be deeply rooted and could not be used simply as a motivational tool to create more profit. Not only did this book remind people why they were at ServiceMaster, but it also became a bestseller. The book was also used in propagating the long-held culture of the company within the Delta group (a group of the top leaders of the company) and in training sessions. The 1995 annual report featured a two-page synopsis of the book.

In 1997, which was the fiftieth anniversary of the company (it was incorporated in 1947), the annual report features remarks from the five CEOs addressing the question of people development through responses to five key statements:

- "People develop by excelling at what they do" (from Wade)
- "People develop and learn as they teach others" (from Hansen)
- "People develop as they invest themselves in others and learn to be as well as to do" (from Wessner)
- "People develop as they serve others" (from Pollard)
- "People develop when they catch a vision and take responsibility for making it happen" (from Cantu)

The wisdom of these leaders (drawing on the writings of Wade, Hansen, and Wessner) demonstrated the complementary perspectives of all five leaders, while each emphasized a different aspect of the development of people.

In 1994, Cantu's initial idea of directly holding on to his past role as CEO for the Consumer Services Division, while at the same time being CEO for all of ServiceMaster, proved more of a load than was reasonable. Thus he began the process of building a new management team. Rob Keith was named president and COO of Consumer Services, Brian Oxley was appointed president and COO of Management Services, Bob Erickson was named president and COO of International and New Business Development, and Chuck Stair was elected as vice chairman of the board. Carlos found, as Bill Pollard had found, that the role of CEO required longer-term strategic attention, which made it impossible to also head an operating unit. His plan of moving to Downers Grove was only partially realized, and he maintained a home in Memphis as well.

As to other parts of his initial plan, Carlos made progress both in international growth and in further acquisitions, as well as some progress toward developing the home healthcare business.

Further Acquisitions

Cantu's goal of further international expansion was realized through several acquisitions. In 1994, the company used its Terminix subsidiary in Europe, TMX Europe, to acquire pest control companies in the United Kingdom, the Netherlands, and Sweden (which worked in both Sweden and Norway). In 1995, TMX Europe also formed a joint venture with Tarmac Facilities Management in the UK.

Other acquisitions were made over this period as well, which added new services and strengthened existing services. In 1996, in addition to smaller acquisitions, the company added new services by acquiring Furniture Medic (on-site furniture repair and restoration), AmeriSpec (home inspection services), and Premier Manufacturing (auto industry custodial services and paint booth maintenance).

In 1997, with the acquisition of Certified Systems (processing for payroll and employee benefit plans), the company formed ServiceMaster Employer Services. But the biggest acquisitions were in the lawn care area: Barefoot (residential lawn care services) and the lawn care and plant services part of Orkin. Combined with TruGreen/ChemLawn, these acquisitions enabled ServiceMaster to become a dominant player in this market.

Also in 1997, the company bought out the remaining 19 percent interest that Waste Management held in the Consumer sector, which cost $626 million in cash.[34] Two months later, Phillip Rooney, the former CEO of Waste Management, was hired as a second vice chairman of the board, which was a newly created position. This hiring created immediate speculation in the press. Casey Burkos of the *Chicago Tribune* interviewed Claire

Buchan, ServiceMaster spokeswoman, and asked for comments about how Rooney fit in. "Waste Management is a service company, as we are," said Buchan. Then Burkos added, thus beginning the speculation, "It is not clear that Rooney is on track to become ServiceMaster's chief executive when the 63-year-old Cantu retires." Buchan replied, "There are probably a lot of people who are in line for Carlos's job."[35]

Expenditures for acquisitions during this period grew significantly: $98 million (1994), $69 million (1995), $124 million (1996), and $459 million (1997), excluding the Waste Management buyout. While these changes created opportunity, leadership also needed to address three significant challenges. First, they wanted to make it easy for customers of one service to learn about another service, and common access to service through 1-800-WE SERVE was one helpful step in this direction. Integration within and across services—requiring collaboration and integration within the company—made progress, however slowly.

Second, since ServiceMaster had rarely hired a person from outside the company into a top leadership position, the addition of Rooney at the senior level was an unusual step. He would need to become immersed in learning and owning the culture.

The third challenge was even more difficult. The ServiceMaster edge was the development, empowering, and finding purpose for people at all levels of the organization. Since many other service rivals treated their employees merely as tools of production, the newly acquired management and workers would all need to be retrained in the ServiceMaster culture and objectives. As Tichy and Cohen state in their book *The Leadership Engine*, "ServiceMaster is a low-tech service company making world-class returns of 25% per year for the past 25 years because it expects all of its workers to lead, and it follows them when they do."[36]

The pursuit of acquisitions during the Cantu period also took some strange trails. In one case, ServiceMaster was looking to acquire a window-washing company, Classic Care. The principal, Coleman Orr, suggested that rather than meeting in the office they should meet with him out on the site where he was working. After several such meetings, the ServiceMaster team realized they always saw the same truck and the same two people. It turned out the company had no office, only one truck, and only two people! In spite of this seeming setback, ServiceMaster Window Cleaning was set up, starting with Classic Care.[37]

The acquisition process did begin to raise again the question Ken Hansen had wrestled with when he was involved in early acquisitions: Do we really know how to manage this kind of business, and can we engage with the people in that business (from the top leadership through every worker) in such a way that they deeply own the ServiceMaster objectives?

External Events

The public availability of the Internet in late 1993 started discussion across the business world. What does it mean to a business to have a presence on the World Wide Web? How might this affect the way we market our services, connect with our customers, and sell to our customers? In 1995, the emphasis was still on older telephone technology, developing and promoting the use of 1-800-WE SERVE, and trying to better connect with customers.[38] Though undoubtedly discussions about the impact of the Internet had taken place earlier, it wasn't until 1998 that the first mention of ServiceMaster's response to it made its way into the annual report: "We have innovated the development of new ways for easy customer access, including 1-800-WE SERVE, and www.servicemaster.com."[39] That is, they added a website to an "800" phone number for customer access. In 1999, this would change dramatically.

Environmental groups were also now raising concerns about the chemicals used on lawns and gardens and the impact on the streams and water tables. While this was not a new issue, the intensity of concern grew at this time, raising issues with the heart of the growing lawn care segment of the ServiceMaster business. Weather patterns were also beginning to change, which could also affect the lawn care business.

In 1997, at the close of the fiftieth anniversary of the incorporation of the company, these new challenges required further adaptation. In the annual report, Carlos Cantu reminded the organization: "Leadership must help anticipate future opportunities and prepare the organization for change. All of the associates share the corresponding responsibility to seize these opportunities. But most of all, we must bring this spirit of responsibility to life with a willingness to serve others."[40]

Internally, ServiceMaster was coming to the end of its limited partnership provision and would revert to corporate form in 1998. As Carlos Cantu and Bill Pollard said to the shareholders, "Many of you eagerly awaited our return to corporate form, which was completed in December. The ServiceMaster Company is the name of the new company which will continue to trade on the New York Stock Exchange under the symbol SVM."[41] Although a publicly traded corporation, rather than a partnership, was something investors better understood, ServiceMaster would now be more subject to day-to-day and minute-by-minute responses to news and rumors. These shortened cycles only accelerated in the age of the Internet, when people received stock prices on their watches.[42]

The building volume of acquisitions created growing debt for the company, and this would need to be managed well. And there was the ongoing need to focus, particularly with growth through acquisition, on instilling the sense of purpose and meaning at every level. As Chairman Pollard reminded the shareholders,

> Yes, we celebrate profits. But as Peter Drucker has said, we are also a firm that "has made a business of the training and developing of people." . . . How then do we unlock the potential of people, empower them for extraordinary service, and in the process find the soul of the firm? It extends beyond the means goal of making money, and allows the firm to value each person as an individual with unique skills and talents, and so to recognize the benefit and reality of diversity within the firm.[43]

Financial Performance

The revenue and profit charts continued as they had since 1971. Growth in revenue (Figure 6.1) and profit (Figure 6.2) continued quarter after quarter, year after year. Again, the transition of leadership seemed almost seamless.

A Turning Point in 1998

Early in 1998, however, a new and significant challenge faced the company when Carlos Cantu was diagnosed with stomach cancer. There was, of course, a very real impact of this news for Carlos and for his family. Life and work would be disrupted by doctor visits and decisions on treatment alternatives, all of which undoubtedly occupied a major part of his mind. While Carlos's health was a high priority for the company, at this crucial point in ServiceMaster's history, this illness also disrupted dealing with the challenges that lay in front of the company.

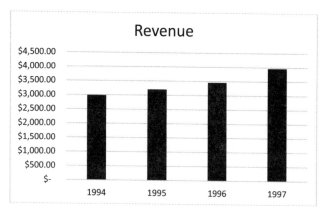

Figure 6.1. Revenue growth in the Cantu years (dollars shown in millions).[44]

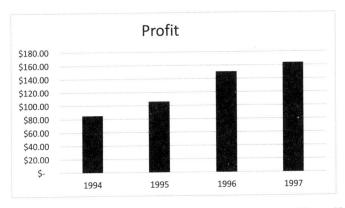

Figure 6.2. Profit growth in the Cantu years (dollars shown in millions).[45]

The situation was stated carefully in the 1998 annual report, which was authored by Carlos and Bill:

> As we came to the close of 1998, your Chairman and your President and CEO found themselves in an expanded partnership relationship. The illness of Cantu has involved Pollard in additional supporting roles, all as part of leading the company and maintaining momentum. We are thankful for the close relationship of trust we have developed over the years, and for God's faithfulness in meeting the changes that have occurred in our lives and in the life of the business. We are thankful for Cantu's response to the care he has received, and we are looking forward to his full recovery. The ServiceMaster management team, especially the senior officers, has provided strong leadership and continuity during this interim period.

The leadership challenge of Cantu's illness, the external factors of "dot coms" and environmental concerns, and the internal challenges of integrating acquired businesses and disseminating the ServiceMaster culture seemed to have no effect on the 1998 numbers. It was more like what happened between 1969 and 1970, when the slowdown was rooted in what happened years earlier and the issues would come together to have an impact on the company in the next several years.

During 1998, standard financial markers were all going in the right direction. Operating revenue grew from $3.9 billion to $4.7 billion, although the change from partnership to a publicly traded corporation made net income comparisons across these years a bit more difficult. The company had recorded a net income of $329 million for 1997 in partnership form.[46] As a publicly traded company, they translated the 1997 net income to $163 million. Against this number, net income grew again to $190 million in

1998.[47] Customer level revenue (adding in the revenues of the various independent franchises) was given as $6.4 billion.

Acquisitions continued as well, and the pace barely slowed from the previous year. ServiceMaster spent $163 million in the landscaping area, including its acquisition of Ruppert Landscape Company. Altogether, they purchased sixteen commercial landscape companies. In the pest control and other lawn services area, they spent $172 million, including the UK pest control company National Britanie. They added Quantum Resources, a temporary technical staffing company, to Employee Services. Finally, they acquired Rescue Industries, a plumbing and drain cleaning service, thus providing a new type of home service, for $74 million. Altogether, 1998 acquisitions totaled $438 million.[48]

The company made some organizational changes as well. Vice Chairman Phil Rooney was given operational responsibility as the COO of the company. This appointment was prefaced by the statement, "ServiceMaster has a tradition of developing people from within and seeking talented individuals from outside the company."[49] Rooney fit the latter category. "There were also questions raised about some past financial dealings that attracted the attention of the press."[50]

Being originally from outside the company, Rooney did begin to wrestle with the meaning of the four objectives. In an essay in the 1998 Annual Report, introduced by Carlos Cantu, Rooney quoted a statement he found from Ken Wessner, who had offered this summary of the objectives:

> They clearly define our philosophy and our character. It is only as we seek to achieve all four of our objectives simultaneously that we will be true to the first objective. . . . If we achieve one objective at the expense of the others, we will not continue to be the significant organization we have been privileged to become.

This was yet another way of stating the challenge of holding the four objectives in tension. Then Rooney added:

> As we continue on this journey, we will be led by those enduring realities, our objectives. We embrace them by our willingness to serve those we lead to accomplish our goals in making the whole worth more than the parts. Servant leadership is at the core of making the objectives come alive in the eyes of our people.[51]

Two other key promotions in 1998 included Joy Flora, who was given responsibility for Merry Maids, and Albert Cantu, who became president of Terminix. Albert, Carlos's second son, had grown in his responsibilities within the company.

Despite these various issues, in 1998, ServiceMaster was recognized by the *Financial Times* as one of the twenty most respected companies in the world, and *Fortune* magazine once again recognized ServiceMaster as the number one outsourcing services company in the country. In their commentary on the year in the annual report, Carlos and Bill reminded the shareholders, "While we are thankful for significant recognition of what we have accomplished, we are also mindful that we cannot rely on yesterday's press clippings. The story will be told by what we are doing today and tomorrow to serve our customers."[52]

Carlos Cantu's Legacy

Unfortunately, Cantu did not get better. The 1999 annual report opens with the statement, "We began the year with the knowledge that we would need to appoint a new CEO." His retirement was announced mid-year, but became official in October 1999.

His impact on the company was significant and during the final years, a number of honors were bestowed on him. In 1997, he received the Horatio Alger Award, which honors outstanding individuals who have succeeded in spite of adversity. Also that year, he was honored with a resolution from the legislature in the State of Tennessee that stated, in part, "We hereby honor and congratulate Mr. Carlos Cantu upon winning the Horatio Alger Award, and thank him for his many selfless contributions to his community and to Tennessee."[53] In May 2000, he was also honored with the Ellis Island Medal of Freedom and as the Society of Entrepreneurs 2000 Entrepreneur of the Year. In 2003, he received the Distinguished Alumni Award from Texas A&M University.[54]

During his tenure at ServiceMaster, he participated as a board member for DePaul University, Exelon Corporation, First Tennessee National Corporation, the Field Museum in Chicago, Christian Brothers University, and the Dixon Gallery and Gardens Museum in Memphis. In 1999, he established the Carlos H. Cantu Hispanic Education and Opportunity Endowment at Texas A&M University, addressing the nation's serious Hispanic student drop-out problem. In 2007, the *Memphis Business Journal* reported, "Chicago Mayor Richard M. Daley and corporate and community leaders dedicated the Carlos H. Cantu Children and Family Center Friday in the Little Village neighborhood."[55]

Even with his illness, Cantu was able to continue in a consulting capacity and as a board member for a time. He died in September 2003. Once again, ServiceMaster faced a leadership question for this now very large company.

7

THE TRANSITION PERIOD

During the transition period after Carlos Cantu's cancer diagnosis in April 1998, Bill Pollard and Carlos worked together to manage the business, to make some hard decisions, and to identify opportunities for the future. The hope was always that Cantu could come back to his leadership role. But in early 1999, it became apparent that he would not be able to return. It was not until July 1999 that ServiceMaster made this official, announcing that Bill Pollard would be stepping back into the position of CEO, effective October 1, 1999, while maintaining his role as chairman.[1] Although this was not an interim appointment, Pollard made it clear to the board that he would serve until a suitable replacement could be found.

While this time was not a part of any long-range plan, it created a helpful pause for the company to consider a number of questions that had arisen during these periods of rapid growth, both internally and externally. Internally, the shape of the company had changed dramatically through the acquisition of businesses, which then led to cultural challenges and the delivery of new products and services. Externally, the business world had gone mad after the introduction of the Internet. "Dot coms" attracted the favor of the analysts along with investment from both venture capitalists and stock purchasers. Weather was also a factor, particularly for lawn care and landscaping, during this period. For example, new weather patterns changed the traditional revenue models for lawn services.

This was not a typical kind of pause, however, since the company continued to grow and serve customers across the world while responding to this changing environment. It was more like what a Boeing executive said during a time of great change in that company: "We can't shut the company down to carry out needed changes. What we need to do is like changing the sparkplugs in the car while driving down the road at sixty miles per hour."[2]

Unlike 1969, ServiceMaster did not record any losses during this period of rapid change. But for the first time in twenty-nine years, profits dropped back a bit from 1998 to 1999 and held even from 1999 to 2000. The graphs for operating revenue and net income for 1996 to 2000 are shown in Figures 7.1 and 7.2 below; the two prior years, 1996 and 1997, are included for comparison.

The twenty-nine years of consecutive growth in both revenue and profit was an unprecedented accomplishment, and it had to end sometime. Yet it was disappointing to the leaders when it did. In 1999, the annual report began with the following: "This past year was a year that we experienced difficulties, change, and some very significant accomplishments." Then in 2000, the annual report opened with, "This was a year when overall performance was below expectations."

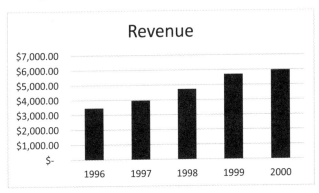

Figure 7.1. Revenue in the Cantu/Pollard years (dollars shown in millions).

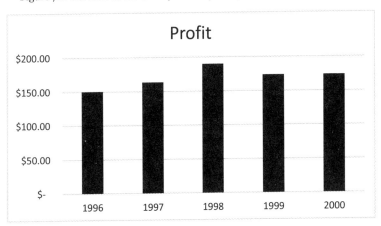

Figure 7.2. Profit in the Cantu/Pollard years (dollars shown in millions).

During this period, the stock price began to flatten and decline, even in the face of a rising overall market. In Figure 7.3, the ServiceMaster stock price low-high range by year is compared with the Dow Averages low-high. While ServiceMaster outperformed the Dow from 1990 to 1998, its value declined in 1999 while the Dow continued to grow, declining further in 2000 while the Dow was close to flat.

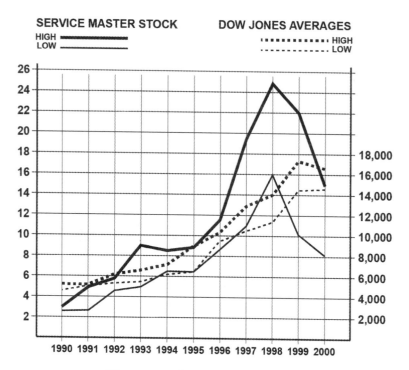

Figure 7.3. Stock price from 1990 to 2000.

The same analysts, who had accepted the "religious" roots of the company because of strong and growing profit, began to point to this now as one source of a major problem. According to writer Mike Schuster, "Some analysts blamed the company's fixation on religion as responsible for the weakening of its business in the 1990s."[3] Shareholders who had loved the stock earlier were now concerned about its flattening. This included the internal shareholders who had banked their retirements on the price of the stock.

Part of the concern of the market was the growing debt of the company (shown in Figure 7.4 below), which increased dramatically in 1997 from historic lows of the early 1990s. It remained high and climbed through the next three years. There was a call for a renewed promise for the future.

In 1969, when a similar but deeper problem had occurred and the company actually went into a loss position, Ken Hansen was able to address the problem. In his case, the company was much smaller, but he did this by drawing on the unique "shingles on a roof" concept of ServiceMaster leadership, working with founder Marion Wade and Ken Wessner. This newer transition period was different. While Bill Pollard had outside board members with whom he could talk (who had no direct operating experience

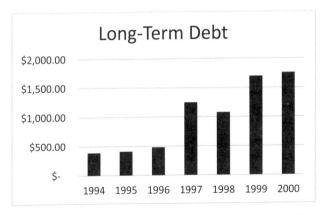

Figure 7.4. Long-term debt during the 1990s (dollars shown in millions).

in the company) and relatively new people in key reporting positions (Phil Rooney and Steve Preston), it was not the same as being able to discuss these issues with the men who had originally built the company. Ken Hansen and Ken Wessner had died, and Carlos had stepped aside.

Assessment

Bill and Carlos, and then primarily Bill himself in his new role as both chairman and CEO, worked with the board and senior leaders and examined a number of key issues. They focused on what was working well and what was not. Even those things that had been done for many years needed to be assessed. This included the following:

- Evaluating market segments in which ServiceMaster did business
- The impacts of technology on both costs and opportunity
- The need to integrate the segments of the company, both for growth and efficiencies
- The growing impact of the company's debt
- The growing complexity of managing a company of this size with its many product lines
- The role of the culture, the four objectives, and the company's commitment to them

The company took some action on these points during this transition period. For other points, Bill made recommendations to the board to create either a plan or alternatives to be carried out by the next leader. As Ken Hansen had observed before, there was no cause for panic, but there was a need to return to the basics and then execute the plan. The company was in need of a younger Bill Pollard, Ken Wessner, or Carlos Cantu who could execute, while at the same time add his or her own insight and take the company to the next level.

Dealing with Challenging Market Segments

In 1983, The ServiceMaster Company focused on its franchises, and Management Services and Consumer Services. In Management Services, their primary customer was hospitals, with the beginning of growth in education and industry. This division had grown from cleaning to equipment care, plant operations, food services, and many other services. Fifteen years later, through the series of acquisitions, a mix of market segments were included under Consumer Services:

- Pest control (from Terminix and other related acquisitions)
- Lawn care and landscaping (from TruGreen/ChemLawn and many smaller acquisitions)
- In-home healthcare (through the Diversified Health Services acquisition and others)
- Home cleaning services (through the acquisition of Merry Maids)
- Commercial cleaning and disaster recovery through ServiceMaster franchises
- Appliance home warranty (through the acquisition of AHS and others)
- Furniture repair (through Furniture Medic)
- Plumbing (through the acquisition of Rescue Rooter)
- HVAC and electrical services (through the acquisition of American Residential Services)
- Home inspection (through AmeriSpec and others)
- Smaller areas, such as window washing

These services were supported by company-owned and franchise businesses, and in some areas both. Cleaning services had once been company owned at ServiceMaster, but then sold off into franchises under Ken Hansen. Many Terminix services were provided through franchises but then consolidated into company-owned services. Merry Maids consisted only of franchises. In addition, International had grown in minor segments such as franchising and through major partners (particularly in Japan and England) across a variety of services.

One question facing the company during this transition period was the health of the individual segments: which segments were working well, which needed attention, which should be further developed, and which should be sold off?

Back in 1993, Carlos Cantu and his team had identified Home Health-care as a likely "third leg of the stool" for the growth of the business, which would balance Consumer Services and Management Services. Late in 1997, however, the company concluded that "without substantial investment, we could not profitably provide home healthcare services in the current regulatory environment. As a result, we are exiting the direct operation of home healthcare agencies."[4] In 1999, ServiceMaster "took a charge against earnings of our long term care business and divested our home healthcare business."[5] This was identified as a major factor in the reduction in profit-ability that year.

The lawn care and landscaping business represented both an opportu-nity and a challenge. In 1998, TruGreen/ChemLawn posted strong revenue and profit growth; and in 1999, the company then made a significant ad-ditional acquisition of LandCare USA for $331 million.[6] Acquisitions for the year totaled almost $1 billion, as almost one hundred smaller acquisi-tions were brought into this part of the business.[7] The 1999 annual report stated, "Unfortunately, this rapid, unintegrated growth, combined with a major drought in the third quarter of 1999 (one of the worst on record in the Northeast and Mid-Atlantic), and the decline in earnings of this unit had a rippling effect on the overall achievements of the company."[8] In 2000, the problems in the lawn care business got only worse.

One approach to making these disparate lawn care businesses more unified came through the creation of a common financial system across the various lawn care and landscaping sectors. This system was complete by the end of the first quarter of 2000. There was, however, an execution problem: "Although the new financial systems had been installed, they were not being effectively used. Labor and other operating costs were not being properly tracked and were significantly over standard."[9] These is-sues led to an increased emphasis on training, particularly in the use of the new systems, and to changes in management. It also led to a major reor-ganization of this business, bringing lawn care and landscaping together as one operation. In the report, Pollard concluded,

> While the process of bringing these two businesses together is taking time and will continue into 2001, it is the right step for the future. Our land-scape business is a good business. It complements our lawn care business. It allows us to grow and expand both these services to the commercial and residential market.[10]

Growth in other segments was important. Though revenue increased, it was noted that operating costs caused margins to decline in American Home Shield and Management Services. It was a good year, however, for ServiceMaster Clean and for Merry Maids. Terminix also had a good growth year, though as Paul Bert stated, "One challenge we had was the defeat of our number one rival, Orkin. It had energized us to pass them and become number one, but having done that, there was no one left to defeat."[11]

Another area Pollard looked at was the relative growth of the different components of the business. He realized that while Management Services for hospitals, businesses, and educational facilities was continuing to do well, its profit margins and growth were less. The company had gone a long way into this market, more competitors had emerged, and they were struggling with margins. With the death of both Kens and Carlos Cantu's retirement, it became increasingly difficult to maintain their idea of "shingles on a roof." Pollard began discussions with leaders both inside the company and outside. One such discussion was with Warren Buffet, one of the most successful investors of all time, who was also a significant investor in ServiceMaster. Pollard wrote,

> I was trying to explain why one of our units was forecasting only ten percent growth for the coming year, when our standard for the overall business was twenty percent. I told him that, before budgets were finalized, I thought I could get the team leading this unit to agree to twelve or fifteen percent growth.[12]

Buffet's response was helpful and immediately meaningful to Pollard. "Bill, why would you do that?" he asked. "The market they are in is not growing. An eight percent growth would be a great result. Remember, it's not how hard you row the boat. It is how fast the stream is moving."[13]

Pollard concluded that ServiceMaster needed to continue with the strength of its Management Services while looking for other areas of growth.

Dealing with Technology

During this period, technology also created some costs, some opportunity, and some distractions. Though the Internet had come on the scene in 1993, the subsequent emergence of the "dot com" boom in the late 1990s affected every company, and ServiceMaster was no exception. Analysts lauded any new idea for an online company, venture capitalists were pouring millions of dollars into this space, and business commentators were questioning the value of brick-and-mortar companies. Many traditional companies struggled with how they could present themselves to the marketplace as a "dot com." The stock market reflected this boom, where the tech-heavy NASDAQ index attracted all of the attention, more than doubling between the beginning of 2000 and the peak in April 2001. The drop was as rapid as the rise (see Figure 7.5 below).

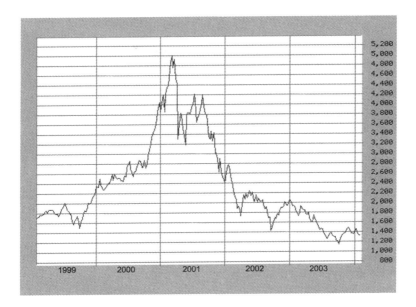

Figure 7.5. NASDAQ stock performance between 1998 and 2002.

Traditional companies were also caught in the hype with multiple motivations. This new capability made possible by the Internet was attracting so much attention, there must be something there to create growth or even assure survival. Perhaps there was an investment opportunity rooted in this change. In addition, tech company leaders were treated like rock stars with recognition, salary, and bonuses. Could leaders of traditional companies get on board?

An illustration of this phenomenon is the icon of old industry, General Electric. In the late 1990s, Jack Welch, then chairman and CEO of GE, sought to identify the company with the new trend. He spent time with a "mentor" during this period, learning from a "twenty-five-year-old kid" in his organization about the "digitization of everything."[14] The company responded, making changes in many ways, including how it sold products on the web. In defending old business in the face of a growing new company, Amazon.com, Welch said, "As far as sales are concerned, we are the biggest 'dot com' by a significant amount."[15]

ServiceMaster also began to explore what this electronic presence might look like. Beyond building a website, ServiceMaster explored a more intriguing opportunity during this period. In the fourth quarter of 1999, the annual report said, "We announced our intention to enter the world of e-commerce through the development of a website to provide homeowners with an entirely new tool to manage their households and purchase home services over the Internet." ServiceMaster wanted this to be more than a website for sales, but rather to create a separate "dot com" company called WeServeHomes.com that would be able to operate independent from the corporate structure.

To accomplish this, ServiceMaster formed a partnership with Kleiner Perkins to "form a separate Internet company. They will bring to the partnership insight and experience of developing a number of successful consumer-oriented companies."[16] Between 2000 and 2001, the company showed costs of $15 million per year in the development of this capability, hoping to achieve a new way of operating in the twenty-first century.

This new subsidiary had lofty ambitions, and its leaders wanted to be the solution to the problem with which ServiceMaster had struggled for a long time: How can we get customers who buy one service from the company to buy other services from the company? At this point, in spite of these efforts, the toll-free service number fell far short of expectations. Although the call center was designed to handle 285,000 calls per month, according to one ServiceMaster manager, by late 1999 it "had become a hodge-podge. Only 25,000 to 30,000 calls a month were coming in and were from local branches or individuals wanting new service, a third was overflow for calls to a specific subsidiary, and the other third were from shareholders calling about dividend checks."[17] In addition, customers still averaged only 1.2 services from ServiceMaster, which did not achieve the company's desired cross-sell goals.[18]

The new subsidiary also faced the challenge of "getting the network of service providers to use the technology and ensuring that they deliver a consistent level of service quality." Culturally, this new Internet start-up looked very different from the old ServiceMaster Company. Ken Hooten, the cofounder of the startup, had to address this question: "How strong a connection should we have with ServiceMaster?"[19]

WeServeHomes.com recruited Diane Primo, "a Harvard MBA with a strong background in the consumer services industry . . . a former senior manager at Quaker Oats and Ameritech,"[20] to shape the company in its early phases. And they moved to their own building across the parking lot from the parent company. "If WeServeHomes.com had continued its growth at ServiceMaster Corporate," a ServiceMaster executive said, "it would never have gotten off the ground. We would have seen it as just another cost center and counted every penny it got—and we're very cost conscious."[21] However, as Hallowell stated, "Hooten and his colleagues . . . were mindful of recent leadership changes."[22] Indeed, at the beginning of 2001, a new ServiceMaster CEO would come on board and there remained a question about how this would fit with the vision of the new leader.

In addition to the subsidiary "dot com" ServiceMaster was setting up, technology affected the company in other ways. As was the case with most large companies at the end of the twentieth century, technology costs increased significantly, leading to both opportunity and a cost drain. Changes to internal software and systems were needed as the year 2000 approached to protect the company, requiring the "Y2K investment." Although these were necessary changes to ward off potential problems, they were simply cost-avoidance investments rather than strategic investments for the future.

Common systems, on the other hand, opened true opportunities for savings and efficiencies. As new acquisitions had been made over the years, each came with its own financial systems, human resource systems, and so forth. Standardizing seemed like a great opportunity. However, such changes carried with them the need for training and for organizations willing to adapt to new systems. The issues of people not using such systems, or working around them, were common among most large companies. ServiceMaster was affected in this way in attempting to bring together its lawn care and landscaping acquisitions through common systems.

Dealing with Integration

We have seen the work on integration within service areas, such as within the lawn care and landscaping collection of acquisitions. But to gain leverage from the many purchases, there was a need to get leverage between service areas as well. A big goal was to see the customer who was buying pest control through Terminix also buy lawn care from TruGreen, appliance warranties from AHS, and home cleaning through Merry Maids. In part, this was the e-commerce goal of WeServeHomes.com. One example of this was the goal that "WeServeHomes.com and American Home Shield will have a closer working relationship, all as part of building coverage and strength in providing multiple service solutions through a single source."[23]

In addition to seeing the integration of services for the customer, there was a need to find ways to share the research done in cleaning processes from Management Services with Merry Maids, for example. It was also necessary to cross-train people who could be moved from one type of service to another.

Another opportunity with integration was in helping people to develop. When a person could readily move from one segment to another, this allowed a person in a slow-growing part of the business to benefit from growth in another part of the business. While this integration goal had been on the table for a long time, new acquisitions had kept challenging it from happening. At this point, it still remained an opportunity for the customer, the employees, and the shareholders.

Dealing with Debt

Figure 7.4 above shows that debt had increased substantially over the period between 1998 and 2000, largely from the major acquisitions ServiceMaster had made. The company had come a long way from 1983, when it was basically debt free. How serious was the problem? Certainly, more borrowing was required, which drew away profit to pay for the loans. "As we look to this new year," the 2000 annual report stated, "we recognize that profit growth will be affected by added interest cost." In the report, Pollard wrote,

> We have been in similar investment cycles in the past. I can assure you that your management team is committed to returning the performance of our company to a consistent pattern of year-over-year growth in profits. It is here for us to do and it represents a focus that extends beyond one year and involves the process of building the next cycle of growth for ServiceMaster.[24]

One board member noted that "Bill was comfortable with a bit more debt than we were."[25]

Managing Complexity

Pollard also explored how to more effectively manage a company the size of ServiceMaster in 2000 with almost $6 billion in operating revenue. He determined that something needed to be done about the effective management of this now enormous company. "During the experience of this last year, we have been reminded once again that we must be both small and big. This is the paradox of service."[26]

To underscore this paradox, the cover of the annual report in 2000 featured the question: "Is Big Better, or Is Small Beautiful?" As the report developed the question, it stated,

> A "yes" to either question may not be the right answer. The tension of opposites often produces the strength and resolve for significant results, especially when there is demand for flexible and responsive solutions. In business, growth in size can bring opportunities for increased shareholder value, economies of scale, and more resources for investment. However, it also can impede innovation, stifle rapid response, and add layers of management that become involved in bureaucracy of review rather than producing measurable results.

In seeking to bridge the two sizes, leadership set a goal of seeking to be small for flexibility and innovation, while still bringing the benefits of size to the customer, employee, and shareholder. To underscore this point, the annual report in 2000 was 5½ inches by 7½ inches in size, rather than the traditional 8½ by 11 inches, with the accompanying note:

Yes, our annual report is smaller in size this year. We have used less paper and reduced our cost. Yet it still contains all the required information and conveys a powerful message. As we continue to rethink and manage our firm, the opportunities to bring more solutions and added benefits are greater than they have ever been before.

Managing the Tension of the Four Objectives

As we have seen all along, what had made the company work was a culture that valued the service worker, providing each person with a sense of meaning and purpose regarding the work. This culture included commitment to integrity and a goal of excellence while growing profitably. Heskett called this the way that ServiceMaster had "cracked the code" on the service business. Indeed, it had been achieved through holding the four objectives in tension all these years.

They now had to assess if there was a valid reason to modify these objectives. They needed to determine whether or not a twenty-first-century global and publicly traded company could still have as its first objective, "To Honor God in All We Do." Could the company continue to make the first two objectives the *ends* goals, and the second two the *means* goals as Ken Hansen, Ken Wessner, and Bill Pollard had so frequently said? Did the leaders of the company still believe they were in the "growing people" business, as Peter Drucker had said, or were they simply in the services, or money-making business? Did the company still want to operate following the "shingles on the roof" philosophy, or were they looking for a new leader who, like so many other companies of this era, would be a strong, single-minded "rock star" CEO? This assessment was a vital part of the plan going forward and the search for the new CEO.

Reassessing Objective 1: "To Honor God in All We Do"

This objective was more than honesty. It was accountability to the highest standard of ethical conduct. It was the recognition that all people are made in the image of God and worthy of being treated with dignity and respect. It was a commitment to the dignity of work being carried out at every level of the organization. Further, since people had aspirations of their own, it was about recognizing these aspirations and helping to create opportunity for growth for each person through growth of the company. It was the recognition that leadership was about serving, not about the leader.

Over the years, critics both from the outside and even the inside the company fought this objective in two ways. Many said that religion had no place in business and that the two could not be mixed. But leadership had always contended that the objective created the highest bar for ethical behavior, for the recognition of the dignity of both the work and the worker and for accountability beyond what would satisfy the letter of the law. While all of the early leaders rooted their own leadership in their Christian faith, they didn't want to impose their faith on others but to create a strong moral standard. While some perceived a religious pressure, the commitment of the leaders was to be inclusive.

The company also took criticism from some Christians who argued that the standard should be more specific, referencing Jesus rather than God. From the beginning, each leader fought back against this suggestion. The company was not a church and was not imposing religion. While the leaders felt the freedom to state clearly their own faith-based opinions, they sought to couch this in less specific language rather than impose their beliefs on others. That being said, Bill Pollard and other leaders wanted "to confront people with the question of God."

Reassessing Objective 2: "To Help People Develop"

This was about providing the tools for each individual to do his or her work. It was about training so that work could be done effectively and well. It was about helping people find the sense of meaning and purpose in their work, connecting the task with the bigger meaning and purpose. It was also about providing opportunity for people to grow in their responsibilities. As Pollard had said many times, "People work for a cause, not just for a paycheck." Again, the company walked a narrow line. What the leaders did through this objective was motivated by the desire to enable people to grow and not to manipulate them into higher performance and efficiency. As Ken Wessner said, "We want to help people *be* something before we ask them to *do* something."[27]

Reassessing Objective 3: "To Pursue Excellence"

The statement "To Pursue Excellence" recognized both the goal of performance at all levels with the recognition that this is carried out by imperfect people. Marion Wade's statement "If you don't live it, you don't believe it" meant that you always pursued excellence; and when you didn't achieve it, you made it right.

Excellence was the goal at many other levels as well. The company had done a good job in achieving excellence at the task level, with its training and task-oriented research. It is less clear if this extended to the tasks of the acquisitions. When it came to the projects, measuring excellence had to be done on the terms of the customer, not on the terms of the provider. Bill Pollard learned this lesson the hard way when he encountered an unhappy customer. While he had all of the internal quality data to demonstrate that the team was doing a good job, the hospital administrator was measuring quality by visual inspection at 6:00 a.m. each Monday morning.[28]

Excellence is also needed at the management level, keeping the organization nimble and free of bureaucracy. It was measured, in an imperfect world, in how they recovered from mistakes. This might be from a personal interaction, an acquisition, or the pursuit of a new market. The guideline to "fail fast" is to try something, and if it doesn't work, admit it and move on quickly. It is a part of excellence.

Reassessing Objective 4: "To Grow Profitably"

Profit was the means by which the company could attract investors. Profit was the means by which the company could invest in innovation, research, and understanding new markets. Profit was the external recognition of doing the business well. Profit was the fuel that provided the growth and the creation of wealth.

Pollard said, "Profit viewed as an end in itself can foster greed and other abuses. It may result in some short-term economic benefits but rarely has long-term benefit."[29] But profit as a means goal creates value. "It was a measurement of the effectiveness of our efforts. It provided a return for our shareholders, which included our employees. . . . Without surplus, there could be no economic growth for the firm. It was not a matter of maximizing profits."[30]

Keeping It All in Balance

As the company grew, particularly through acquisition, there was a growing number of people who had come from different business environments. Few businesses truly captured the magic of holding these different objectives in tension. The image of the balance beam, introduced in 1989, shows the last three company objectives being balanced on a fulcrum of "To Honor God in All We Do." Keeping this balance was a challenge, but it was also what had allowed the company to "break the code" in the service industry. New people, at all levels, needed to be trained—not just to practice these objectives because they were expected to do so by ServiceMaster leadership, but so they would own these objectives at a deep level.

There was an important reason that ServiceMaster leaders made the distinction between end goals and means goals. If, as in many companies, maximizing profit is the end goal, then treating workers well is in the company's best interest because that will cause them to work harder and the company will make more money. But ServiceMaster recognized that philosophy as exploitive rather than truly valuing the worker. Pollard had stated many times, "People are the subject of work, not the object of work." The worker is not merely another tool of production. To honestly care about the person who works, as an end goal as captured in the first two objectives, changes all of that.

The second related concept that had been a part of ServiceMaster was their adherence to the practice of "shingles on a roof." This played a vital role in two ways. The first was a level of accountability, since, as imperfect leaders, it is so easy to move from valuing people to exploiting them. Having another person who could point this out and create the needed conversation is vital. The second reason is for succession. Creating that working arrangement allows the next person to learn from the previous one, thus helping avoid the problem of each new leader making the same mistakes as the previous one. In the role of a coach, this keeps the culture on track.

A third practice was servant leadership. Marion Wade had reminded Ken Hansen of the importance of this, and Bill Pollard has given a number of talks over the years titled "The Awesome Responsibility of Leadership."[31] Leadership is not about the power, perks, or status of the position but about being a servant, helping and preparing the way for others to grow. He likes to say, "As Peter Drucker reminded us, 'A leader has only one choice to make—to lead or mislead.'"[32] Servant leadership was also marked as a fundamental aspect of the type of leader the company needed.

Presentation to the Board for Go-Forward Plan

Pollard and the board concluded that these four objectives and ways of operating had been key to past success and would remain relevant and vital to ServiceMaster in the twenty-first century. Having these at the heart of decision-making and rooted in management practice would continue to be important. The challenge, of course, was the tension of holding multiple objectives together and the differing ways individuals can interpret a situation. Interestingly, when Bill Pollard wrote *The Soul of the Firm*, at least one board member questioned whether a company could even have a soul.

But there were still issues to be worked out. Pollard stated, "It was my judgment that, with the current direction and structure, we could not maintain growth in value creation we had achieved in the past. I felt we could either become an integrated operation company or a holding company with separate subsidiary units."[33] He therefore offered additional insight. By choosing the integrated model, the company could find substantial cost savings through consolidating what many companies call Shared Services: for example, contracts, finance, computing, research, branding, and other needs into a single-shared organization. In this case, the benefits of consolidation include cost, standardization, and the ability of making it easy for people to move from one area to another.

As an alternative, they could create a holding company for the various businesses that were acquired. Pollard wrote, "The holding company model would give us more flexibility in adding new businesses and spinning off existing businesses to our shareholders, creating separate public companies and providing the potential of a new dimension of value."[34] In this case, the "company" would act as a banker for the corporation and the four objectives would be a representation of the brand. At that time, General Electric and Berkshire Hathaway were two examples of this way of doing business.

The disadvantage of standardization for some companies is that one size may not fit all when there is very little to share. Jack Welch at GE used to talk about the reason why they standardized very few practices. Between two of GE's major divisions, NBC television and aircraft engines, there was almost nothing in common about the business processes, marketing, customers, or suppliers. By keeping them separate, they were able to allow each to be more innovative and nimble in their own markets.

The tradeoff between the models is to make sure that the benefits of sharing resources, which requires that both divisions have the same processes, must be greater than the benefits of each being flexible to adapt at their own pace to meet their own needs.

Pollard laid out the general way that both models could bring value to ServiceMaster. The board agreed that the two represented the best plan for the company but decided to allow the new CEO to make the final call as he or she brought experience and insight to the plan.

Board Plan for the New CEO

The "dot com" world of that day created a distraction for hiring a CEO. The high-flying tech CEOs often came with high salaries, lots of stock options, and isolated leadership. This had a huge impact on CEO searches at that time. In many cases, technology, salary, and options dominated the discussion of values, history, and earnings growth in the hiring process. This impacted not just the "dot coms," but also long-standing companies in many fields.

Hewlett-Packard—an early tech company in Silicon Valley founded in 1947 by Bill Hewlett and David Packard in a garage, literally—represents an example of a long-established company known for its "HP Way." Lew Platt was the fourth CEO of the company and was known as a down-to-earth leader who frequently ate lunch in the employee cafeteria with HP engineers. He and the company were deeply committed to the company values that were written and understood as part of the HP Way.[35] As a result, the company had a strong, loyal employee base. In an interview with Platt at the end of 1999, he said, "There isn't a single person at HP who couldn't make more money elsewhere. I mean every single person—whether it's an administrative assistant or our brightest engineer or the president of the company. They stay here because they like the environment."[36]

But Lew Platt, like Bill Pollard, faced a dilemma. What needed to be done going forward was to make changes in HP that would take longer than he felt he could commit to stay. In an interview with Platt shortly before he retired in 2000, he talked about how to preserve the HP Way.

> I like to describe the HP Way as consisting of three concentric circles. The inner circle contains our values. The next circle out contains our objectives. The outer circle contains our practices. The values in the center circle (the importance of making a contribution, of good citizenship in the community, of valuing, trusting, and respecting people) are timeless. They've worked great for the company so far and it's hard to imagine that they won't work at any point in time over the next hundred years. We also have objectives. These are not timeless, but they change slowly. In the Fifties we wrote down our objectives for the first time. We've had seven since the beginning but there is nothing magical about seven; it could be five, it could be eight. Finally, we have practices, and these change quickly. The pace of change in business forces us to change these practices even more quickly now than we did in the past. When we hold on to old practices and don't change them fast enough we get in trouble. You can have any new objectives and practices you want, so long as they are consistent with the values.[37]

The four objectives of ServiceMaster played the same role that the values of HP did for that company. The goal for ServiceMaster, like HP, was to make the adaptations needed for the changing business realities of the early twenty-first century, while remaining rooted in their established values.

When Platt announced his intent to retire, he assessed the needs of the company, and his board was given the task of hiring a new CEO. They identified Carly Fiorino, someone who was high profile, "a business rock star who could charm and dazzle and whose very presence created a media onslaught."[38]

ServiceMaster Selection Process

Early in 2000, the ServiceMaster board created a selection committee, which was chaired by Herb Hess, a longtime outside director and a managing director at Berents and Hess Capital Management, Inc., in Boston. Other outside directors on this committee included Sidney Harris, dean of the College of Business at Georgia State University; Dave Wessner, president and chief executive officer of Park Nicollet Health Services in Minneapolis; and Don Soderquist, senior vice chairman (retired) of Walmart Stores, Inc., in Bentonville, Arkansas. Carlos Cantu and Bill Pollard were also on the committee.

They interviewed twenty internal senior leaders, considering internal candidates and looking for insight on what was needed in terms of skills and qualities for the next CEO. After a nine-month process, the board made the decision to go outside the company for the next leader and selected Jonathan P. Ward. Jon had had a twenty-three-year career at R. R. Donnelly, an integrated communications company that provides marketing and business communications. Donnelly was also a Fortune 500 company. Jon's background was in sales, operations, and marketing, and he had been the president and COO at Donnelly. Bill stayed on as chairman. In the 2000 annual report, Pollard stated, "He is a team builder with a high energy level and a focus to help us achieve our growth goals for the future. He is a person of integrity with a commitment to people and he enthusiastically embraces our four corporate objectives."[39]

Jon was forty-six years old when he began his role as CEO in January 2001, about the same age Bill Pollard was when he stepped into the lead position in 1983. The difference was that Bill had five years working inside the company before the promotion and the company was significantly smaller.

With some level of turbulence in the outside business world, economic turbulence ahead, and an outside leader for the first time, ServiceMaster prepared for continued growth in the twenty-first century.

8

POST-2000

When Jon Ward stepped into leadership, The ServiceMaster Company was in a delicate position. The company had grown and refined its mission over many years, but it still operated on the premise that the company was in the "people development" business, as Peter Drucker had observed. Accomplishing this mission meant a focus on the end goals of honoring God and helping people develop. Pursuing excellence and growing profitably were absolutely necessary, and these were the means by which the company achieved its mission.

Tied to the first two objectives, ServiceMaster leadership recognized that service workers were often treated as expendable low-cost labor. When they were given a sense of purpose and mission, they approached their work with a passion that moved them from a job to a purpose. This was transforming for the service worker, and in turn, this created value for the customer and profits for the company.

There is a strange and easily misunderstood relationship between honestly caring about the worker as a person and seeing that care reflected in the bottom line of the company. Wayne Alderson, the vice president of a steel company in the late 1960s and early 1970s, had a way of putting this that helps explain the important distinction. In the early 1970s, Alderson had turned around his company, which was rooted in what he called the "Value of the Person." Understanding and valuing the work of the steelworkers, which included creating a work environment where they could thrive, led to the settling of a strike and major progress by many measures for Pittron Steel.[1] He once said, "If you treat people with love, dignity, and respect, they will work harder and the company will do well. But if you treat people with love, dignity, and respect *so that* they will work harder, they will see through you in an instant."[2] The line between these is subtle and fragile, and it goes to the very heart of how ServiceMaster had been built. For ServiceMaster, the anchors had always been the first two objectives, and it was these anchors that allowed them to withstand the buffeting of internal and external pressures over the years. Even when this focus was imperfectly executed, it was noticed and it made a difference in the lives of the workers and in the company.

To manage this transition, Ward had some help. If the concept of "shingles on a roof" was to continue, then Bill Pollard would be there to work with him from his role as chairman. Ernie Mrozek, who had been with the company since 1987, had moved to Memphis and was the president of the fastest growing part of the company, the Consumer Services Division, for the past several years. In talking about this transition later, Mrozek said,

> Jon Ward's background was more in sales and marketing; mine was in operations for eight years. Though, if you look at the totality of my career, I was more financially oriented. I was probably viewed more as a financially oriented control guy; he was more of a sales and marketing guy. And I guess, ultimately, the judgment was made at that time that we needed to regain our growth momentum and that Jon was a stronger bet. They tried to make it attractive for me to stay. And I just loved the company, loved the people, I loved the opportunity, and I considered it, prayed about it, and ultimately said I would stay and try to make it work.[3]

In 2001, there were strong pressures from inside the company because of the debt and because some business areas were underperforming. Further, in some of the acquisitions, the culture had not fully captured the hearts and minds of the leaders and employees of those companies. While those who had never worked in such an environment before gave assent to this way of operating, they didn't necessarily own it.

There were also strong pressures from outside the company. The crash of the tech-heavy NASDAQ in April 2001 (see Figure 7.5), combined with a growing economic recession, affected all companies, including Service-Master. The company was also more vulnerable to these forces as a standard corporation and challenged by the market every day. Between 1987 and 1997, they had been protected from some of this turbulence when they operated as a limited partnership. Then in 1999, for the first time in thirty years, profit numbers declined. The external voices called for a focus on the bottom line and also looked for places to point the finger for the recent downturn. The "religious" culture and the internally developed leadership were two such places. These voices generally cheered the hiring of someone from outside the company.

How would Jon Ward, an outsider with little experience dealing with the four objectives or managing in the service industry, respond? Key events in the first year, 2001, set the tone for the new direction.

Jon Ward Takes Charge

Ward was greeted with enthusiasm from some reporters and analysts. In November 2001, *The New York Times* reported,

> Mr. Ward, who took charge in January, is treading carefully. He calls meetings to order by quoting the book of Isaiah, but he is also heeding calls to change corporate priorities. "He made it clear that his first

principle is to increase shareholder value," said John Miller, an assistant portfolio manager at Ariel Capital Management, a large shareholder. No one is attributing the company's woes solely to its religious orientation; indeed, though religion might be a distraction from focusing on improving ServiceMaster's financial situation, it might be an asset in other ways, like fostering a strong work ethic. And other culprits exist: an expansion that was too rapid and a weak, in-bred leadership lead the list.[4]

Similarly, Lewis Solomon wrote of Jon Ward's efforts to improve the company through cost controls, financial incentives at the top, and quality programs (such as Six Sigma[5]) to improve customer satisfaction:

> In the early years of the 21st century, we can only conjecture about the impact of ServiceMaster turning away from Wade's devotion to honoring God and promoting evangelical Christianity to become an inclusive, more spiritual business organization. Similar to many other corporations, the Firm recognized the need to be more customer focused to ensure its survival and continued success. Under a modern CEO, it implemented the Six Sigma process, rather than looking to biblical principles, as Wade and others would likely have done.[6]

Neither of these observers seemed to grasp the connection between the four objectives and the past success of the company. Putting the singular focus on shareholder value takes the focus off the employee and, at best, makes the employee a tool for economic gain. Solomon missed something else as well. The company did, indeed, focus on biblical principles and also carried out research projects creating moth killers, better cleaning chemicals, and better cleaning techniques. Had Solomon understood this, he would have known that the leaders of the past would have used modern methods, while *at the same time* looking to biblical principles.

These voices were effectively calling for a switch between the end goals and the means goals, reducing the development of people and honorable dealings to the role of improving financial goals and excellence. This is a subtle but powerful distinction.

In his first year, Jon Ward signaled a new direction in small and big ways.[7] Shifting his focus to increasing shareholder value was at least the way one analyst heard his remarks. In his first annual report, Ward laid out his goals.[8] He focused on the business, its growth, execution, and Six Sigma, and only tangentially mentioned the workers. He said nothing about helping them develop. He closed this first-year letter with this comment, "From time to time, someone will advise us that to reach our goals, we must jettison one objective or another. I believe we are fully capable of meeting all four objectives with equal intensity as we shall demonstrate."[9] Numerous interviewees who were present at that time, however, report that Ward indeed raised the idea of eliminating the first objective on many occasions.

Ward was met internally with more skepticism. Part of this came from his unfamiliarity with the nuances of the ServiceMaster culture. Two examples, chosen from many, are cited by internal leaders. One longtime ServiceMaster leader first met Jon Ward in the boardroom at corporate headquarters. To him, the boardroom was the hallowed ground in which the passion and purpose of the company was worked out, "and there was Jon with his feet on the table." A little thing, for sure, but he remembered it eighteen years later as if it were yesterday. Mike Mack was one of the leaders of the Seattle franchise in 2001, at the time the revenue leader among franchises. He and Wes Mitchell attended a ServiceMaster awards gathering that first year. When they met Ward, they expected him to be interested in what made the top franchise in the company tick. Rather, Ward greeted Mitchell without looking him in the eye, peering over his shoulder at someone else. After Ward's assistant whispered in his ear, he said, "So you have a little business in Seattle."[10]

Perhaps he could have avoided these little things if he had continued the "shingles on a roof" style of leadership. Or if he had spent six weeks doing front-line work as other leaders had done. Neither, however, happened. Ward wanted to establish his own leadership and put his own stamp on the company. One board member from that period commented that he understood Ward's desire to make his own mark and to be different from Pollard: "Bill can be a bit intimidating, you know."[11] While that is likely true, it was also true of all of the previous leaders, who had been challenged by the leaders who went before. All of them acknowledged that this process of "shingles on a roof" was sometimes difficult, but it made them and the company better.

In a smaller 2001 decision, the company acknowledged that the ServiceMaster Home Service Center, including WeServeHomes.com, was going to be rolled back into the company. The dream of this "dot com" spin-off had failed, as the e-commerce investment had not come close to its revenue projections. After the collapse of the "dot com" market, it looked best to use this e-commerce site from inside the company.

First Major Changes

The first major action Jon Ward took was to make a decision on the direction of the company. He chose not to follow one of the two paths the company had laid out before he came. Rather, within that first year, he made the call, with the board's approval, to sell a significant and traditional part of the company. On October 5, 2001, the *Chicago Tribune* reported,

> ServiceMaster said Thursday it would sell its Management Services business, which assists institutional customers, to Aramark Corporation for $800 million. With the sale, the Downers-Grove based household services

company will be focused primarily on U.S. consumer markets, said Chief Executive Jonathan Ward. Proceeds from the deal, about $600 million after tax, will be used to pay down debt. ServiceMaster also announced it would close some unprofitable businesses, including TruGreenLandCare, which provides landscaping services. The company expects to record a restructuring charge of $300 million to $365 million in the fourth quarter as a result.[12]

Along with the sale, Ward made another significant decision to move the company headquarters, along with the statue of Jesus washing the feet of the disciple, to Memphis, where the consumer groups were located. As part of the Management Services deal with Aramark, the Downers Grove headquarters was sold. Concerns were raised by employees, thinking this move from the roots of the company signaled something bigger. *The New York Times* reported, "'I don't know how you can believe that they're not throwing out the old stuff and the old ways,' said one longtime executive, who insisted on anonymity. 'For God's sake, they're moving Jesus to Memphis.'"[13]

Although it was not referenced in the announcements or in the annual report, the sale of the Management Services business included the sale of the research department. After the sale, Bill Bond, the director of research at the time, said, "I got the very distinct feeling that Aramark had no need for research. I knew I could retire, so I was trying to protect my people, to find places for them. In two or three years, the whole department was gone, and I retired."[14] The patents on the cleaning agents that had been developed by the research department were also sold as part of the Aramark deal. For the franchises, this meant they would no longer get rebates on the purchase of cleaning supplies from the ServiceMaster distribution centers.

Patricia Asp was also involved in this deal:

> I was executive vice president of Strategic Development, including Management Services, and was told I was going to be going with the divestiture of Management Services. And then Jon Ward asked me to stay and lead the Six Sigma "voice of the customer" and "voice of the employees," basically the transformational initiative corporately, for what remained of ServiceMaster at that time. I stayed through my two-year commitment.[15]

The deal "significantly strengthens our financial flexibility," Ward said, adding that it gave the company greater latitude in investment in its core businesses.[16] Begun under Ken Wessner as a service to hospitals, the Management Services division had added educational and industrial clients. Through the 1970s until 1986, this was the heart of the company, along with the franchises, and was where the four objectives were tested and made real. While this division's profitability had declined due to competition and maturity, Warren Buffet had advised Bill Pollard to recognize the lower profitability targets rather than try to set more challenging goals. Ward's statements suggest that the sale was a financial decision, and nothing was said about the impact on the culture.

In the 2001 annual report, Jon Ward talked about the sale of Management Services as a part of achieving focus and growth in the business, but did not mention the people. In his letter as chairman in the same annual report, Bill Pollard acknowledged the Management Services group:

> We are grateful for the way the people of Management Services have carried this decision of change and we thank them for their many contributions to our company and for their continued gift of friendship. As they join the Aramark team, we encourage them to continue their focus on service to the customer and to live and practice the values that have been an integral part of their training and life at ServiceMaster.[17]

Pollard also expressed gratitude to Rob Keith, who was leading Management Services at the time it was sold and who went with the group to join Aramark. Keith had joined the company in 1985, although he had known Bill Pollard (as his youth group leader) from the time he was eleven years old. He started in the finance area and worked closely with Pollard on the move to limited partnership. Keith said, "I initially thought that idea was impossible, but Bill taught me, 'There is always another way to solve a problem.'" Through his time at the company, he had fully bought in to the four objectives. "They were integral to the success of the company. Everybody in the organization knew them and talked about them. They impacted everything we did."[18]

When Ward took over, Keith observed that his focus was more on getting value from Management Services and less on the employee side. But in making the transition with the organization to Aramark, he said,

> I realized we had a missionary role in the new organization. Our people, and the people we managed in Management Services, had never known how important their work was before they came to ServiceMaster. We wanted to take that with us. I agreed to stay with the organization for two years, and I did. It was not the same, but we tried to deliver value and support our employees and the people we managed.[19]

Parallels with Other Companies

The transition of leadership in a company, from a strong leader to someone coming in from the outside, is generally difficult, particularly for a company with a strong internal culture. ServiceMaster was no exception. The following examples demonstrate how difficult this move was for three different companies.

Hewlett-Packard

Earlier we cited Hewlett-Packard's decision, also in 2001, to seek outside their company for a new CEO. Like ServiceMaster, HP also had a deep and vital culture, founded in its five principles called "The HP Way":20

1. We have trust and respect for individuals.
2. We focus on a high level of achievement and contribution.
3. We conduct our business with uncompromising integrity.
4. We achieve our common objectives through teamwork.
5. We encourage flexibility and innovation.

Also similar to ServiceMaster, the principles were practiced first by the founders, David Packard and Bill Hewlett, and then formalized when the company went public in 1957.21 Even in the 1940s, this way of thinking was countercultural.

In 1942, at age 29, [David Packard] attended a Stanford conference on wartime production. Dominated by industrialists from giants like Standard Oil and Westinghouse Electric, it was presided over by business school professor Paul Holden, a major management guru of the day. "Somehow, we got into a discussion of the responsibility of management," Packard later told Peninsula journalist and historian Ward Winslow, '52, "Holden made the point that management's responsibility is to the shareholders—that's the end of it. And I objected. I said, 'I think you're absolutely wrong. Management has a responsibility to its employees, it has a responsibility to its customers, it has a responsibility to the community at large.' And they almost laughed me out of the room."22

Over the decades since HP's founding in 1947, David Packard (1947–68), Bill Hewlett (1969–77), John Young (1978–92), and Lew Platt (1992–99) had shepherded and adapted the HP way. After the founders, both Young and Platt started their careers with the company and rose through the ranks to their leadership roles. In the 1990s, some accused Platt of being outdated, too focused on the long term, and not solely focused on profit. In 1999, when Carly Fiorina stepped in, she was the first to come from the outside and offered little insight about their original five principles.

Jim Collins, noted business writer, countered, "While Packard's values have since waned within HP [after Lew Platt], he [Packard] did more to create the DNA of Silicon Valley than perhaps any other CEO. Like the heritage left by the architects of democracy in ancient Athens, the spirit of his and Hewlett's system lives on, far beyond the walls of the institution they built."23

It didn't take long for Fiorina to make her mark with a major move. Over the objection of the founding family, she pushed ahead with the major acquisition of Compaq Computer early in her leadership. Collins wrote:

Hailed as a wunderkind just two years ago, when she was wooed to take the top job, she has been through a firestorm of criticism over the past year and is now in danger of being ousted as a result of her ill-fated merger with Compaq. Members of both the founding families of HP have come out against the deal, and the company's stock has tanked. In fact, shares of Hewlett-Packard only began to rebound when it looked like the deal was in jeopardy.[24]

Under the heading, "Hewlett-Packard, 1938–2002, R.I.P.," David Packard, son of the founder, said,

> The HP Way touched many people's lives. Most of us expected that it would last forever—that it would prove as timeless as a Frank Capra movie. But those entrusted with the duty to safeguard it have exercised their legal right to make another choice. *Dura lex, sed lex.* The law is harsh, but it is the law. HP employees are now on a new ship, being taken on a new voyage. The company has even changed its stock symbol to HPQ to stress that the "old" HP is gone. For the sake of the surviving employees, of course I hope for a good outcome. But it is hard to imagine that their leaders can invent something better than what they left behind.[25]

Carly Fiorina lasted until February 2005, and ten different CEOs have held the leadership role since then. Though still a good company, it is not the same.

Starbucks

Like ServiceMaster and Hewlett-Packard, Starbucks faced a similar dilemma. Orin Smith, who had joined Starbucks in 1990, was appointed CEO in 2000 and worked with the chairman and founder Howard Schultz. Orin Smith announced his plan to retire in 2005, and the company had determined no internal candidate was ready to take the lead. Starbucks also was a company with a strong culture, as Smith explained it:

> Our competitors come in and they take pictures of the stores, they read the menu board, and they sample the beverages. Then they go out and knock us off—all around the world. What differentiates us, at the end of the day, is that we provide the best experience of any competitor of scale out there. And that's because we're able to inspire our people to be passionate and committed to this company, to what they do, for the customer. So when we say we value our people, they are the reason for the success of this company.[26]

Unlike HP and ServiceMaster, however, the outgoing CEO was able to work with the new one during a time of transition. Smith continued:

> I had hoped that I would be able to bring along somebody who was already in the organization. In the end, while I know that there are future successors in this organization, they were still young enough and inexperienced

enough that we didn't think they could make the jump. When a company grows as fast as we do, it's hard to keep up with the increased complexity and responsibilities in your own job, much less jump to a higher level. We avoided my worst fear: that we would find my successor in an overnight transaction, like so many companies do. My experience in hiring from the outside is that you don't know who you hired. And I think that is really, really dangerous, especially for a company that doesn't need to be fixed. This is a high-performing company.

While we looked at the other experiences the individual had, and the functional skills, and of course the results, the big issue was: is he going to work out here? We didn't really know. But we said, "This is going to be at least a two-year process and we're going to take you through the various parts of the organization. We'll give you one set of responsibilities and then we'll add to it over time."[27]

The outside CEO, Jim Donald, had two and a half years to work everywhere from barista to warehouse to international sales before stepping into the position in 2005 when Smith retired.

In 2007, Chairman Howard Schultz sent a memo to Donald "warning of what he called 'the commoditization of the Starbucks experience.'" Ultimately, Howard Schultz stepped back into the CEO role in early 2008. According to a company statement, Schultz would be "refocusing the company on providing customers with the distinctive Starbucks experience, and building on Starbucks' legacy of innovation."[28]

Nordstrom

Nordstrom started as a family shoe company in 1901 and had grown into a national high-end clothing store across the United States. Until the 1990s, the stated responsibility of employees was "to use good judgment in all situations" and front-line employees were empowered to make decisions. The empowerment of front-line employees is illustrated by the following story. A customer in Fairbanks, Alaska, brought a set of tires to Nordstrom without a receipt and asked for his money back. The employee, without asking, reasoned the tires had been purchased from a store that Nordstrom had acquired earlier, and he refunded the customer money.[29] Nordstrom had never sold tires and had closed out that area in the acquired business. Employees were the decision-makers at Nordstrom and were valued.

In the 1990s, the family that had founded and managed Nordstrom Company went outside the family for the first time, bringing in a modern CEO with the goal of improving shareholder value. In 2000, Nordstrom's board made the decision to return to family leadership with, initially, co-CEOs appointed from the Nordstrom family and a stated direction to return to the focus on the employees. The analysts did not like this direction and stated so in no uncertain terms with comments such as the following report from Carol Tice:

> Investors worry that the Nordstrom family is overly concerned with building customer service at the expense of company profits. The fear can be boiled down to the feeling that the family's philosophy was weighted more to other factors besides the shareholders, more than maybe the Street liked.[30]

In 2001, Blake Nordstrom commented, "In the 1990s, Nordstrom lost its way when it put its focus on shareholder value. Only when we got our focus back where it belongs, on our employees and our customers, have we begun to restore shareholder value."[31] Indeed, Nordstrom restored its edge, improved its performance, and its stock rose more rapidly than the market over the next decade. The board, dominated by the family, didn't make this call to raise stock price but to restore the cultural edge that they believed in.

Each of these companies, in its own way, was built on the importance of a culture that values people. Each demonstrated the challenge of bringing in someone who did not know the culture at a deep level. Shifting away from this focus—whether for ServiceMaster, HP, Starbucks, or Nordstrom—would have longer-term consequences.

New Directions

On September 12, 2002, Bill Pollard wrote a letter to Jon Ward, with copies to the ServiceMaster board of directors, announcing his retirement from the board. At the board's request, this was made effective after the January 2003 board meeting. Pollard had been frustrated in his concern over the drift of the culture in the company, as embodied by the four objectives, and felt he could no longer have an effective voice in redirecting the company. His letter was positive, affirming, and challenging.

Pollard expressed gratitude for the opportunity to serve and gratitude for the faithful service of so many who were continuing. But he challenged Jon Ward.

> As you lead for the future and continue to make the necessary and needed changes that are all part of the new ServiceMaster, don't lose the continuity with the past. . . . I have found within this culture certain timeless values and principles that are the ServiceMaster way. This, of course, includes the four objectives. No matter what changes are made, keep before our people the importance of the principle of "service" and the need for a source of moral authority.

In raising concerns about leadership and the development of their employees, Pollard added,

> There is no end to the requirement of people development from within. This should be a priority. . . . There was a gap in this area as I came back into the business (in 1999) and there is a need for much improvement in this area. . . . Some of the fresh blood you have brought to the leadership team is healthy but, for the long term, there needs to be more focus on our second objective—the development of people.
>
> You have made some key decisions. You have moved us past the fork in the road. I commend you for the energy and enthusiasm you have brought to this change. Keep at it. Keep clarifying your strategy and direction for the next phase of our growth. . . . Jon, I believe that God has given you—entrusted you—with the platform of leadership at ServiceMaster to raise the "Question of God" in the marketplace and also to be a beacon of light to a needed and sometimes dark world. . . . The results of your leadership will be measured beyond the workplace. The story will be told in the changed lives of people.[32]

By this time, however, Jon Ward had made it clear that he was going his own direction. "Shingles on a roof" was not his style and Pollard's letter was largely ignored.

The Rest of the Jon Ward Leadership Period

Starting in 2002, the annual reports reflect a change in emphasis consistent with the new leadership of the company. The focus on the dignity of the work, and the dignity and importance of the worker, was primarily gone from discussions of the business. The focus instead shifted to financial growth and the importance of the customer.

At the January 2003 board meeting, Bill Pollard, Carlos Cantu, Chuck Stair, and Vincent Nelson all retired from serving on the board. All four had been on the board since the late 1980s, and Pollard and Nelson since the late 1970s. All but Nelson had significant roles and experience leading within the company. This meant that when these men stepped down, a large part of the history and connection to the founding of the company left the board at the same time.

Steve Preston had joined ServiceMaster in 1997, reporting to Carlos Cantu as chief financial officer and executive vice president. An early assignment was supporting Carlos and Bill in the move back to a public company from the limited partnership. He observed, "We had a pretty big company with a lot of small company ways."[33] Now he was executive vice president working with Jon Ward, who was now chairman and CEO. Preston said,

I really wanted him to be successful. Jon brought strong knowledge of sales, knew how to build a communications team, had good operational instincts, and good business fundamentals. He came at leadership differently from Pollard and Cantu, who both had significant strengths, but he didn't work to diminish the cultural history. Jon found that a number of leaders had difficulty conveying the first objective, so he undertook a study to make the objectives practical.

Unfortunately, many of the senior leaders were new, with many from outside the company, and no one seems to have looked back at all of the writings left by the previous leaders or to think to bring in Bill Pollard, who had spoken on these for years.

Over the next three years, Jon Ward took deliberate steps to refocus the company toward the customer. In the 2004 annual report, he proposed the first change in the four objectives in thirty years. The comment in the annual report states the reason for the change: "Associates and leaders agreed that we should clearly state that we value our customers and that our pursuit of excellence should be outwardly focused; so as you read our proxy statement, we propose to replace 'Pursue Excellence' with 'Excel with Customers.'" An essay on each of the four objectives was published in the annual report, with a statement from the chairman that "we want to be consistent with making our values more apparent in our day-to-day business." Nothing was said about the order of the objectives, but the essays had "Excel with Customers" in the second position.

In the annual report for 2005, the chairman's summary of the year emphasized performance and growth, with one comment on the objectives: "In 2005, we launched an initiative designed to help all of our employees use the Objectives as the context for basic, regular decisions." The objectives were listed in the back of the report.

We are accountable to:

- Honor God in All We Do
- Excel with Customers
- Help People Develop
- Grow Profitably

For the first time ever, the annual report did not contain a Scripture reference.

For many followers of business, these changes were not surprising. Critics had pushed back on the "religious" influences on the company, and the emphasis on the customer seemed to many as a previously missing ingredient. Missed, however, was the foundation of ServiceMaster on the value and dignity of the work and the worker. With this small change, people were more likely to be seen as a means to achieve customer satisfaction, not as a value themselves. Ken Wessner had frequently commented that "we need to help a person *be* before we help them *do*."[34] Focusing excellence outward on the customer meant taking emphasis away from the inward focus on the employee.

The foundation for the growth of the company had been that Service-Master could engage service workers in a mission beyond a mere job, which provided almost unique pride in what many thought was demeaning work. As we have seen, this created a culture of excellence that resulted in satisfaction from the customer and profitable growth. Now, with these new changes, the earlier distinction between end goals and means goals was lost.

Solomon, who had lauded the transition of leadership to a "modern CEO," noted in the introduction to his 2004 book, "More recently, this transitional firm, now led by a non-evangelical CEO, follows an inclusive, non-sectarian approach. Coincidentally with this transition, the company's legal difficulties mounted, and its financial results stagnated."[35]

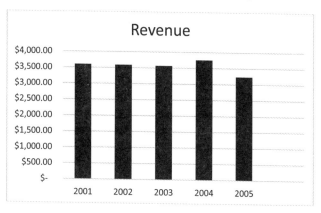

Figure 8.1. Revenue in the Ward years (dollars shown in millions). The lower numbers compared with earlier include the sale of Management Services.[36]

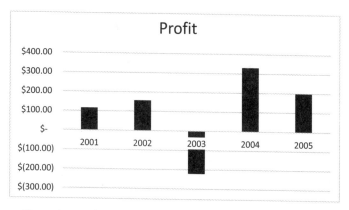

Figure 8.2. Profit in the Ward years (dollars shown in millions).[37]

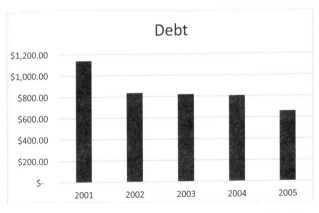

Figure 8.3. Debt in the Ward years (dollars shown in millions).

In 2005 and 2006, the rockiness continued. Early in 2005, Jon Ward promoted Albert Cantu, son of Carlos Cantu, from his position as leader of Terminix to group business president of ServiceMaster with responsibility for American Residential Services (ARS), ServiceMaster Clean, Merry Maids, and Furniture Medic. Ward said,

> Albert has done a remarkable job of growing the business and building the Terminix brand. His proven skills and ability to lead a field service organization will be very important as ARS works to take full advantage of the HVAC and plumbing markets. Those same skills will help our ServiceMaster Clean, Merry Maids and Furniture Medic franchisees continue to grow and develop.[38]

But by late 2005, "In a little-noticed Securities and Exchange Commission filing on Nov. 4, 2005, ServiceMaster said it was thinking about selling its American Residential Services and American Mechanical Services operations."[39] The report said, "ServiceMaster CEO Jonathan P. Ward told an interviewer on the CNBC cable network Nov. 3 that the plumbing and HVAC operations were not for sale. '[N]one of our companies at this point are quote, unquote on the block,' he had said."

This report referred to an SEC Form 8K filing on November 7 by ServiceMaster Senior Vice President and General Counsel Jim L. Kaput, who wrote,

> Mr. Ward's response was incomplete. Mr. Ward should have added, "While no decision has been made, as part of its regular portfolio review process the company has been and continues to explore strategic alternatives with respect to American Residential Services and American Mechanical Services, which among other alternatives could include a sale of all or a portion of those businesses."[40]

On December 13, 2005, Albert Cantu left ServiceMaster.

> ServiceMaster said Monday that Mr. Cantu "is leaving the company to pursue other interests," but declined to offer any specific cause for his departure. But in a written statement issued by Mr. Cantu, he indicated his departure was not voluntary, but stopped short of saying he was fired. "I did not retire from ServiceMaster," said Mr. Cantu, who had spent his entire 20-year career with the company. "I am disappointed to no longer be with the company and this is a process that I did not initiate."[41]

Albert attributed his departure to disagreements over company strategy. In May of 2006, Jon Ward also left the company.

> Jonathan Ward said on Tuesday his resignation from the company stemmed from differences with the Board on strategic issues and had nothing to do with matters of performance or governance. "It kind of came about suddenly," Ward told Reuters shortly after the company announced what it described as his mutually agreed-upon resignation. "The Board always has the right to have whoever in the corner office they want."[42]

Steve Preston said, "I was in the process of leaving at this time for an opportunity in Washington DC, where I felt very much called. But things changed a lot in a short period, and it was a confusing time for the company."[43] In April 2006, Preston accepted a position as administrator of the US Small Business Administration (SBA) under President George W. Bush. On April 18, 2008, he became the fourteenth US Housing and Urban Development (HUD) secretary and served until President Bush left the White House.

Transition

Board member J. Patrick Spainhour was appointed interim chairman and CEO, and the company issued a statement, "ServiceMaster is looking for a new growth-oriented CEO to capitalize on our brands and our markets." Almost immediately, the rumors started that Albert Cantu would be brought back as CEO.

> Wall Street analysts and some of ServiceMaster's biggest shareholders are speculating that Albert Cantu, who once headed ServiceMaster's Terminix pest control division, will emerge as one of the leading candidates to replace Mr. Ward, who also was the company's Chairman. "Without a doubt, Albert has to top that list" of candidates, said analyst Alexander Paris Jr. of Chicago-based Barrington Research. "He has great support within the company and on Wall Street."[44]

Spainhour announced that the board would look at both internal and external candidates and that Ernie Mrozek, president and chief financial officer, would be given consideration. Journalist Bob Tita added in his article, "It could be difficult for ServiceMaster to find a new CEO, given the challenges of improving some of its slow-growth businesses and the company's religious culture." Of Spainhour, Tita said, "Spainhour was known to read the Bible in his office and discouraged employees from using profanity."

On July 1, 2006, Spainhour was named the permanent CEO and chairman. In discussion of his compensation package, there was press speculation about whether the company would be sold to a private equity firm. But analyst Alexander Paris Jr. of Barrington Research Associates, Inc., in Chicago said that, if ServiceMaster directors were contemplating such a move, the change-of-control provisions in Mr. Spainhour's work agreement would likely have been altered. "I don't think the company is contemplating selling itself," he said. "I think it's the Board's intent to stay a public company."[45]

Then on May 1, 2007, ServiceMaster was sold to the New York-based private equity firm Clayton Dubilier & Rice (CD&R) and was no longer a public company.

> Bowing to pressure from large shareholders, ServiceMaster in November announced plans to look at "strategic alternatives." In March, the company turned to CD&R, which agreed to pay $15.63 in cash for each share—16 percent above ServiceMaster's stock price on March 16—while assuming existing ServiceMaster debt. In announcing the deal, ServiceMaster CEO J. Patrick Spainhour said the new owners would be free to make improvements without the burdens of satisfying Wall Street investors as a public entity.[46]

One longtime ServiceMaster leader liked the prospects:

> "We really are very excited about CD&R's purchase," said Mike Isakson, president and chief operating officer of ServiceMaster Clean and current chair of the International Franchise Association. "They have owned franchise businesses in the past. They understand franchising. As we have visited them, we feel good about them."[47]

Since CD&R had recently purchased and reinvested in another franchise business, the Culligan Company, this seemed like a good opportunity for ServiceMaster to get back on its feet. Ernie Mrozek agreed that this was the best solution, given the circumstances:

> Our two largest business units, lawn care and pest control, both had some significant things going on in their industries which could cause some short-term turbulence and disrupt our pattern of predictability and require some investment. There was a concern about how the market would react if we had to make those investments and impede growth for a period

of time. We went for about 12.5 times EBITDA [Earnings Before Interest, Tax, Depreciation, and Amortization], which was considered a high multiple at the time, and we concluded that at that price we should not turn it down. Flying under the radar as a private entity seemed like the right answer.[48]

Before coming to ServiceMaster, Spainhour had been the CEO of the Ann Taylor Stores Corporation from 1996 to 2005. He served as CEO and chairman of ServiceMaster until his retirement on March 31, 2011.

In 2011, Hank Mullany, a former Walmart executive vice president, was brought in to lead the company. His first task was to finish the job that Spainhour had started, spinning off the TruGreenLandCare business. His second task was to try to get the TruGreen lawn care business back into profitability. He appointed a new TruGreen president, who lasted less than a year. According to industry writer Chuck Bowen, "In 2012, [TruGreen] reported an 11 percent drop in revenue, and operated at a loss of $805 million."[49] On April 12, 2013, after having three presidents in three years for TruGreen and the resignation of the president of Terminix as well, Mullany resigned. John Krenicki had joined CD&R after a twenty-nine-year career with GE, where he had recently been the CEO of its $50 billion energy division. When Mullany resigned, Krenicki stepped in as interim chairman and CEO of ServiceMaster and announced a search for a new full-time CEO.

Rob Gillette Named Chairman, ServiceMaster Goes Public Again

The search for a new permanent CEO didn't take long. John Krenicki reached back into his GE contacts and recruited Rob Gillette. While Gillette came from the position of CEO of Honeywell Aerospace, before that he had held a number of senior management positions at General Electric. He was brought in with two priorities: to take ServiceMaster public again and to fix TruGreen. Going public again became a priority for CD&R, since the investment firm had other companies it had acquired during the economic downturn. Since ServiceMaster was generating revenue and profit, going public would provide more investment for the other CD&R companies that were still struggling.

> The company still had the stated objectives, including 'To Honor God in All We Do,' but they weren't acting this way. The worst way to lead people in an organization is to say you stand for something, and then do something else. People watch what you do, not what you say.[50]

At his first open meeting after coming on board, Rob Gillette said he was confronted by an employee who wanted to know where he stood on the objectives, and in particular on the first objective. He recalled replying, "I think you should honor all religions of all people. That's all I'm saying about that." Later, he worked with the communications people and HR to draw up a set of behaviors, not far removed from the four objectives, that they could use going forward. But he didn't believe he could use "God language."[51]

TruGreen had been a major disappointment for the company, and the original leaders left. Under Mullany, there had been a high turnover of leaders without solving the fundamental economic problem. Some observers concluded that lawn care was not a good choice for ServiceMaster. There was a growing concern by the public about the chemicals used in lawn care, according to Robert Palmer.[52] The business was also weather-dependent and, hence, cyclical. It also tended to be local because of the variety of climates; for example, lawn services in Phoenix look very different from lawn services in Maine—both in the type of services and in the seasonal nature of these services.

At this point, Gillette made the call to spin off TruGreen from Service-Master. According to writer Brian Horn,

> After Rob Gillette, ServiceMaster CEO, called TruGreenLawnCare a distraction during an earnings call in December [2013], announcing TruGreen's spin-off from the parent company, it gave a peek into the not-so-sound relationship between the two companies.

> TruGreen was separated from ServiceMaster and is now owned by the private equity firm Clayton, Dubilier & Rice, who also owns ServiceMaster. "Being a part of ServiceMaster offered meaningful advantages in terms of scale and also provided the opportunity to continually vet our ideas with a talented management team leading diverse businesses," Alexander [TruGreen's president David Alexander] wrote in an email to *Lawn & Landscape*.

> "On the other hand, by necessity, many decisions were made based on the overall good of the enterprise rather than on the specific needs of TruGreen. We believe that this opportunity allows us take control of our destiny and to be far more nimble, focused and responsive to our customers' needs, while allowing ServiceMaster to move forward on their own timeline for an IPO." Alexander says a major problem with the Service-Master [Company] . . . was the operating system TruGreen shared with ServiceMaster's structural pest control company, Terminix.

> "The challenge came in the fact that they are not a weather-dependent business and we are," he says. "So, the flexibility needs are drastically different. To use a football analogy, from a scheduling standpoint, they are able to run the play they call the vast majority of the time, while we have to be very, very good at calling an audible."[53]

A month after the sale, ServiceMaster had its initial public offering (IPO) and went public again on June 26, 2014. In the 2014 annual report, Gillette wrote,

> When I joined ServiceMaster as CEO in 2013, one of the things that struck me immediately was the company's rich history. In the 86 years since being founded, the company had achieved something most service companies would envy—the trust of customers who literally invite us into their homes and businesses.[54]

He reached back to Bill Pollard for a conversation, trying to understand what had made ServiceMaster work so well in the 1980s and 1990s. He was the first leader of the company since Jon Ward to reach out to Bill. Gillette learned the history of the four objectives, and he learned about helping the worker bring purpose and meaning to his or her work. According to Gillette, "Bill said he knew we would be better run as one company. But we have got to give people a reason to work here that is greater than themselves. It's almost an evangelistic mission that you have to inspire them to pursue." Gillette remembered asking Pollard why this had not been carried on in the same way after he left and was told, "Jon just said it was too hard to do this."[55]

On June 3, 2016, ServiceMaster announced it was moving its headquarters into the vacant Peabody Center in downtown Memphis.

> "We're thrilled to be joining the downtown business community and being a part of the city's ongoing downtown revitalization efforts," said Service-Master Chief Executive Officer Rob Gillette. "We're excited to start the process of creating a new headquarters that reflects our winning culture and will help us attract and retain great talent in Memphis."[56]

In that same year, ServiceMaster was named to the *Fortune* list of most admired service companies,[57] although it was not the top service company.

But before the move to downtown was completed, ServiceMaster made two more announcements on July 26, 2017: American Home Shield would be spun off as its own public company sometime in 2018; and Rob Gillette was out, effective immediately, replaced as CEO by Nikhil Varty.[58] Reflecting on that time, Gillette said,

> We then needed to build a better board. Too many people were there who were making sure we didn't get into trouble, but not engaging enough in the direction of the company. We didn't have the advantage that Pollard had, with a board that understood what the company was about. I was in awe of what the company had done, and all the money they had made, when they were on the same page about direction. The board wasn't knowledgeable enough in the service industry and relented to activist in-

vestors whose only goal was short-term profit/benefit versus Pollard's board focused on a mission. My biggest failing at ServiceMaster was not building a good board. The rest I am very proud of.[59]

Before joining ServiceMaster, Varty had been president of the Americas and vice president of mergers and acquisitions at WABCO, a Brussels-based intelligent vehicle company. On October 1, 2018, ServiceMaster completed the spin-off of Frontdoor, the parent company of its American Home Shield business, now a separately traded public company. Revenue and profit numbers are shown in Figures 8.4 and 8.5 below from 2013 (the year before going public) through 2018.

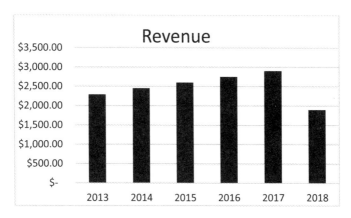

Figure 8.4. Revenue in the Gillette years. The lower numbers compared with the 1990s reflect in part the pieces of the company that had been sold or spun out (dollars shown in billions).[60]

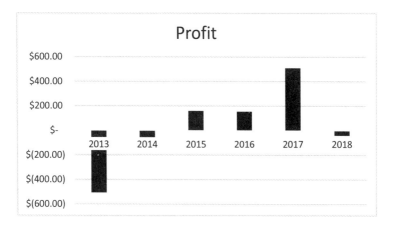

Figure 8.5. Profit in the Gillette years (dollars shown in millions).[61]

On the current ServiceMaster website, the company summarizes its connection to its founder Marion Wade with the following words:

> Today, ServiceMaster operates under many of the same tenets of Marion Wade's original purpose: to deliver exceptional service and quality to customers. Like our company's founder, we believe in being:
>
> - Dependable
> - Accountable
> - Expert
> - Responsible
> - Respectful
> - Accessible
>
> When we do these things well, we're living up to the ServiceMaster legacy.[62]

Interestingly, when examining the various franchise sites of Service-Master Clean or Restore, some franchises continue to identify with the objectives in their original form,[63] some display them in the revised form (with "Excel with Customers" in the second position),[64] and some do not display the objectives at all. The various franchises seem to have a significant amount of autonomy.

More recently, ServiceMaster announced that it "is currently in a cultural transformation, which includes the adoption of a new set of corporate values—one of which is now innovation."[65] This step is consistent with their roots, since innovation, from Marion Wade to the research lab to the innovative changes in products and customers, was a part of what made the company successful. Here is how the company currently lists its values:

INTEGRITY–Lives up to the trust others place in us through consistent honesty, reliability and transparency in all interactions.

HUMILITY–Is not afraid to admit what he or she doesn't understand and is comfortable sharing knowledge. Respects and empowers others and maintains a humble demeanor.

PASSION–Is willing to do what it takes to deliver an exceptional customer experience. Demonstrates initiative, creativity and drive.

ACCOUNTABILITY–Delivers on all commitments and takes responsibility for decisions, actions and results.

PERSEVERANCE–Adapts and maintains effectiveness in the face of obstacles, ambiguity and change.

INNOVATION–Challenges the status quo and generates creative solutions that achieve sustainable business results.

TEAMWORK–Collaborates and works effectively with others to achieve common goals and objectives.[66]

The earlier foundational elements that were tied to a higher authority for integrity and the deep commitment to the value of the worker and his or her development are still not present. This was the area Harvard professor James Heskett noted, as discussed in chapter 1, that had been key to breaking the cycle of failure in the service industry. In those past years, ServiceMaster had "basically reengineered jobs, provided training to people, and attempted to deliver a level of self-esteem that many workers have never had in the past."[67]

ServiceMaster remains a respected company, but the uniqueness from that early foundation is gone. Perhaps companies, like people, have life cycles. But maybe it is not that simple. The foundation of ServiceMaster continues in surprising ways, and this is the subject of the next chapter.

9

SERVICEMASTER'S LONG-TERM IMPACT

For many years, ServiceMaster operated from a unique foundation, set in place by Marion Wade and transformed through the leadership of Ken Hansen, Ken Wessner, Bill Pollard, and Carlos Cantu. Though the foundational elements—"To Honor God in All We Do" and "To Help People Develop"—are no longer the foundation of the company, they are not gone.

Many franchises within ServiceMaster continue to hold onto the four objectives within their domain. They carry this on without much support from the corporation. In addition, there are leaders who were shaped by their time with the company, who are now leading other organizations and guiding them by what they learned during their time with ServiceMaster. The story, therefore, continues.

In this chapter are some of those stories that highlight the present reality of these objectives both inside and outside the company. Perhaps this is what Marion Wade had in mind when he said,

> I was not asking for personal success as an individual or merely material success as a corporation. I do not equate this kind of success with Christianity. Whatever God wants is what I want. But I did try to build a business that would live longer than I would in the marketplace, that would be a witness to Jesus Christ in the way the business was conducted.[1]

Within the Franchises

Today, franchises in ServiceMaster are independently owned and operated. Although they pay a fee to corporate as a percent of revenue, they have a great deal of autonomy. Some, though not all, continue to carry out the foundations of what made ServiceMaster work over the earlier years. Several of these franchise leaders, starting with Mike Mack in Seattle, capture the picture of the continued influence of the ServiceMaster way.

Mike Mack, Seattle Franchise

Mike Mack is the president and owner of the Seattle franchise, and his partner and executive vice president is Richard Barr. Hired as a sales manager twenty-five years ago, Barr now has multiple people in the sales group and owns 25 percent of the company. Mike Mack started with ServiceMaster Seattle in 1989, hired by first-generation franchise owners Wes and Barbara Mitchell. In 2005, Mike and Dan Olson, who had joined the team in 1992, bought the franchise from the Mitchells, and in 1994, Barr became part of the team. Today, the franchise employs 165 people in four locations.

During his time in the company, Mack had the opportunity to meet many of the CEOs, starting with Ken Wessner, "though Ken Wessner was mainly retired when I met him," he said.[2] In his office are the four objectives of ServiceMaster. There is a plastic model of the original headquarters wall representing the much larger wall in Downers Grove. Employees with twenty-five years of experience no longer have their names carved on the corporate wall, but in Seattle they receive a copy of this model to commemorate their twenty-five years of service. Also in his office are two bookends with the "servant leadership" model etched in glass, recalling the larger model of the statue of Jesus washing the feet of the disciple that used to be displayed at corporate headquarters to remind ServiceMaster people of the importance of servant leadership. Between the bookends are two of Bill Pollard's books on the company. The training room downstairs has the four objectives prominently displayed on the wall.

Having all of these items is not nostalgic for Mack. Rather, they are reminders to him that the corporate objectives still matter every day and that the way the company was run in the past remains effective in the twenty-first century.

> I have some guys in production who have worked here for thirty years. Creating that sense of purpose and meaning for the workers, and providing the career opportunity for individual workers, has helped us make this a good place to work. I sit down with every person who works here, whether in sales, operations, or administration, and talk with them about a career path.[3]

It isn't only the executives who have a long career at ServiceMaster. Incidentally, the Seattle franchise has been the number one franchise for the company in twenty-three of the last thirty years.

This Seattle business consists of ServiceMaster Clean (providing commercial janitorial services), ServiceMaster Restore (restoration and insurance repair), and Pack Out, a storage service for household goods and clothes when fire or water damage requires removing these things while repairs are made. A more recent innovation called ServiceMaster Recovery Management (SRM) is a collaboration between ten large franchises across the country, which allows them to bring resources together in times of major disasters. Mack said,

This started in an informal way after a major flood in St. Louis in the 1990s. But in the last eight years, with the help of Mike Isakson and Doug Pound, it was formalized into a quick way to draw on people and equipment across the country, with pre-signed contracts.

This enabled the Seattle ServiceMaster team to help in Alaska recently after an earthquake there.

For a number of crucial years, Mack added, Mike Isakson was president and COO of the Franchise Group and instrumental in helping the franchises navigate the changing corporate directions.

Mike Isakson and Doug Pound played key roles both in protecting the franchises from corporate changes, and advocated for the franchises. They filled the gap after Bill Pollard left, when the emphasis on the ServiceMaster way lessened from the top. They were also helpful in keeping the way of doing business in front of the franchises.

Although Pound and Isakson are no longer in that position at corporate, since they are running their own franchises, their franchises do continue to collaborate. Mike Mack said,

In the early 2000s, I fought the formal organization of franchises, stating we didn't really need this. But four years ago, when Isakson was gone and those leading the franchises from corporate started making unreasonable demands, we did formally organize. We now have funding and legal support, and the association is helping to calm the waters.

When asked how many of the franchises continue to promote the ServiceMaster way, Mack replied,

A number of them do, particularly the more successful franchises that are second- and third-generation family owned. But some of the ones that have been sold to those newer to the business have less regard for the foundation. Undoubtedly it will lessen over time, without the reinforcement from the top.[4]

Bob Smith, St. Louis Franchise

After Bob Smith graduated from college in 1977, he started his career with ServiceMaster as a hospital manager in Grand Island, Nebraska. Ken Wessner was CEO at the time, and Bob loved the philosophy of the company. Smith said, "I remember to this day the passion he had for the four objectives, and for why we existed as a business."[5] After his assignment in Nebraska, he transferred to St. Louis where he led the ServiceMaster hospital work there. He was then promoted to regional manager, responsible for hospitals and school programs in St. Louis and southern Missouri.

When Bill Pollard took over in 1983, Smith felt the transition was seamless:

> Bill not only continued to utilize our corporate objectives as the foundation for how we did business, but defended this foundation as we continued our rapid growth. Bill was responsible for connecting ServiceMaster, including our Christian foundation, to the broader business community and to Wall Street. Mr. Pollard was very well spoken and respected in the business community. He was a demanding leader, but led ServiceMaster through a period of unprecedented growth.

In 1984, Bob began to put his dream into motion to own his own business. He had met with a variety of franchise owners since he had been at ServiceMaster, and it seemed that this was a course he wanted to follow.

> In those early years, I knew if I stayed in corporate, I would be moving. We were at a stage in the family where I wanted to stay in one place. I remember flying up to Chicago to meet with Mr. Pollard to discuss my decision to leave the corporate role and become a franchise owner. He wanted me to stay, suggesting a great opportunity for growth within corporate. But he was very gracious, and he respected my decision. He said he would love to have me come back to corporate if it didn't work out. What I heard from Mr. Pollard said a lot to me about the value of what I had done in the company. I found that very encouraging.[6]

This gave Bob the opportunity to build his business under the umbrella of ServiceMaster, with the same objectives and in the same spirit. "As a franchise owner, I was privileged to have Richard Armstrong and Brian Oxley as leaders of the ServiceMaster Franchise Division. They were instrumental in helping me develop my business through the ServiceMaster support system."

"Carlos embraced what we did and what we stood for," Bob said of the leadership change. When Jon Ward took over, "there was more of a distancing of corporate leadership from the franchises. The direction was more about revenue and Wall Street, less about a way of doing business. It was a different path."

Changes on the board and in leadership meant it was tougher to see strong support for the franchise owners' way of doing business. Smith recalled:

> We were forceful in wanting to keep the four corporate objectives as they were, but from corporate there was a "watering down" of the emphasis. A new breed of leaders came into the company, many without ServiceMaster experience, or even experience in the service area. The focus from corporate became more about fees and demand for growth, with almost a "take it or leave" kind of tone. Fortunately, Mike Isakson took over the corporate responsibility for franchises, and he sought to make this a true partnership.

He was a strong proponent of our foundational corporate objectives and developing strong collaborative relationships with the franchises.

When Mike left, there was a real change. Our relationship with corporate became adversarial. On the disaster restoration side of the business, we used to have a partnership with the national insurance companies, but now we were treated more as a vendor. With corporate turnover, we no longer had the key relationships with our insurance partners, and this made it more challenging for us.

For us, the ServiceMaster way continues as an integral part of what we do. We have about 160 people in our janitorial service, and about 65 in disaster recovery. Who we are and what we stand for is something we share with every new employee, every new customer. We have a big sign in the training room featuring the four objectives as they were written in 1973. This is where we host training sessions for employees, customers, insurance adjusters, and agents. We go over these objectives, explaining unapologetically that this is the basis of how we do business. We will honor God in the way we do business, honor diversity, and treat people with respect. When we do all these, our customers benefit as well. When we do all these things right, we also grow profitably and will be here next year providing jobs and serving our community. All of these things translate into better customer performance and better employee experience. This is what we stand for. This is what makes us a stronger company.[7]

The older franchise leaders find it sad to see the support for the ServiceMaster way disappear from corporate. Some franchises are being sold within the family, however, and so the old model continues. But then, many newer franchise owners know nothing about these commitments. Bob said, "Without the support from the top, we know we are a generation away from this being totally gone."

On a personal note, he added,

I went to ServiceMaster because I wanted to be in an organization where people wanted to work together, not destroying each other, where fairness and hard work were valued. It has been a very rewarding career for me. I believe that our way of doing business, consistently reinforced in our training, has encouraged our own growth and our customer satisfaction. It has been a great opportunity to run a company, and I never regretted moving from corporate to own a franchise. I have learned to be a servant leader, to manage finances, to run a business, and at the same time honor God in the way we do business. This way of thinking about people overflows to how we interact with employees, customers, and in our daily lives. I have never regretted the move from corporate.

After forty years of doing this, we will continue the janitorial services part of our business, as we have been developing good leadership there. We are selling the disaster recovery part to our son-in-law Josh and our daughter Nikki. That is the time-sensitive part of the business, requiring 24/7 response, and we believe it is time to move on from that. Josh has been involved in the business for thirteen years. We are pleased that they will carry on the four corporate objectives.[8]

Dave Moore, Wheaton Franchise

Dave Moore may have more time with ServiceMaster than almost anyone in the company—because he started early:

> My dad was reading yellow ServiceMaster manuals while I was arriving in the delivery room. He was working for the company in the early days when many of the carpets were sent out for cleaning. Our basement always had rugs in it. My first job, at age five, was washing, drying and folding towels, and I got paid a nickel a load.[9]

By age ten, Dave was involved in selling spotting kits door to door. "My sales territory was limited to our neighborhood, so I wasn't particularly successful." He also went out with his father on weekends to hang advertising flyers on doors.

In high school, Dave started working three to four hours after school cleaning buildings in the Wheaton area, still working for ServiceMaster. He said, "I got to know Bill Pollard from those early days, since I was a classmate with his son. I ended up hanging out at their house in those days."[10] In 1981, Moore went away to college at Taylor University to study business and computer science. "I was a bit of a rebel, since everyone expected me to go to Wheaton College." His dad had sold his cleaning franchise and became a distributor, a regional manager for franchises, so Dave worked with other franchise owners in the Wheaton area during the summers. After graduating, he bought his own franchise in the Wheaton area and operated it for almost three years.

Then he was asked if he would consider selling his franchise and moving to corporate in a training position. That launched a fifteen-year career at corporate where he worked in "about twenty different jobs" over the period, ending as vice president of operations for the International Division. His background from college allowed him to develop systems that helped standardize and automate processes.

"In 2000, I decided it was time to stop traveling so much and be home with a growing family. So, I bought another franchise, and that's the business I own now." The decision, for Moore, involved considering what was right by God, family, and work.

> We had two young boys at home, and I was gone a lot. I loved what I did, including the travel, but wanted to do what was right. I considered leaving the company, but I remember meeting with Mike Isakson, who at the time was responsible for franchises. He took me for a walk, showed me a path for the future, and at the end of that, I decided to buy a franchise and to stay.

Today, Dave's franchise is solely a part of ServiceMaster Clean, cleaning office buildings, small schools, and medical facilities. When he trained his employees, he taught the four objectives every day.

> It ingrained in me the simplicity of a way of doing business. When I taught what it meant "to honor God in all we do," it was not teaching you in an exclusive way what you should believe. Rather, it meant there was an authority for right and wrong that went beyond our own opinions. Everything I do, from a business decision to a hard conversation with an employee, gets focused through this understanding. Just fifteen minutes ago, a sales guy came in and told me we have the opportunity to charge a customer a lot more money because of the circumstances of the job. What should we do? we asked. What was the right thing to do both for us and the customer? No spreadsheets, just a conversation about what is right and wrong.[11]

After 2001, the company went through some major changes, which Moore observed. One was when the Management Services division was sold. The primary way this sale affected franchises is that it took away the buying power for equipment and supplies. A second change was "downgrading the four objectives, minimizing 'to honor God.' Though we felt uncomfortable hearing about these changes, as franchise owners we didn't allow that to affect us. Most of the time, the franchisees came away with the understanding that we could operate as we always had." Third, he had grown up in an era of expansion and growth. "Selling off pieces of the company seemed like trying to create the biggest return for certain leaders."

To keep together, franchise owners met for workshops and training.

> We are also a part of a ten-group network that meets twice per year. We continue to support each other in the four objectives. As changes happen in corporate, we always have a way of communicating from the franchises, helping them understand what we are doing. I believe the culture among the franchises is still strong.

There is also some pressure for growth.

> A lot of it is about the money. But we believe that if we do excellent work, the money will follow. As before, we start from doing the right thing and pursuing excellence; we don't start with the focus on money.

Moore said the work he has done over the years has had a strong impact on him personally.

> All day, every day, you think about doing things right and taking care of people. So, when I go home and coach a soccer team, this way of thinking applies there also. I may not have had the same outlook on life if I had been in a different company.[12]

Dave Moore is cautiously optimistic about the future of his franchise. His oldest son recently moved back from Dallas to be near family and to be a part of the business. As already mentioned, his younger son and daughter-in-law are also part of the business. "They are learning the business from the inside, and we will see where this goes."

Mike Isakson, Multiple Franchise Owner

Between 1990 and 2012, Mike Isakson may have been the franchise "dean" of ServiceMaster, and he has a long history with the company that continues to the present.

In high school, he worked for a ServiceMaster franchise owner in Minnesota. After graduating from college, he worked for a trucking company in marketing and sales but, after a couple of years, he and his wife Jinny decided they would like to own and run their own company. A friend and mentor, Dave Thiessen, recommended they buy a ServiceMaster franchise. So, in June 1977, they bought a franchise in Bismarck, North Dakota, starting with no revenue.

Over the next few years, they built it into a thriving business, landing in the top 10 percent of franchises by 1980 when they won the Marion E. Wade Award of Honor. In the 1980s, they bought a second ServiceMaster franchise. Performing both janitorial services and restoration, they built their franchise to the point where they employed thirty full-time and one hundred fifty part-time people by 1990. In 1988, when ServiceMaster bought Merry Maids, the Isaksons decided that was an interesting business, "so we bought a Merry Maids franchise as well."[13]

Corporate leaders had their eyes on Mike, and in 1990, Bill Pollard called him to see if he would be willing to move to corporate as vice president of market expansion, selling franchises for Merry Maids. At that point, the Isaksons sold their franchises to managers of the businesses, moved to Downers Grove, and began a corporate career. "I am grateful for the strong leadership and mentorship from Bill Pollard, Brain Oxley, and Don Parker, three important people who really helped me in my career."[14]

After a year, Isakson became president and chief operating officer of Merry Maids, overseeing about three hundred franchise owners. Four years later, he said,

Rob Keith asked me to become the president of the ServiceMaster Franchise Division, and then we moved to Memphis and had responsibility for franchises in both Merry Maids and ServiceMaster. Over the next twenty-five years, I was privileged to be the chief operating officer of the franchise businesses. When I left in 2012, ServiceMaster Clean had, give or take, about five thousand franchises worldwide in about thirty-four different countries and did about $2.5 billion in consumer level revenue. We had

about three hundred and fifty staff members across the globe—primarily
in the United States, Canada, and the UK—who supported our franchise
owners in marketing and systems, finance and sales, innovation and market expansion.[15]

It was in this capacity that Mike became the advocate for the franchise
business owners across the country, supporting their training and development, as well as creating a positive environment for franchises within the
corporate structure. He played a key role in focusing the franchise owners
on the value and application of the four objectives.

After stepping away in 2012, Isakson and two of his colleagues decided
to buy Merry Maids franchises in Ohio, Arkansas, and Iowa.

Today I'm not involved day-to-day in our Merry Maids businesses, but I
serve on three corporate boards and do a fair amount of consulting and
then speaking in the franchise industry. I've been chairman of the International Franchise Association and am still very involved in that part of
the whole franchise world.

Reflecting on his time with the company, he said, "It has been a privilege to have guys like Bill Pollard, Ernie Mrozek, and Rob Keith as key
mentors in this whole process. It has been a wonderful ride. But things
changed a lot over the time." He said that working with Bill Pollard was
quite an experience.

Bill was very visionary, very explosive. Bill could erupt with incredible
excitement about opportunities and visions of where we were going. He
also could grind you into the ground with very tough questions, but he
always picked you back up.

[By contrast, Cantu was] very, very measured in his responses. There were
times where it was easy to see that there was tension building for Carlos,
but he was just very solid. He came from a different faith background than
Bill, but he clearly understood, accepted, and interpreted those objectives.
Bill and Carlos worked very well together and there wasn't much light
between their shoulders.

Jon [Ward] made a decision, with the board's approval, to sell the Management Services Group to Aramark. He really believed that we could become
a consumer company as opposed to the business-to-business work we
did with Management Services. His vision was to add some other large
platforms onto the consumer side of the business. However, selling to
Aramark really changed the face of our company, because that was where
the objectives had really taken root.

Another part of the change was due to bringing in lots of people from
outside the company. I remember meeting with our new vice president of
human resources, and I asked her, "What do you think of the corporate

objectives?" She had never heard of them! Right then, I knew that we were losing part of our culture and I needed to step into the advocacy role, working with franchise owners.

After leaving corporate in 2012, Mike didn't want to retire, so he became a franchise owner again.

As a Merry Maids franchise owner, I was just at our National Convention in Phoenix last week. At the same time, the ServiceMaster franchise owners were there also. I was honored and privileged to have virtually hundreds and hundreds of franchise owners come up and talk about the period where my team had franchise leadership over those twenty-five years. Many of them said, "It doesn't matter what's on the corporate wall today. Those objectives are alive and real in my business today and they're, if you will, chiseled in the business."

The ServiceMaster objectives needed to be shared, experienced, taught, and discussed to keep them alive. Given that they are no longer a part of the fabric of the current ServiceMaster, it will take more effort by individuals to keep them alive in their businesses. I have often said that culture eats strategy for lunch and that the culture of those objectives is much more important in determining performance than pages and pages of strategy. Strategy is important, but it must be combined with culture and trust.[16]

Outside the Company

The longer-term impact of the earlier period at ServiceMaster not only continues to be felt within the company, but it also radiates out to the rest of the world through people who were trained, shaped, and developed during their time of working in the company. Some were there for a long period and others just a short time. But ServiceMaster left a mark on all of them and these ideas now reach across the world.

Matt Edwards, Chief Operating Officer, Pine Cove Camps

Matt Edwards is the chief operating officer of Pine Cove Christian Camps, based in Tyler, Texas, with camps in multiple Texas locations and South Carolina. They have an annual budget of $45 million and serve 100,000 campers per year. He got his start at ServiceMaster.

He described his early days as "a young guy out of high school who had lost his way."[17] He was working in a hospital in Lorain, Ohio, when two major turning points changed his life. First, he had an encounter with God and committed his life to Christ. And, second, he met someone from ServiceMaster who was overseeing the maintenance and housekeeping at the hospital. The ServiceMaster leader, Brett Baird, took an interest in him and put him through the training program. Then, in 1984, he was sent to manage housekeeping in a hospital in Detroit.

In Detroit, he started by cleaning toilets, emergency rooms, and stairwells, learning the work of front-line employees during the ServiceMaster "We Serve" program. Following the ServiceMaster plan of "promoting for potential, paying for performance," Edwards became the environmental services director at Sinai Hospital. He fully embraced the four objectives, grew as a servant leader, and found a career he had never thought possible. While in Detroit, he also had the opportunity to complete a degree from William Tyndale College.

In 1997, Matt was asked to move to Texas to work in Integrated Services, coordinating the seventeen departments of service at Mother Frances Hospital in Tyler. Again, two major turning points happened. First, he had prayed for an older mentor who would be a help to him, both in his life as a Christian and in his career. Before leaving Detroit, he received a phone call from Francis Galloway, the person who had opened up the Southwest Region for ServiceMaster in the early days.

> He had heard I was coming to Texas, and he just wanted to reach out to me and help in the transition. He was the mentor I was looking for, and he, too, helped shape my life.

Second,

> Between 1997 and 2004, I received several inquiries from Pine Cove Camps to come and join them. But I loved what I did and felt a strong calling to ServiceMaster. Further, the company encouraged my development through assignments and training.

While in Texas, he was able to get his master's degree at the University of Texas, which was also encouraged by the company.

After his assignment in Integrated Services, he became director of hospitality services for Mother Francis Hospital, leading housekeeping, grounds, laundry, patient transportation, and so forth.

> Over those years, I made numerous trips to Chicago for training, and on one occasion I had the opportunity to meet with Bill Pollard in his office, to hear his heart, to develop my passion and understanding for the business. His passion for the business and interest in me was inspiring.

But things began to change in 2001 after Jon Ward came in.

> The family feeling was gone. It was less about passion and calling, and more about business and the bottom line. It just wasn't the same. I was in Chicago to visit Jon Ward, when I first heard the rumor (from a colleague there) of the sale of our division.

When Management Services was sold to Aramark, things changed even more.

> I had been participating in annual meetings at ServiceMaster where we were encouraged, challenged, and inspired by the objectives of honoring God and helping people develop. Our first Aramark gathering was in Las Vegas. The CEO arrived in a limousine with a collection of show girls. It was night and day. I finally left to join Pine Cove in 2004.

At Pine Cove, Edwards realized that his business training, vision, focus, and preparation had all come from ServiceMaster. The connection to ServiceMaster, however, was more than his preparation for the work. When Pine Cove was going through its strategic planning, Edwards reached out once again to Bill Pollard to ask for guidance.

> Bill came down for two days of work with the senior leadership team, challenging us, pushing us, focusing us on what we needed to do to prepare for our next growth. He went through our finances and encouraged us to eliminate some things, focusing on what we did well. And he paid for his own airline ticket. His time here fundamentally changed our direction and focus.

As Pine Cove grew, Edwards also reached out to ServiceMaster for some services help. He now has a crew of people from the company who take care of the grounds. He also went to ServiceMaster with an interesting problem.

> Our camp week ends with one group on Saturday morning, and the next group arrives on Saturday afternoon. Our goal was to end the experience for each group with a hot meal as a sendoff, but we didn't have time. Our people needed to clean up the cabins in preparation for the next group. So, I went to ServiceMaster to see if they could apply their skills organizing the work to free up some time.[18]

They used their disciplined training to help restructure the cleanup, allowing time for camp staff to clean *and* to serve the closing hot breakfast.

As Matt drove around the camps in his pickup truck, he frequently stopped to talk with the ServiceMaster people who were working on the grounds. He called them by name, asked about their families, and clearly honored them in their work. He lived, as well as talked about, ServiceMaster. From cleaning disciplines to business disciplines to managing and leading people, Matt Edwards acknowledges a debt to ServiceMaster. "The only reason I can do what I do today is because of what I learned at ServiceMaster." In his office, he has a lithograph on the wall, a gift from Frances Galloway. On it is written the well-known quote from Marion Wade, "If you don't live it, you don't believe it."

Joy Flora, Budget Liaison, University of North Carolina, Asheville

"In my first job out of college in 1977," Joy Flora shared, "I was involved in limited real estate partnerships. Unfortunately, I encountered some ethical issues there and decided I needed to leave. What attracted me to ServiceMaster was its ethical framework and commitment, though I was not a Christian when I joined."[19] In 1986, she started as a regional manager in the franchise business and then held several finance positions, including international controller. In 1998, she became president of Merry Maids. "This was a great opportunity to be in the operations of the business."

Dallen Peterson, the founder of Merry Maids, which was sold to ServiceMaster in 1988, talked about servant leadership, using Joy as the exemplar: "It is the responsibility of the leader to serve his or her people by instilling that sense of passion and excitement." This happens when the people in the organization are "in touch with the leader, seeing his or her own excitement, integrity, and commitment. Joy Flora is a great example of this." Peterson described her this way:

> Joy has considerable management and corporate experience through her work with ServiceMaster. She is also a former Merry Maids franchise owner, so she knows the day-in, day-out joys and trials of the business. She has a leader's sense of passion and excitement about the big picture, and staff and owners also know that she can identify with the small daily challenges they face.[20]

Not only did Joy contribute significantly to the company, but it also shaped her. She said,

> I learned a lot about leadership. We talked about not just walking the talk, but also talking the walk. We wanted to make sure that people knew the reasons why we did things the way we did. Through this hard work, we all became the people we are today. No one aspires to be a maid, but when you are doing ordinary work, extraordinary things happen in your life. I also became a Christian while at ServiceMaster. The four objectives not only shaped our work; they shaped my life.

> One of the foundational things I learned came through a discussion Peter Drucker had with the ServiceMaster leadership team. He had asked the leaders what their business was, and they responded with the things they did, whether pest control, cleaning, or lawn care. But he said, "No! You are in the people-training business," and we took that very seriously.

> When Jon Ward took over in 2001, there was a shift. The emphasis on Six Sigma was good and helpful, but there was less emphasis on the development of people.

But when the company was sold in 2007, there was a more radical shift, as she perceived it.

> After CD&R bought the company, there was a meeting where it became clear that senior leadership of ServiceMaster was being asked to "buy in" to their new direction. I was just not comfortable doing that. When I told our new leader that, he said, "Your last day is a week from today." It was December 11, 2007, just before Christmas.

> I had a great career. The work I am now doing at the university is driven by "To Honor God in All We Do." ServiceMaster was not a job, it was life changing. The time at ServiceMaster was great with experiences, great financially, and impacted me to be the person I am today. I am grateful.[21]

Hassan Moharrak, Businesses in Saudi Arabia

We met Hassan Moharrak in chapter 5 when, under Bill Pollard's guidance, he opened up the ServiceMaster market in Saudi Arabia, Lebanon, Sudan, and Egypt. By 1998, his company, Al Majal ServiceMaster, had grown to $250 million in revenue.[22] It would be hard to overstate Moharrak's enthusiasm for what he learned at ServiceMaster:

> When I was doing training at ServiceMaster, I one time told the teacher, "If you have any extra papers that you are thinking of throwing in the garbage, set them aside for us. We will hang them on the wall of the office!" Everybody laughed, but that was how much we valued what we learned.

Al Majal was owned by four people, with Moharrak as the operating head. Then in 1998, one of the partners, Prince Muhammad bin Nayef, became an official part of the government as minister of the interior and the company was sold.

> But ServiceMaster, and Bill Pollard, shaped my life. The ServiceMaster way also shaped the lives of many young men who had been a part of the company. When we left, we went on to other roles in business, either our own businesses, or being a part of another business. We took the ServiceMaster way with us. And we are still drawing on these concepts as we shape business in Saudi Arabia, Egypt, Sudan, and Lebanon as well. We start with "To Honor God in All We Do," and then go on to the other objectives. It is a great way to do business, and this is transforming our people every day. We carry these principles in our heads and our hearts.[23]

Ming Lo Shao, Business in China

In the 1990s, Ming Lo Shao became a ServiceMaster partner in China. Of him, Bill Pollard said, "Ming Lo had a great respect for the objectives and values of ServiceMaster, and sought to implement those values in the business in China."[24] Pollard also introduced Ming Lo to Peter Drucker, which led to a partnership resulting in the establishment of Drucker Academies in China. According to Pollard, the Drucker Academies have had a strong influence on thousands of developing leaders in China.

In addition to working together at ServiceMaster, Bill Pollard and Ming Lo Shao became friends and continued to work together in other ways beyond ServiceMaster. Pollard said,

> I have had the opportunity to participate in teaching at some of the management seminars conducted by the Drucker Academies and have seen firsthand what is being accomplished in China. Ming Lo has taught me, as he has taken an idea and then created something of significance and value. He is a great example of an entrepreneur with a servant's heart and a focus on results.[25]

Shao said, "My involvement with ServiceMaster, as a licensee in China, began in 1998 and continued until 2004 to 2005, though some of this was with Aramark after the sale of Management Services."[26] Currently he is promoting Peter Drucker's teaching in China, drawing on Drucker's teaching of management as a liberal art, which focuses on the responsibility of leadership. "The ethical responsibility of management recognizes the humanness of those in the organization," said Shao, "and the responsibility of the leader to develop people." The academies are located in many cities of China, Hong Kong, Taiwan, and the United States. Although Ming Lo operates this organization as a nonprofit, he is also involved in investment management, where the profits from that work support nonprofit management education. Shao shared:

> Much of what I do was inspired from my time with ServiceMaster and learning from Peter Drucker and Bill Pollard. The most important thing I learned at ServiceMaster was the breadth of application of the principles of management. Whether a for-profit enterprise or a nonprofit, or indeed any organization, its purpose is to create value for customers while, at the same time and with the same process, to create value for every individual in the organization. Our goal is to create the opportunity for every individual to grow in capability and confidence. We should elevate everybody into a better version of themselves. Sadly, many organizations from enterprises to government don't pay enough attention to the development of people.

> Learning about developing people was a vital part of my learning at ServiceMaster, primarily through the four objectives. And we continue to focus on the end objectives of the first two: "To Honor God in All We Do" and "To Help People Develop."

> It is difficult to adapt this to China, but it is very important. That is why we have developed the leadership training work that we do in China. Even though it is hard, it is not impossible. We found that, when running Ser-

viceMaster in China, we needed to adapt the message for the Chinese culture. We changed, for China, the first objective from "To Honor God" to "To Honor Truth," because most in China don't have a religious background. We tried to adapt this in such a way that it would communicate in a language that was understood.

After our business with ServiceMaster was sold to Aramark in China, I personally continued to consult with the company. The current CEO is the person who started with me back in 1998, and he continues with the same teaching and objectives. He continues to invite me to share these values with his organization (four hundred to five hundred people). The truth, responsibility, and human dignity, helping people develop, remains vital for the company and they continue to want to pursue this.

We are continuing to try to combine the Chinese culture, and those traditions, with what we do. We have found that the Confucian religion has kindness, thoughtfulness, equality with others, and "do unto others as you would want them to do to you" as familiar teaching for those in China. So, we are looking to create shared values in a Chinese context as a means of valuing the workers. All of this foundation came from ServiceMaster. And through the academy, we want this to be a part of leadership development for the Chinese entrepreneurs who are increasing here. Through this work, we are growing in confidence that this is the right thing to do and can be done effectively in China.

Manny Mill, Koinonia House National Ministries

Although Manny Mill never worked for ServiceMaster, his life was profoundly changed by his interactions with it. It all started in what might look like an accident.[27]

Born in Cuba, he immigrated to the United States as a child. He was an outgoing, risk-taking young person who was a natural salesperson. He was challenged early to live a life of faith, but he tended to live life on the edge, whether playing baseball or selling insurance. He did not do well in school, but he did do well making money by multiple schemes. After marrying and having a child, he pushed the boundary one time too many and found himself on the run from authorities, trying to escape a fraudulent check-cashing scheme. Hiding out in Venezuela with his son and pregnant wife, he received a call from his father saying that he should come home and come clean. At the same time, he underwent a radical conversion. Committing his life to Christ, he returned home and was sentenced to a prison for white-collar criminals.

The new Manny knew more about acting in the right way, but he continued his entrepreneurial bent. While serving time in Allenwood Federal Prison in Montgomery, Pennsylvania, he applied for permission to attend a Discipleship Seminar in Washington, DC, sponsored by Prison Fellowship

Ministries. Against all odds, he was allowed to leave the prison for two weeks to attend the seminar with five hundred other people. Manny knew no one. At a dinner event with Billy Graham as a guest speaker, seating was assigned and Manny found himself at the same table as Ken Wessner. Manny later wrote, "Not just at the same table, but right next to the man."[28] That encounter changed his life.

Not only did Ken Wessner take an interest in Manny, but he also said he would follow up with him after the seminar. Although Manny admits he wasn't sure that would happen, he soon received a letter from Ken Wessner that ultimately led to Manny applying to Wheaton College. Since Wessner was the chairman of the board of the college, he was able to arrange some scholarship funding for him.

When Manny became a student, the two began meeting on campus. Manny wrote, "Talk about taking a chance—he loved me without really knowing me. He went to bat for me with the scholarship committee. He also put the fear of God in me like no one else could."[29] Over a meal one day in the campus cafeteria, Manny said, "He looked me right in the eyes, pointed his finger close to my nose, and said, 'Manny, you have no room to fail. You have no choice but to make it.' Those words have rung in my ears ever since. He was like a father to me."[30]

Ken Wessner took him to visit ServiceMaster. Though Manny was never employed there, he later sent people to work at the company who were coming out of his programs. Others from ServiceMaster, including Dick Armstrong and Bill Pollard, had a significant role in his life. After Wessner died, Wessner's brother-in-law, Bob Cook, stepped into the mentorship role in his life, helping him found the Koinonia House National Ministries, a group that helps people transition to society after being released from prison.

While he was in prison, Manny's wife left him. He later married Barbara and they had two sons. The first was named Howard Kenneth Mill, with the middle name for Ken Wessner. The second son was named Kenneth James Mill, also for Ken Wessner. Manny said, "The man changed my life."[31]

Greg Leith, CEO, Convene

Greg Leith is CEO of Convene, an organization with a mission to connect, equip, and inspire Christian CEOs and business owners to grow exceptional businesses and become higher-impact leaders to honor God.[32] Leith is involved in supporting, teaching, and coaching hundreds of Christian CEOs with businesses totaling more than $7 billion in revenue and serving over 45,000 employees. The foundations for the work he is doing came from his time at ServiceMaster between 1978 and 1998.

His ServiceMaster tenure included ten years in various assignments at corporate (finance, personnel, and area management), five years as a distributor and franchise owner (1988–1993) in Vancouver, BC, and then six years representing ServiceMaster in British Columbia where he worked to open the healthcare management market in Canada. During that period, he said:

> I was shaped as a young leader. I was privileged to work in a company that was not only traded on the New York Stock Exchange, but at a company that was firmly rooted in Christian principles. We were readily able to say that we sought "to honor God in all we do, to help people develop, to pursue excellence, and to grow profitably." That shaped my understanding that people have value and dignity and you needed to treat them that way. All of this is integral to the work I do now, working with business leaders from all parts of the country.

> What we called the four objectives were actually etched in stone outside of the corporate offices, but were also figuratively etched on the hearts and minds of all of us as leaders.

Fred Smith, President, The Gathering

Fred Smith served as president of the Gathering, an association of individuals, families and private foundations who give to Christian causes around the world. The Gathering holds regular conferences, including two a year where a group of people go into a city to understand its leaders, its culture, and the needs of that particular city.

As a leader of leaders, Fred Smith got some of his foundation from the work he did at ServiceMaster between 1974 and 1976 while a student at Harvard Divinity School. He needed to work through school and was introduced to Allan Emery, who at that time ran the Northwest Region of ServiceMaster's Hospital Services business. Smith remembers Emery as a highly disciplined person. One time, he heard Emery say, "I have never wasted a minute in my life."[33]

Emery was always looking for talent, and when Fred met him at church in Boston, Allan and his wife invited Fred and his wife to dinner to talk about working at ServiceMaster. Smith was given the opportunity to take a job scrubbing out the operating room after surgeries, because he had said he wanted to get over his fear of blood. He also spent time buffing the floors of the hospital in Summerville:

> The great thing about being at ServiceMaster is they helped me take pride in my work. The ServiceMaster leadership was very intentional about how work was done and about developing leadership, even for people mopping the floor. My experience there was extraordinary, a wonderful experience.

That short experience a long time ago still shows in the work I do with the Gathering. Seeing it played out in leading leaders today, I am grateful for what could have been just a job, instead of an opportunity to grow and develop.[34]

Conclusions

It would be too easy to look at The ServiceMaster Company and conclude that a great set of foundational ideas, developed by early leaders, could not go on forever. In fact, some have said that perhaps companies, like people, have life cycles. They grow and they die. While ServiceMaster certainly has not died, the goal of developing people is no longer a part of its corporate goals.

But even these principles continue to develop and blossom, as demonstrated by this small sample of stories that continue on inside and outside the company. There is something important about honoring people in their work, about respecting the dignity of the worker, and about seeking to support the growth and development of each employee. Employees are not tools of production but are unique and important individuals worthy of respect. In Christian language, this is because they are made in the image of God. Leaders with this insight, courage, and commitment can indeed live this out in business—even in the twenty-first century.

10

Reflections

When scientists try to understand a complex object, they carefully change one variable at a time, learning the impact of that particular variable. While the ServiceMaster case does not quite constitute a scientific experiment, it is close. The variable that changed was the company's commitment to the four objectives both in word and in action. Importantly, what changed was the company's commitment to the first two objectives, which it had originally called "end goals." Yes, there were changes in external environments as well, but this had been the case for seventy years.

The order of succession by the founding leaders proved vital in building the kind of company ServiceMaster became. The graph of revenue over the years between 1957 when Ken Hansen took over for Marion Wade through Bill Pollard's final year in 2000 shows an astounding picture (see Figure 10.1 below). It would be easy to conclude that not much happened through the years of the leadership of Wade and Hansen between 1929 and 1973.

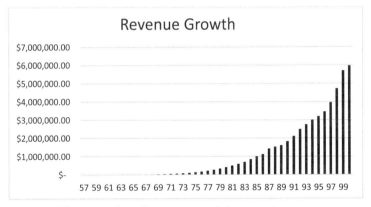

Figure 10.1. Overall revenue growth from 1957 to 2000.

That, however, would be the wrong conclusion. The foundation of ethics and purpose as laid down by Marion Wade was of great fundamental importance and extended throughout all of the years. The foundation from

Ken Hansen in establishing good business practices was also vital. It was also critical that the foundations where laid in this order.

Some would say that starting with ethics rather than business skills might seem strange, but I believe it to be foundational. In 2005, I was speaking to a large audience of government officials, business leaders, and entrepreneurs in Beijing. I had made the case for the importance of ethics in business, when a young entrepreneur responded, "I am starting a small business. It is tough to get started with so many obstacles. Wouldn't it be okay for me to put off looking at ethics until I have established my business? Do I need to consider ethics now?"

I asked him to think about these questions:

- What does success mean? If you mean profit, at what level? Is success only financial? You need to establish this now because otherwise it will change as you grow.
- Who will retrain all your leaders, including yourself, to start acting ethically if you have arrived a point of success without acting ethically?
- As a customer, do you like to do business with someone who you know is trying to take advantage of you and cheat you at every turn?

He smiled and said, "You win," and sat down.[1]

After the foundation of ethics, other layers were added to the company in just the right order. Ken Hansen brought in business disciplines, while holding to and developing the ethical foundation. Ken Wessner developed the foundation further, adding processes and systems. Only then were Bill Pollard and Carlos Cantu able to add acquisitions to continue the growth.

Starting with Bill Pollard, and later with Carlos Cantu, the company wanted to extend this opportunity to groups of workers who came to ServiceMaster through acquisitions, rather than simply to individual workers who hired on in the existing company. This proposition was more difficult, because it required retraining and reorienting multiple levels of management and workers at the same time. For this reason, it could be expected to take longer. It is interesting to observe that the earlier acquisitions (Terminix and Merry Maid) became foundational within ServiceMaster, while some later acquisitions were ultimately spun off.

When Bill Pollard and Carlos Cantu purchased service companies for ServiceMaster, they weren't just adding companies or revenues. They believed in and were committed to the workers, to help them understand the purpose and meaning of their work, to train them, to watch the way they rose to the occasion, and then to give them the chance to grow. Great value to the person and great value to the company. Would TruGreen have

thrived if the focus on training and empowering the workers had continued? If continued emphasis for understanding a sense of purpose and
meaning in work had continued to unfold?

As we have seen in this book, the first two objectives, which Service-
Master treated as end goals, did not simply hang on a wall. They were
important to the leaders and important to the workers, and they became
foundational for the success of the company. Here, once again, are the two
objectives that were so important:

- "To Honor God in All We Do." This provided a strong sense of ethics and integrity, a clear understanding of the dignity and worth
  of each individual, and a clear understanding of the dignity of the
  work itself.
- "To Help People Develop." This provided a commitment to the
  training and development of each worker and a focus on helping
  workers find the meaning and purpose in their work, and the opportunity to develop a career beyond a job.

Of all of these commitments, only "integrity" from the first objective remains in the published statements by the company today.

As we have seen, size became a challenge for ServiceMaster, which
they recognized and mentioned in the 2000 annual report. But it wasn't
just an issue of managing a company that was so large and diverse. It was
also a matter of finding people capable of carrying out this leadership on
this large scale—who would also be willing to truly understand the service
business.

In the late 1990s, ServiceMaster hired two strong, experienced leaders from outside the company, Phil Rooney and Steve Preston. Then in
2001, they brought in Jon Ward as CEO. I have not found evidence that
any of these leaders spent their time doing the physical labor involved in
the services provided by the company, thereby helping them understand
what life was like for the people doing the work. All of the earlier leaders had done this. Perhaps hiring senior leaders for a $6 billion company
meant it was not possible to have them engage in service as Bill Pollard
when he was hired into a $200 million company—or Carlos Cantu when
he began working at Terminix. Of course, Marion Wade, Ken Hansen, and
Ken Wessner all grew in responsibility in the company while doing the
actual work of service.

Another key lesson from this story, which is applicable to any company, is the importance of commitment to the mission at all levels of the
organization, including the board of directors. Rob Gillette's comment
about having a board that focused on financial results without being deeply
engaged with the mission of the company is important and telling. He

needed a board that understood and cared about the service business and the commitment to develop the workers. Without this, oversight tilts toward viewing the company only as a large money machine to generate cash.

Sadly, this same failing can be seen in many other companies. While a singular focus on profit in the short term may produce short term results, this focus generally fails for the long term. A more detailed version of this case was developed with David Gautschi in a book we edited, *The Purpose of Business: Contemporary Perspectives from Many Walks of Life.*[2]

ServiceMaster and Its Christian Roots

A foundational part of this story, which may be difficult for some, is the strength of the Christian commitment of its early leaders. Some decry the mixing of religion and business, while some Christians say this mixing should be more overt.

What I found in this story is the imperfect walking of a narrow line between what motivated a leader and what was demanded of others. The leaders focused on integrity, the value of every person, the need to help people grow, and the dignity of work—all rooted in their own foundation of Christian faith. They were relentless about training and teaching, wanting each person to know how to do their job well and why it mattered. Not always successfully, the leaders drew on their own Christian faith to make this the anchor of the right way to do business, while not imposing that foundational belief on others. Pollard often said, "I want to have every person confronted with the question of God. They must decide how to answer that question."

I know there will be those who read this story and say it is not for them because they don't have a Christian faith. Yet there is broad agreement that the principles derived from this faith are foundational in what made the company work. In the course of my own study of successful companies, I have found many public and private companies with similar foundations without any faith connections, though none with the longevity of growth and commitment to such principles as ServiceMaster.

Critics of the company also provide a lens through which to understand it. Many writers poked at the Christian roots as a source of challenge in a pluralistic age. The company was too religious, they thought. For example,

> During this time, ServiceMaster's Christian motif became ever more pronounced: Outside corporate headquarters stood an 11-foot statue of Jesus washing a disciple's feet, the company's stated objectives began with the maxim "To Honor God in All We Do," and employees regularly held Bible study groups. Some analysts blamed the company's fixation on religion as responsible for the weakening of its business in the 1990s.[3]

This theme was echoed by Darren Grem, who was critical of any form of mixing religion and business. He wrote strongly on this in his own book, *The Blessings of Business*,[4] and as an editor and contributor to another book, *The Business Turn in American Religious History*.[5] I don't believe any of these writers looked deeply enough into the company to see what really made it work.

Others, however, said the company was not religious enough, and they criticized it for straying from its evangelical roots when it sought to be more inclusive. But we see from this history that the goal was always to be inclusive. Starting with Marion Wade, the theme of bringing Christian faith to business was about a foundation of ethics and honoring and valuing people, motivated by the strong Christian foundation of the leader.

From the earliest days, clear statements came from each leader that the Christian faith provided a deep anchor to their commitment to do the right thing even in turbulent times. Anyone can treat employees well and maintain ethics during easy times, but what about when the pressure is on? This is what compelled and propelled ServiceMaster's early leaders.

Perhaps it is the Christian foundation for leaders through 2000 that gave them the anchors to stick with their commitments even when times were turbulent. But it wasn't just that they were Christians. They were also Christians who saw a deep connection between their faith and their work, through which they recognized their work as a "high calling." Some employees, and even some leaders, who arrived in the late 1990s and beyond did not seem to understand this important connection.

I am certain that, while this line was sometimes walked imperfectly, it ultimately became the foundation for the company. Lewis Solomon's observation, mentioned earlier, is particularly relevant here and worth repeating. He wrote about the company, often in a critical way, when discussing its Christian foundations. But he also acknowledged that, after the evangelical leadership of the company disappeared. "Coincidentally with this transition, the company's legal difficulties mounted and its financial results stagnated."[6]

No model for a company, however lofty, is helpful if it requires perfect execution by perfect workers. This will never happen in practice. Only when leadership believes deeply enough in what they are doing, that it is not a program but a commitment, can it resiliently respond to the inevitable failings along the way, from outside forces and from bad choices.

The Long-Term Impact

Early in 2019, after more than a year of working on this story of ServiceMaster, I realized I had never visited a ServiceMaster facility. I had been reading books, papers, and annual reports, and I had more than sixty telephone or personal interviews. I knew ServiceMaster had changed over the years, so I wasn't sure what I would find in a modern-day version of the company.

On January 17, 2019, I decided to visit a ServiceMaster franchise in the Seattle area to meet current leaders, hear their stories, and see the facility. What I heard, and what I saw, was not what I was expecting. It was like being transported back in time. I was surprised to find the four objectives proudly displayed, just as Ken Wessner and Ken Hansen had developed them. This franchise was pursuing its business in the same way as one of the early franchises. And this franchise was doing great business.[7]

The real impact of the ServiceMaster story is how well it worked for so long in the face of changing times and imperfect workers, and how much it continues through the lives of workers both inside and outside the company.

We end with a telling observation made by twenty-five-year executive Patricia Asp:

> The ServiceMaster objectives were not only a way of working, but a way of living. When I left, I took the objectives with me and they will remain in my leadership DNA.[8]

Acknowledgments

In the spring of 2017, I had a phone call with Bill Pollard relating to a project he was supporting at Seattle Pacific University. At the end of the conversation, he told me he had another matter to discuss with me: "I would like you to write a book on the history of The ServiceMaster Company. There have been a few books written on the company, but none has rightly captured the contributions of Ken Hansen and Ken Wessner." My immediate response was to decline, as I had a full plate of things to do and this seemed like a daunting task. But Bill is persistent. He sent me some material to read, and he asked if we could talk about this again in two weeks. Over that period, my interest in the project grew.

For the past twenty years, I have been studying what makes a successful company in this rapidly changing world of technology. I have interviewed more than one hundred leaders from around the world, exploring what it means to value employees, engage them purposefully, and to create a thriving culture. These interviews are archived on my website www.ethix .org. In fact, Bill Pollard was one of the people I interviewed because I was intrigued by ServiceMaster. In this book, I have quoted from eight other interviews.

In parallel, over a long period of time reaching back into my days as a Boeing Company executive, I have been developing my understanding of what my Christian faith has to do with business. How does Christian faith affect the way we do our work, even what work we do? How do we live this out in a pluralistic world, not by imposing faith on others but drawing from our faith to help create a great organization? For the past twelve years, I have been involved with the Theology of Work Project, where we have written a commentary (published by Hendrickson) that draws out what the Bible has to say about daily work (www.theologyofwork.org). Several years ago, I wrote *The Accidental Executive* (also published by Hendrickson) on the life of Joseph from the book of Genesis in the Bible, looking at this story through a career lens. The study of ServiceMaster seemed to align with the things I cared about.

When I talked with Bill two weeks later, I told him "You have stolen real estate in my brain." I agreed to do this project with some conditions. First, I would not accept payment for the project. If this was going to be my perspective on the story, then it could not be seen as distorted by an economic objective. Second, I would value his input in identifying and connecting with resources, even in checking facts, but the final decisions on content and selection of material would need to be mine. Third, I had some other obligations, and the work would need to be done at a pace I could sustain.

With that agreement, we went forward. We did test these boundaries. More than a year later, I remember a delightful dinner with Bill and his wife Judy, when my wife Nancy and I were in the Chicago area. At one point, Bill asked me what he could do to help the project along. I told him my one request was "patience," and everybody laughed. I am grateful for his prodding and have deeply enjoyed this project.

One motivating factor for Bill's call about the book was the death of Bob Erickson. Bob had played a vital role in the company, as chief financial officer, as the president of international, and as a board member. His death was a reminder that those with direct knowledge of what the company had done would not be around forever. It was time to get this recorded.

Bill provided me with many valuable ideas and connections that made this project possible. First, he connected me with his network. It started with a spreadsheet containing forty key ServiceMaster people with contact information. This opened the doors to many, many conversations. Second, he provided me with papers and even a transcript of a private book that Ken Hansen had written. Although Hansen's family did not want the personal parts of the book made public, they agreed to have Bill glean from Ken's life and views regarding his time at ServiceMaster. Third, he gave me lots of time for questions, discussions, and his insight. He even hosted me in his home once when I was passing near Lake Geneva, Wisconsin. On a number of occasions, he would push back on something until I reminded him of our agreement: This had to be my view of the company, not his. The acceptance of this was not easy for him. In the end, I very much appreciated his role in the project and could not have done it without him. I am grateful for the confidence he placed in me to do this work and for his friendship.

Bill also introduced me to Dave Baseler, who for many years had worked with Bill at ServiceMaster in a marketing capacity. Dave had produced most of the annual reports while he was there, and he also had a strong role in Pollard's books. He has been an invaluable resource in making connections and gaining understanding. Dave had his own network, resources, and stories that have all had an influence. He provided me with a stack of annual reports (1983–2005), files of talks and articles, introductions to key people at just the right time, and a collection of pictures. Dave also pointed me to various books such as Marion Wade's biography (*The Lord Is My Counsel*) and a small booklet Ken Hansen had written (*Reality*).

I had already read Pollard's books. Each offered great insight and stories. Dave Baseler even found four pages of handwritten notes from reporter Bruce Hansen (*Memphis Business Journal*) that filled in some of the early background for Carlos Cantu. These notes were written in late 1993 as Cantu was transitioning into the leadership position. Both the book list and the interview list grew as I found other books and people that brought independent insight on the company. My one regret was the many, many insightful comments and stories that I ultimately was not able to include in the book.

This book would not have been possible without Dave's support, insight, suggestions, or time. He also carefully read through the document at several points through the project, suggesting stories or people while finding many small and large errors. And he always said, "But it is your book." I am very grateful for all that he has done and for my growing friendship with him.

History professor Shelton Woods of Boise State University graciously met with me early in the project and provided some helpful ways of thinking about this history project. I knew there was a great deal of information out there, and I wanted to not simply pick and choose to create the story I wanted. Shelton was very helpful and patient. Reading history books by David McCullough, Jon Meacham, Walter Isaacson, and Doris Kearns Goodwin provided some helpful models. Friend Mark Neuenschwander recommended John McPhee's book *Draft No. 4: On the Writing Process*, which offered great insight on organizing the large amount of information going into the book—because the information for the project kept growing!

Filling in information from earlier annual reports proved more difficult as they were hard to find. Some emerged from a request to the various people on the contact list. In particular, Dave Moore, ServiceMaster franchise owner in Wheaton, found the 1971 twenty-fifth anniversary issue and scanned it for me. Some were found in the National Archives in Washington, DC, after I filed a freedom of information request. Tom McAnear, at the National Archives in College Park in Maryland, and Felicia Taylor, at the Securities and Exchange Commission in Washington, DC, provided helpful assistance in accessing archives of early ServiceMaster material. Thanks go also to Darrel Cosden, who was living in the area and who drove over to go through the boxes, so I didn't have to make a trip to Washington. He created some important and insightful scans for me.

Unfortunately, the early annual reports (1963–1967) were missing from the archives. But another contact found these in his attic and scanned them for me, along with some very early articles from *Fortune* and *The Wall Street Journal*. He chose not to be identified, but I thank him. This filled in some of the early history and the early numbers.

Since Ken Hansen, Ken Wessner, and Bill Pollard all graduated from Wheaton College, I found some early papers, letters, and articles in the archives of the Billy Graham Center at Wheaton. Thanks to Sarah Stanley and David Osielski at the Graham Center for their work in assembling boxes for me to go through when I was on campus.

Vince Nelson, Ken Hansen's stepson, provided some wonderful insight on Ken in his thoughtful recollections. David Wessner and Barbara Wessner Anderson were also very helpful in adding to the background on their father. Both Vince and David have served on the board. Karen Troutman, director of public relations at the Wilson School District in West Lawn, Pennsylvania, was also helpful in finding some early material on Ken Wessner from his high school yearbooks. Albert Cantu, Carlos Cantu's son who also worked at ServiceMaster, was also helpful as were Walter Hansen (Ken's son) and Chip Pollard (Bill's son).

Dave Baseler set up two meetings, one in Memphis and one in Wheaton, with former ServiceMaster employees who gathered over lunch for group discussions about their experiences with the company. I was able to watch them interact with each other, hear their pride of having been a part of the company, hear their passion about the company, and observe their friendships that have continued. Many arrived early and stayed around to share with each other.

Beyond this information, I learned a great deal about the company simply from the willingness of so many former employees and leaders to talk about their experiences there. Almost all of the conversations led with insights that people offered about the four objectives of the company. If I had thought that the objectives were simply statements hanging on a wall, this removed all doubt. It also became clear that the company was not perfect and its leaders made mistakes. Instead of detracting from the story, however, this added reality. There are no perfect companies and no perfect people. How leaders respond to mistakes is a vital part of what makes a good company. I admit my admiration for these leaders grew as I saw who they really were.

Starting with the original list given to me by Bill Pollard, I am grateful to the following thirty-nine people who spent time with me on the phone to explain their perspective of ServiceMaster. Some are quoted in the book, but all provided helpful background in framing the discussion. From corporate, Dave Aldridge, Patricia Asp, Susan Baker, Bill Bond, Bruce Duncan, Jim Goetz, Bill Hargreaves, Ken Hooten, Rob Keith, Jane McGuffey, Hassan Moharrak, Ernie Mrozek, Bisher Mufti, and Vern Squires. From the Management Service Group, James Huse and Chuck Stair. From the Consumer Services Group, Dick Armstrong, Paul Bert, Albert Cantu, David Crawford, Scott Cromie, Joy Flora, Brian Oxley, Dave Slott, Dallen

Peterson, and Tom Scherer. Board members interviewed included Lord Brian Griffiths, Herbert Hess, Gunther (Bud) Knoedler, Vincent Nelson, and David Wessner. Franchise owners include Mike Isakson, Tom Little, Mike Mack, Dave Moore, Doug Pound, and Bob Smith. Three others include Sandy Jett (information technology), Dan Kellow (ServiceMaster Clean), and Rob Gillette (recent ServiceMaster CEO). In addition, I had discussions with current or former ServiceMaster people Greg Leith, John Bigelow (Furniture Medic franchise owner), Phil Foxwell (Japan), Scott Heise, Steve Preston, Fred Smith, Mary Bennet, Bob Groff, Matt Edwards, Richard Barr, Ming Lo Shao (with translator Phillip Pan), and Brian Miller. Jon Ward (CEO 2001–6) was the only one who specifically declined to talk with me, sending me a simple e-mail stating, "I decline." Several requests to more recent leaders went unanswered.

I also talked with observers of ServiceMaster including Dick Hattwick (professor at Western Illinois University who wrote on the company), Steve Hoke (son of a former roommate of Ken Hansen), David Woodward (Seattle Pacific University), Laura Nash (author), and Manny Mill (friend of Ken Wessner).

In addition to careful reading by Dave Baseler, I am grateful to several colleagues who read parts of the book and made suggestions on specific chapters. These include Helen Chung, Ryan LaBrie, and Laura Singleton.

My thanks also go to Seattle Pacific University (from both me and my wife). Their library houses the largest collection of resources anywhere on the broad issues of work and faith. They also have archived Bill Pollard's speeches throughout the years. They will take the collection of books, annual reports, papers, and videos I have collected during the project (which are now in piles all over my den!) and make them available to others who want to do further research. In particular, Michael Paulus (university librarian), Cindy Strong (education librarian), and Janet Hauck (business and social sciences librarian) have been working with me on the plan to archive these materials. Janet has also helped me track down a number of sources. I am grateful to them all.

Thanks also to Edward Isaac at InteleANTS Transcription Service, who turned hours of interview recordings into text, which allowed ready access to the many conversations I had. To Matthew Kaemingk, who found the reference to the Van Dyke poem in chapter 1. To Cinda Peters at Cinda Peters Design, LLC, who created three of the figures and helped me with others. Dan Hallack introduced me to his ServiceMaster provider, opening the door to my visit to the Seattle franchise.

This book would not have been possible without the good work of Hendrickson Publishers and their general manager Paul Hendrickson. I have worked with many editors in my writing days, and none compare with editorial director Patricia Anders and her insight and thoughtful work. Ultimately, the final responsibility is mine, but I acknowledge with gratitude her good work.

Finally, a very special thanks to my wife Nancy. She has not only put up with the clutter and distraction of the project, but she has also put up with me. And she has applied her journalistic skills to making my writing more clear. We met working together on the student newspaper at Northern Illinois University in 1960, so she has edited my writings for many years. She committed then "to a lifetime of managing the editor." More importantly, as my wife for more than fifty-seven years, she is the love of my life, my best friend, and a wonderful companion.

Al Erisman
Bellevue, Washington
September 2019

Appendix A

The Twenty-One Principles of Leadership at ServiceMaster

In the mid-1980s, ServiceMaster leaders went through historical and recent practices and created these Principles of Leadership that became a part of training and development.

1. We are opportunity seekers, not entitlement takers. We create and earn and cannot afford to sit and inherit.
2. We are value driven and performance oriented.
3. We eat our own cooking. We bet the egg money on our own performance.
4. We train and run for both the sprint and marathon. We rest, have fun, never quit, and always seek to learn.
5. We plan for succession and develop our future leaders.
6. The truth of what we say is told by what we do. "If you don't live it, you don't believe it."
7. If we cannot serve and sell with a passion for excellence, we cannot lead.
8. We believe in what we sell and deliver.
9. As we provide extraordinary service, we bring value-added to the customer that cannot be duplicated.
10. There are no friendly competitors.
11. We believe in a lean and disciplined organization. We would rather buy a grand piano than employ or assign one unnecessary person.
12. We pay based on performance and promote based on potential, not belief, tenure, gender, race, or friendships.
13. Those who produce the profits should share in the profits. Those who produce more should share more.
14. We make and beat budgets.
15. We seek to know and increase our market share so that we can grow and increase the profitability and value of our business. If we ignore our market share, we run the risk of losing our market and our business.

16. When we are wrong or fail, we admit it. Truth cannot be compromised. We report on what has occurred or is anticipated, not on what will make us look good.

17. We promote others, not ourselves. We shoot against par.

18. We must have a spirit of independence without the malady of autonomy.

19. The customer comes first and should be our friend.

20. We are all prisoners of our hope. It is our hope that sustains us, and it is our vision for what could be that inspires us and those we lead. "Don't doubt in the dark what you have seen in the light."

21. We have all been created in God's image, and the results of our leadership will be measured beyond the workplace. The story will be told in the changed lives of people.

Appendix B

Key Dates for ServiceMaster

1929 Marion Wade founds moth-proofing business in Chicago

1945 Marion Wade opens office on Austin Avenue in Chicago

1946 Ken Hansen hired

1947 Company incorporates as Wade, Wenger and Associates

1952 First residential/commercial franchise is sold

1954 Ken Wessner hired

1957 Ken Hansen named CEO
Marion Wade named chairman
Revenue reaches $1 million

1958 ServiceMaster banner adopted as a trademark

1961 Company name changed to Wade, Wenger ServiceMaster Co.
First foreign agreement is signed as operations begin in Great Britain

1962 Corporation goes public and stock sold over the counter
ServiceMaster begins housekeeping service at Lutheran General Hospital,
    Park Ridge, IL

1963 Corporate offices move to ten-acre site in Downers Grove, IL

1966 Revenue reaches $10 million

1970 ServiceMaster begins twenty-nine years of consecutive growth in revenue
    and profit

1973 Marion Wade dies
Ken Wessner promoted to CEO
Ken Hansen named chairman of the board of directors
Four company objectives first established: To honor God in all you do, to
    help people develop, to pursue excellence, and to grow profitably

1974 Revenue reaches $100 million

1977 C. William Pollard hired as executive vice president

1981 First hospital served in Japan

1983 Pollard promoted to CEO
Ken Wessner becomes chairman
Ken Hansen becomes chairman emeritus

1984 *Fortune* magazine rates ServiceMaster #1 among the "Service 500"

1985 Lawn care added as a franchise with purchase of Village Green
Revenue reaches $1 billion

1986 Terminix acquired
Carlos Cantu joins ServiceMaster as president of Terminix
Company enters master limited partnership arrangement and becomes
    The ServiceMaster Company Limited Partnership

1988   Merry Maids acquired

1989   Consumer Services established in Memphis, combining Terminix and
        ServiceMaster residential/commercial activities
        American Home Shields acquired

1990   Bill Pollard named chairman

1991   TruGreen acquired
        Revenue reaches $2 billion

1992   TruGreen purchases ChemLawn

1993   Carlos Cantu named CEO

1994   Ken Wessner and Ken Hansen die
        Company enters home healthcare field with several acquisitions

1995   Revenue reaches $3 billion

1997   Company makes significant investments in the landscaping business
        Company returns from limited partnership status to corporation status
        Revenue reaches $4 billion

1998   Rescue Industries acquired to enter plumbing business

1999   Carlos Cantu steps down as CEO and Bill Pollard is named CEO and
        continues as chairman
        LandCare acquired
        Company exits home healthcare business
        First year since 1970 that profits do not increase
        Revenue reaches $5 billion

2001   Jon Ward, first CEO brought in from outside the company, hired
        Bill Pollard continues as chairman
        Management Services Division sold to Aramark
        Company focuses on consumer businesses
        TruGreenLandCare sold

2003   Bill Pollard resigns as chairman

2006   Jon Ward resigns
        Patrick Spainhour named interim CEO

2007   Patrick Spainhour named CEO
        ServiceMaster sold to private equity firm CD&R

2011   Patrick Spainhour retires
        Hank Mullany is named CEO

2013   TruGreen/ChemLawn sold
        Hank Mullany resigns
        John Krenicki named interim CEO and chairman
        Rob Gillette named CEO and chairman

2014   Company goes public again

2017   Rob Gillette terminated
        Nikhil Varty named CEO
        Company adopts a new set of values:

Dependable	Accountable
Expert	Responsible
Respectful	Accessible

2018   Frontdoor, parent company of American Home Shield, becomes separate
        company

NOTES

Chapter 1

1. James Heskett, "ServiceMaster: We Serve," HBS Case Study N9-900-030, Harvard Business School (June 6, 2000).

2. See Lewis D. Solomon, *Evangelical Christian Executives: A New Model for Business Corporations*; and Amanda Porterfield, Darren E. Grem, and John Corrigan, *The Business Turn in American Religious History* (New York: Oxford University Press, 2017).

3. C. William Pollard, *The Soul of the Firm* (New York: HarperBusiness, 1996), 56.

4. Ibid.

5. Heskett, "ServiceMaster."

6. Pollard, *Soul of the Firm*, 13.

7. James L. Heskett, W. Earl Sassar, and Christopher W. L. Hart, *Service Breakthrough: Changing the Rules of the Games* (New York: The Free Press, 1990), 201.

8. John Medina, noted brain scientist and best-selling author, has been tracking the literature on experiments related to people being given the "types of control normally seen in a promotion, then measuring their responses." He concluded, "Granting someone a new level of authority and control—such as what happens when someone experiences a promotion—causes a person to become isolated." John Medina in conversation with the author, March 2019. Perhaps, without knowing about the research, ServiceMaster had found the key to avoiding executive isolation by having them spend time doing the work of a front-line worker.

9. Mike Isakson in conversation with the author, fall 2017. Throughout the book, conversations will be referenced with various people associated with ServiceMaster. These took place, primarily by telephone, in the time period between summer 2017 and spring 2019. Some of these discussions represent more than one conversation.

10. Kenneth Hansen, *Reality: That Which Gives Purpose, Zest, and Motive Power to Life*, foreword by Ken Wessner (Downers Grove, IL: ServiceMaster, 1979). Hattwick identifies this as a 1979 publication. But the foreword identifies Ken Wessner as chairman of the board and Ken Hansen as vice chairman, a move that occurred in 1983. The booklet itself is undated.

11. Pollard, *Soul of the Firm*, 108.

12. David McCullough, *The Spirit of America: Who We Are and What We Stand For* (New York: Simon & Schuster, 2017), 28.

13. Dave Baseler in conversation with the author.

14. Greg Leith in conversation with the author.

15. The common idea of managing a business by focusing only on increasing shareholder value is analyzed more completely by the author in a chapter titled "Profit Maximization Must Fail," in *The Purpose of Business*, ed. Albert M. Erisman and David Gautschi (New York: Palgrave Macmillan, 2015), 53–84. More recently, the Business Roundtable issued a statement stating that they are endorsing stakeholder capitalism. See Rick Wartzman, "America's Top CEOS Say They Are No Longer Putting Shareholders before Everyone Else," *Fast Company*, August 19, 2019, https://www.fastcompany.com/90391743/top-ceo-group -business-roundtable-drops-shareholder-primacy.

16. Pollard, *Soul of the Firm*, 45.

17. Barry Schwartz, *Why We Work* (New York: Simon and Schuster, 2015).

18. Ibid., 20.

19. "Don Flow: Ethics Flow at Flow Automotive," *Ethix* (April 1, 2004), https://ethix.org/2004/04/01/ethics-at-flow-automotive.

20. "Don Flow: Maintaining Ethics in a Downturn: Auto Sales, Real Estate, Home Building," *Ethix* (June 1, 2009), https://ethix.org/2009/06/01 /maintaining-ethics-in-a-downturn-auto-sales.

21. "Cheryl Broetje: An Orchard with Fruit That Lasts," *Ethix* (December 1, 2005), https://ethix.org/2005/12/01/an-orchard-with-fruit-that-lasts.

22. "Dennis Bakke: Creating Real Fun at Work," *Ethix* (June 1, 2004), https://ethix.org/2004/06/01/creating-real-fun-at-work.

23. Max DePree, *Leadership Is an Art* (New York: Doubleday Dell, 1989).

24. "James D. Sinegal: A Long-Term Business Perspective in a Short -Term World," *Ethix* (April 1, 2003), https://ethix.org/2003/04/01/a-long -term-business-perspective-in-a-short-term-world.

25. Solomon, *Evangelical Christian Executives,* 78.

26. Jeff Haanen, "God of the Second Shift," *Christianity Today* (September 20, 2018).

27. Marion Wade, *The Lord Is My Counsel: A Businessman's Experiences with the Bible* (New York: Prentice Hall, 1966), 88.

28. Henry Van Dyke, "The Toiling of Felix," *Now First Collected and Revised with Many Hitherto Unpublished* (New York: Charles Scribner's Sons, 1911), 67. Matthew Kaemingk identified the source of this poem.

29. Dave Baseler in conversation with the author.

Chapter 2

1. Wade, *The Lord Is My Counsel*, 77.

2. Ibid.

3. Ibid.

4. Ibid.

5. Richard Hattwick, "Marion Wade, Ken Hansen, Ken Wessner," October 24, 2014, American National Business Hall of Fame, http://anbhf.org /laureates/servicemaster/.

6. Wade, *The Lord Is My Counsel*, 83.

7. Ibid., 13.

8. Ibid.

9. Ibid., 16.

10. Ibid., 22.

11. Ibid., 56.

12. Ibid., 60.

13. Ibid., 62.

14. Ibid., 77.

15. Ibid., 75.

16. "This book was Marion Wade's record of service calls for 1947. . . . A similar book was kept for each year since 1929 when he began selling his services." *ServiceMaster Annual Report* (1971), 3.

17. Wade, *The Lord Is My Counsel*, 73.

18. Ibid., 76.

19. From a skit written by Tom Nast and Carl Wilke, performed in the 1980s for ServiceMaster leadership. Text provided by Scott Heise.

20. This story was told by Ken Hansen in a ServiceMaster video created in the early 1990s, which was a part of the leadership development process throughout the twentieth century.

21. Wade, *The Lord Is My Counsel*, 94.

22. Ibid.

23. *ServiceMaster Annual Report* (1971), 19.

24. Ibid., 80.

25. Ibid.

26. Ibid., 82.

27. Nast and Wilke skit.

28. Ken and Jean Hansen Lectureship Series, The Marion E. Wade Center, Wheaton College, Wheaton, IL, https://www.wheaton.edu/academics/academic-centers/wadecenter/events/ken-and-jean-hansen-lectureship/.

29. Wade, *The Lord Is My Counsel*, 95.

30. Ibid., 96.

31. Summary of the first twenty-five years of the company, *ServiceMaster Annual Report* (1971), 3.

32. Wade, *The Lord Is My Counsel*, 100.

33. Bill Pollard interview with Kuno Laren, "Lightposts of Our Heritage," a video series of ServiceMaster interviews in 1995 by Bill Pollard, archived at Seattle Pacific University in Seattle, Washington.

34. Ibid.

35. Ken Hansen in conversation with Dave Baseler.

36. Wade, *The Lord Is My Counsel*, 97.

37. Ibid., 98.

38. Summary, *ServiceMaster Annual Report* (1971).

39. One report suggested a franchise in 1942 (http://www.fundinguniverse.com/company-histories/the-servicemaster-company-history/), but there is no other evidence of this and it is likely a transcription error.

40. Bob Groff, who later owned the Seattle distributorship, in conversation with the author.

41. Pollard, "Lightposts of Our Heritage" video.

42. Ibid.

43. Ken Wessner, "Turning Crisis into Personal Growth," *CBMC Management Memo*, 6–9.

44. Wade, *The Lord Is My Counsel*, 7.

45. Ibid., 119.

46. *Fortune,* "Scrubbing up for the Lord" (January 1956).

47. Wade, *The Lord Is My Counsel*, 119.
48. Richard E. Hattwick, "Vision and Control: Interview with Kenneth N. Hansen," September 16, 1990. Hattwick personal archives.
49. As an executive at The Boeing Company, the author observed that women in leadership were rare at the executive level before the 1990s.
50. Wade, *The Lord Is My Counsel*, 108.
51. Ibid., 134, 138.
52. Ibid., 133.
53. Ibid., 154.
54. Ibid., 144.
55. Ibid., 147–48.
56. Ibid., 146.
57. "Barry Rowan: Bringing Meaning to Work," *Ethix* (July 27, 2011), https://ethix.org/2011/07/27/telecommunications-barry-rowan.
58. Wade, *The Lord Is My Counsel*, 145–46.
59. The author has observed family engagement in hiring and termination practices in many places in Southeast Asia, for example.
60. The author has a training document from The Boeing Company on dealing with women in the workplace, dated from the early 1960s. Comments there make Marion Wade look like a progressive.
61. This is reflected in some of the franchise stories in chapter 9, as well as in the ServiceMaster stories, in Elyse Fitzpatrick, *Believers in Business: Stories from the ServiceMaster Family* (Downers Grove, IL: ServiceMaster Clean, 2001).
62. Ibid., 144.
63. Ibid., 134.
64. Ibid., 123.
65. Ibid., 129.
66. *Book of Remembrances* (September 2001), Marion E. Wade Center, Wheaton College, Wheaton, IL.
67. Wade, *The Lord Is My Counsel*, 57.
68. Ibid., 57.
69. Ibid., 102–3.
70. Ibid., 109.
71. Dick Armstrong in conversation with the author.
72. Wade, *The Lord Is My Counsel*, 142.
73. Ibid., 105–6.
74. Hattwick, "Vision and Control."
75. C. William Pollard, *Serving Two Masters? Reflections on God and Profit* (New York: HarperCollins, 2006), 27.
76. Wade, *The Lord Is My Counsel*, 103.
77. Dick Armstrong in conversation with the author.
78. American National Business Hall of Fame, http://anbhf.org/.
79. *Book of Remembrances*.
80. Wade, *The Lord Is My Counsel*, 2.

Chapter 3

1. The family of Ken Hansen gave permission to Bill Pollard to extract material about Ken's life from a private autobiography Ken had written. Much of

the material about Ken's early life comes from Bill's notes from that document. References will refer to this writing as "Pollard, *Hansen*."

2. Pollard, *Hansen,* 2.

3. Wheaton College Archives, The Billy Graham Center, Wheaton College, Wheaton, IL.

4. Ibid.

5. Pollard, *Hansen.*

6. Wade, *The Lord Is My Counsel*, 96.

7. Ibid., 96.

8. Pollard, *Hansen*, 4.

9. Dave Baseler in conversation with the author.

10. Vince Nelson in conversation with the author, 2018.

11. Dave Baseler, recalling his own conversation with Ken Hansen, in conversation with the author.

12. Richard E. Hattwick, "Wade, Hansen, Wessner: ServiceMaster" (October 24, 2014), http://anbhf.org/laureates/servicemaster/.

13. *ServiceMaster Annual Report* (1971).

14. Hattwick, "Wade, Hansen, Wessner."

15. Wade, *The Lord Is My Counsel*, 97–98.

16. Hattwick, "Wade, Hansen, Wessner."

17. Pollard, *Hansen,* 6.

18. Ibid.

19. Wade, *The Lord Is My Counsel*, 126.

20. Elyse Fitzpatrick, *Believers in Business: Stories from the ServiceMaster Family* (Downers Grove, IL: ServiceMaster Clean, 2001), 36.

21. Ken Watt interview with Ken Hansen and Ken Wessner, *Daily Herald* (1991).

22. Hattwick, "Wade, Hansen, Wessner."

23. Wade, *The Lord Is My Counsel*, 139.

24. Ibid.

25. Pollard, "Lightposts of Our Heritage" video.

26. *ServiceMaster Annual Report* (1963).

27. Ibid.

28. Hattwick. "Wade, Hansen, Wessner."

29. Pollard, "Lightposts of Our Heritage" video.

30. Ibid.

31. Hattwick, "Wade, Hansen, Wessner."

32. Ken Wessner, "Vitality Means Joy" (address, Delta Lambda Kappa, Lake of the Ozarks, MO, September 29, 1977). Available through the Work and Faith Collection of the Seattle Pacific University Library.

33. *Wheaton College News Service* (April 1993), from collected papers in the Billy Graham Center, Wheaton College, Wheaton, IL. Degree confirmed in e-mail correspondence from Beth Daily, Registrar's Office, Booth School of Business, University of Chicago, October 25, 2017.

34. *ServiceMaster Annual Report* (1969), 5.

35. *Popular Mechanics* (March 1966), 5, https://archive.org/stream/PopularMechanics1966/Popular%20mechanics-03-1966#page/n57/mode/2up.

36. Allan C. Emery, *A Turtle on a Fencepost* (Minneapolis: WorldWide, 1979).

37. Ibid., 95.

38. Ibid., 96.

39. Ibid.

40. Jim Huse in conversation with the author.

41. Emery, *A Turtle on a Fencepost*, 97.

42. Hattwick, "Wade, Hansen, Wessner."

43. Hansen, *Reality*.

44. Ken Wessner on "Lightposts of Our Heritage" video.

45. Hansen, *Reality*, 5.

46. *Wheaton College News Service* (May 1966), from collected papers in the Billy Graham Center, Wheaton College, Wheaton, IL.

47. H. Howard Fuller, "My Pilgrimage in Mission," *International Bulletin of Missionary Research* 34 (January 2010): 37–40.

48. *ServiceMaster Annual Report* (1967).

49. *ServiceMaster Annual Report* (1971/1975).

50. Rob Gillette in conversation with the author.

51. Ibid.

52. *ServiceMaster Annual Report* (1969).

53. Bisher Mufti in conversation with author, July 2018.

54. Ken Hansen application to Wheaton College (April 20, 1971), from collected papers in the Billy Graham Center, Wheaton College, Wheaton, IL.

55. Howard Gelfand, *Wall Street Journal* (January 23, 1973), from collected papers in the Billy Graham Center, Wheaton College, Wheaton, IL.

56. Doug Pound in conversation with the author.

57. Fitzpatrick, *Believers in Business*, 102.

58. C. William Pollard, *Tides of Life: Learning to Lead and Serve as You Navigate the Currents of Life* (Wheaton, IL: Crossway, 2014), 115.

59. Ibid.

60. Ibid., 115, 116.

61. C. William Pollard, Kenneth Hansen Memorial Service at College Church, Wheaton, IL, May 14, 1994.

62. Hansen, *Reality*.

63. Ken Hansen speaking on "Lightposts of Our Heritage" video.

64. Doug Pound in conversation with the author.

65. Fitzpatrick, *Believers in Business*, 117.

66. Richard Chase (Wheaton College president) and Ken Hansen correspondence (1984), the Billy Graham Center Archives, Wheaton College, Wheaton, IL.

67. Pollard, Kenneth Hansen Memorial Service.

Chapter 4

1. Wessner, "Turning Crisis into Personal Growth."

2. Hattwick, "Vision and Control."

3. Material for the early days of Ken Wessner is drawn from a variety of sources including: Kenneth T. Wessner, in chapter 52 of Gloria Gaither, *What My Parents Did Right* (West Monroe, LA: Howard, 1993), 211–13; author interviews with David Wessner and Barbara Wessner Anderson (October 2018); archived letters and author's communications with the Alumni Association at Wheaton College, Wheaton, IL; and Wilson High School 1940 Yearbook (West Lawn, PA), retrieved by Karen L. Troutman, director of Public Relations, Wilson School District.

4. Wessner in *What My Parents Did Right*.

5. Ibid.

6. Karen Troutman, public relations director, Wilson High School, in conversation with the author, October 2018.

7. Ken Wessner, "Building a Winning Team" (address, Delta Lambda Kappa Address, White Sulphur Springs, WV, September 23, 1986).

8. The US Air Force did not become a separate military service until 1947. Prior to this time it was part of the US Army (for land operations) and the US Navy (for sea operations).

9. See https://www.northcharleston.org/visitors/attractions/greater -charleston-naval-base-memorial/naval-base-history. The Navy Yard became a first-class national defense activity during this expansion period (1941–45) with a mission to provide construction, repair, and logistic support to the operating forces. Thousands of soldiers, sailor, and airmen passed through its military facilities on their way to war.

10. Wessner, "Turning Crisis into Personal Growth."

11. Ibid.

12. Bob Groff in conversation with the author.

13. Ken Watt, "Values Take Company to the Top," *Daily Herald*, 1991.

14. Dave Baseler, in conversation with the author, based on his conversations with the two Kens.

15. Heskett, Sasser, Jr., and Hart, *Service Breakthroughs*, 48.

16. "ServiceMaster Industries," HBS Case Study No. 9-388-064, Harvard Business School (rev. June 27, 1988), 2.

17. Howard Rudnitsky with Christine Miles, "Who Help Themselves," *Forbes* (March 3, 1980), 56–57.

18. Norma Wessner letter, 3 June 1962, to the *Wheaton College Alumni Magazine*, The Billy Graham Center Archives, Wheaton College, Wheaton, IL.

19. Rudnitsky with Miles, "Who Help Themselves."

20. Pollard, *Soul of the Firm*, 76.

21. See *Healthcare Hall of Fame* for description of past inductees, https:// www.modernhealthcare.com/awards/health-care-hall-fame-inductees -kenneth-t-wessner.

22. Barbara Wessner Anderson in conversation with the author, November 1, 2018.

23. Hattwick, "Vision and Control."

24. Ibid.

25. *ServiceMaster Annual Report* (1971).

26. Kenneth T. Wessner, "Vitality Means Joy" (speech, Delta Lambda Kappa Group, Lake Ozark, MO, September 29, 1977).

27. Wessner, "Turning Crisis into Personal Growth."

28. Wessner on "Lightposts of Our Heritage" video.

29. Malcom Guite is an Anglican priest, poet, lecturer at the Cambridge Theological Foundation, musician, and current chaplain at Girton College, Cambridge. This quote is taken from a talk he gave on virtue ethics at an OxCam C. S. Lewis conference in 2015.

30. Kimberly Amadeo, "History of Recessions in the United States," *The Balance* (August 07, 2018), https://www.thebalance.com/the-history-of -recessions-in-the-united-states-3306011.

31. Michael Hammer and James Champy, *Reengineering the Corporation: A Manifesto for Business Revolution*, Collins Business Essentials (New

York: HarperBusiness, 2006); and Thomas H. Davenport, *Process Innovation: Reengineering Work through Information Technology* (Boston: Harvard Business Review Press, 1992).

32. *ServiceMaster Annual Report* (1983).

33. Ibid.

34. *The Evangelical Beacon* 59, no. 13 (June 23, 1986), contained a brief comment on Ken Wessner's commencement speech at Trinity College, May 10, 1986, http://collections.carli.illinois.edu/cdm/ref/collection/tiu_beacon/id/273.

35. I. Ansoff, "Strategies for Diversification," *Harvard Business Review* 35, no. 5 (September-October 1957): 113–24.

36. Laura L. Nash, *Believers in Business* (Nashville: Thomas Nelson, 1994), 107.

37. *The Wall Street Transcript* (TWST), "TWST Names Wessner Best Chief Executive—Services Industry," July 6, 1981.

38. The Delta Group is the short name for the Delta Lambda Kappa Group that brought leaders of ServiceMaster together to shape what ServiceMaster became.

39. Patricia Asp in conversation with the author.

40. *Funding Universe*, "The ServiceMaster Company History" (2004), http://www.fundinguniverse.com/company-histories/the-servicemaster-company-history/.

41. Heskett, Sasser, and Hart, *Service Breakthroughs*, 49.

42. Pollard, *Soul of the Firm*, 88.

43. Ibid., 89.

44. Ibid.

45. Ibid.

46. Bisher Mufti in conversation with the author.

47. Phil Foxwell in conversation with the author, December 6, 2018.

48. Ibid.

49. Bill Bond in conversation with the author.

50. *Healthcare Management Review*, "HCMR Interview: Kenneth Wessner, Bill Pollard and Alex Balc, Jr. of ServiceMaster Industries, Inc.," vol. 5, no. 1 (1980): 93–100.

51. Ibid.

52. Edwin Darby, "ServiceMaster Cleans Up in a Big Way," *The Chicago Sun Times*, October 2, 1986.

53. Bill Bond in conversation with the author, November 2018.

54. Hattwick, "Vision and Control."

55. Kenneth T. Wessner, R. Daniel Claud, and C. William Pollard (presentation, New York Society of Security Analysts, October 16, 1978).

56. Heskett, Sasser, and Hart, *Service Breakthroughs*, 183.

57. Nash, *Believers in Business*, 110.

58. Ken Wessner, "Building a Winning Team" (presentation, Delta Lambda Kappa, September 23, 1986, White Sulphur Springs, WV).

59. *The Wall Street Transcript*, July 6, 1981.

60. Hansen, *Reality*, 11.

61. Ken Wessner, "Vitality Means Joy" (address, Delta group, September 29, 1977).

62. Fitzpatrick, *Believers in Business*, 125.

63. Wessner, "Building a Winning Team."

64. Remarks by President Ken Wessner (May 1978).

65. *Healthcare Management Review*, 94.

66. Heskett, Sassar, and Hart, *Service Breakthroughs*, 183.

67. *ServiceMaster Annual Report* (1983), 26.

68. Wessner, "Vitality Means Joy."

69. Pollard, *Tides of Life*, 93.

70. Patricia Asp in conversation with the author.

71. Ibid.

72. Nash, *Believers in Business*, 174.

73. Ken Wessner, Next CORP Rolling Quarter Meeting (May 27, 1983).

74. Fitzpatrick, *Believers in Business*, 119.

75. Ken Wessner, "On Such a Full Sea Are We Now" (address, Delta group, September 28, 1978), 12.

76. Wessner, "Vitality Means Joy."

77. Hattwick, "Vision and Control."

78. Kenneth T. Wessner, *Vision and Control* (Downers Grove, IL: ServiceMaster, 1983), referenced by Hattwick in his 1990 interview with Hansen, "Vision and Control."

79. Nash, *Believers in Business*, 117–18.

80. Ibid.

81. *The Wall Street Transcript*, July 6, 1981.

82 *Modern Healthcare Weekly Business News*, September 14, 1992.

83. Manny Mill in conversation with the author, November 2018.

84. Manny Mill with Jude Skallerup, *Radical Redemption: The Real Story of Manny Mill* (Chicago: Moody, 2003).

85. Norma Wessner letter, May 1979, to the *Wheaton College Alumni News*, Wheaton College Archives, Wheaton, IL.

86. C. William Pollard (Kenneth T. Wessner memorial service, April 2, 1994, College Church, Wheaton, IL).

Chapter 5

1. Carol Loomis, "How the Service Stars Managed to Sparkle," *Fortune* (June 11, 1986).

2. Jay McCormick, "Amazing Grace: ServiceMaster Industries, Inc.," *Forbes* (June 17, 1985), 83.

3. Pollard, *Tides of Life*, 142.

4. Ibid., 142–43.

5. H. Lee Murphy, "ServiceMaster Keys on Hospital Frugality," *Crain's Chicago Business* (May 12, 1986), 90.

6. McCormick, "Amazing Grace," 83.

7. Ibid.

8. Murphy, "ServiceMaster Keys on Hospital Frugality," 90.

9. James Heskett, *The Culture Cycle: How to Shape the Unseen Force That Transforms Performance* (Upper Saddle River, NJ: FT Press, 2015), 76.

10. Pollard, *Tides of Life*, 22.

11. Ibid., 45.

12. Ibid., 198.

13. Ibid., 199.

14. Ibid., 54.

15. Ibid., 56.

16. Ibid., 225.

17. Ibid., 112.

18. Pollard, *Serving Two Masters*, 217.

19. Pollard, *Tides of Life*, 112.

20. Ibid., 113.

21. Ibid., 114.

22. Ibid.

23. Ibid., 151.

24. Registration Statement 2-41059, Securities and Exchange Commission (August 7, 1973).

25. Pollard, *Tides of Life*, 117.

26. Ibid., 94.

27. Ibid.

28. Pollard, *Soul of the Firm*, 14–15.

29. Dave Baseler in conversation with the author.

30. Pollard, *Soul of the Firm*, 73.

31. Susan Baker in conversation with the author.

32. Ibid.

33. Ed Catmull with Amy Wallace, *Creativity, Inc.: Overcoming the Unseen Forces That Stand in the Way of True Inspiration* (New York: Random House, 2014), 108–9.

34. Pollard, *Serving Two Masters*, 13.

35. Hassan Moharrak in conversation with the author.

36. Ibid.

37. Pollard, *Tides of Life*, 105.

38. Ibid., 119–20.

39. Susan Baker in conversation with the author.

40. Dave Baseler in conversation with the author.

41. Bill Pollard in conversation with the author.

42. Pollard, *Soul of the Firm*, 154.

43. Pollard, *Serving Two Masters*, 102–3.

44. Ibid., 103.

45. Bill Pollard in conversation with the author.

46. Pollard, *Soul of the Firm*, 9.

47. Ibid.

48. Ibid., 10.

49. Bill Pollard and Charlie Hromada interview, "Lightposts of Our Heritage" video.

50. Pollard, *Serving Two Masters*, 195.

51. *Funding Universe*, "The ServiceMaster Company History."

52. Pollard, *Soul of the Firm*, 151.

53. Pollard, *Serving Two Masters*, 71–72. This quote is originally attributed to Clarence Francis, former chair of the board, General Foods Corporation, who retired in 1954.

54. Pollard, *Soul of the Firm*, 46–47.

55. Ibid., 106.

56. The title of this book also tells something about Bill Pollard. The publisher wanted the title to be *Serving Two Masters: God and Profit*. But Bill replied, "Jesus said, 'You can't serve two masters,' Matthew 6:24, Luke 16:13." He offered a compromise with the addition of the "?"

57. Pollard, *Soul of the Firm*, 76.

58. Bill Pollard in conversation with the author.

59. Pollard, *Soul of the Firm*, 77.

60. Ibid., 142–43.

61. Tom Little, current franchise owner in Kalamazoo, Michigan, had a picture of the balance and the note hanging in his training room. He provided the description and history of this visual device.

62. C. W. Pollard, letter to Dale Sheets, October 17, 1989. A copy of the letter was provided by Tom Little.

63. Pollard, *Soul of the Firm*, 18.

64. *ServiceMaster Annual Report* (1991).

65. Pollard, *Soul of the Firm*, 131.

66. Dave Baseler in conversation with the author.

67. Pollard, *Serving Two Masters*, 34.

68. Ernie Mrozek in conversation with the author.

69. Pollard, *Serving Two Masters*, 52–53.

70. Ibid., 155.

71. Dan Kellow in conversation with the author.

72. Drawn from former ServiceMaster employees in conversation with the author.

73. Pollard, *Soul of the Firm*, 27.

74. Doug Pound, current Merry Maids franchise owner, in conversation with the author.

75. Brian Griffiths, former ServiceMaster board member, in conversation with the author.

76. Bill Pollard and Dale Peterson, "Lightposts of Our Heritage" video.

77. D. W. Crawford in conversation with the author.

78. Ibid.

79. Scott Cromie in conversation with the author.

80. Pollard interview with Mark Lightfoot, "Lightposts of Our Heritage" video.

81. Don Hill, "What Now, TruGreen?," *Turf Magazine* (December 6, 2013), https://www.turfmagazine.com/viewpoints/what-now-trugreen/.

82. Robert Palmer, "Whatever Happened to ChemLawn?," *Weedpro* (blog), February 27, 2015, https://www.weed-pro.com/blog/lawn-care-company -chemlawn.

83. Bill Pollard and Ron Anderegg interview, "Lightposts of Our Heritage" video.

84. Ibid.

85. Dave Slott in conversation with the author.

86. Pollard, *Tides of Life*, 131.

87. Ibid., 132.

88. Ibid., 170.

89. David Young, "Flat Stock Makes a Convert out of ServiceMaster," *Chicago Tribune*, December 16, 1991.

90. Bill Pollard in conversation with the author.

91. *ServiceMaster Annual Report* (1992).

92. Carol J. Loomis, with William Sheeline, "Stars of the Service 500: Strict Attention to Costs and a Passion for Satisfying the Customer Have Kept Profits Blazing at Nine Standout Companies," *Fortune* (June 5, 1989).

93. Pollard, *Tides of Life*, 213.

94. David Miller in conversation with the author.

95. Scott Cromie in conversation with the author.

96. Pollard, *Tides of Life*, 174.

97. Jane McGuffey in conversation with the author.

98. Patricia Asp in conversation with the author.

99. Bill Pollard in conversation with the author.

100. Heskett, *The Culture Cycle*.

101. C. William Pollard, "The Leader Who Serves" (speech, Windsor, England, April 23, 1994), accessible through the Seattle Pacific University Commons.

102. C. William Pollard, "The Servant Leader" (speech, August 18, 1994), accessible through the Seattle Pacific University Commons.

Chapter 6

1. In September 1993, when Carlos Cantu was preparing to step into the role as CEO of ServiceMaster, Bruce Hansen, from the *Memphis Business Journal*, had a lengthy interview with Carlos and wrote a story for the paper. He gave his detailed, handwritten notes to Dave Baseler. These 1993 notes contain what he learned from Carlos, though much of the material never appeared in print. This material is the source of information about his childhood, growing up years, and some early thoughts as he stepped into the new position. It will be referenced below as "Hansen, handwritten notes."

2. Hansen, handwritten notes.

3. David Young, "New Leader at ServiceMaster," *Chicago Tribune*, September 2, 1993, https://www.chicagotribune.com/news/ct-xpm-1993-09 -02-9309020125-story.html.

4. Hansen, handwritten notes.

5. Pollard, *Soul of the Firm*, 139–42.

6. Ibid.

7. *ServiceMaster Annual Report* (1993).

8. Ibid., 8.

9. Hansen, handwritten notes.

10. See https://horatioalger.org/members/member-detail/carlos-h-cantu/#.

11. Ibid.

12. Hansen, handwritten notes.

13. Albert Cantu, Carlos's son, in conversation with the author.

14. Hansen, handwritten notes.

15. Dave Baseler in conversation with the author.

16. Hansen, handwritten notes.

17. Donna Chavez, "No Challenge Has Been Too Great for Carlos Cantu," *Chicago Tribune*, May 19, 1996.

18. Hansen, handwritten notes.

19. Ibid.

20. Proclamation by the State of Tennessee, April 29, 1997.

21. Hansen, handwritten notes.

22. Albert Cantu, son of Carlos and Gloria Cantu, in conversation with the author.

23. Hansen, handwritten notes.

24. Ibid.

25. Ibid.

26. Brad Harbison, "ServiceMaster's Carlos Cantu Passes Away at 69," *Pest Control Technology* (September 22, 2003).

27. Paul Bert in conversation with the author.

28. Hansen, handwritten notes.

29. Paul Bert in conversation with the author.

30. Patricia Asp in conversation with the author.

31. Cushing Memorial Library & Archives, Texas A&M University Libraries, http://archiveexhibits.library.tamu.edu/siempre/index217f.html ?pg=41&nav=5.

32. Augusto Failde and William Doyle, *Latino Success: Insights from 100 of America's Most Powerful Latino Business Professionals* (New York: Fireside, 1996), 228–29.

33. Bob Groff in conversation with the author.

34. SEC 8K Report (February 1997), https://sec.report/Document /0000806027-97-000007.

35. Casey Burko, "WMX Chief to Become Vice Chairman of ServiceMaster," *Chicago Tribune*, April 29, 1997.

36. Noel H. Tichey with Eli Cohen, *The Leadership Engine: How Winning Companies Build Leaders at Every Level* (New York: Harper, 1997).

37. Dave Baseler in conversation with the author.

38. *ServiceMaster Annual Report* (1995), 3.

39. *ServiceMaster Annual Report* (1998), 4.

40. *ServiceMaster Annual Report* (1997).

41. Ibid.

42. In the late 1990s, the author recalls meetings with IBM leadership in which executives tracked stock prices on their watches. It seemed novel at the time.

43. *ServiceMaster Annual Report* (1997).

44. Ibid.

45. Ibid.

46. Ibid.

47. *ServiceMaster Annual Report* (1998).

48. Harvard Business School Case Study (1999); *ServiceMaster Annual Report* (1998).

49. *ServiceMaster Annual Report* (1998).

50. Steve Daniels, "At ServiceMaster, a Reformation for Phil Rooney," *Crain's Chicago Business* (April 10, 1999).

51. Phillip P. Rooney, "Reflections on a Journey: Serving and Leading at ServiceMaster," *ServiceMaster Annual Report* (1998).

52. Ibid.

53. State of Tennessee House Resolution 70, April 29, 1997, http://www .legislature.state.tn.us/bills/100/Bill/HR0070.pdf.

54. *Brownsville Herald*, "Carlos Cantu, Retired Senior Chairman of The ServiceMaster Company, Dies at Age 69," September 22, 2003.

55. *Memphis Business Journal*, "Cantu Center Dedicated in Chicago," October 1, 2007, https://www.bizjournals.com/memphis/stories/2007/10 /01/daily29.html.

Chapter 7

1. George Gunset, "William Pollard Returns to ServiceMaster Chief Executive," *Chicago Tribune*, July 27, 1999.
2. The author recalled Art Hitsman, president of the Boeing Computer Services division, saying this in a meeting.
3. Mike Schuster, "The Gods of Retail: ServiceMaster," *Minyanville* (blog), March 24, 2009, http://www.minyanville.com/investing/articles /ServiceMaster-retail/3/24/2009/id/21539#ixzz4qWqbN8a7.
4. *ServiceMaster Annual Report* (1998).
5. *ServiceMaster Annual Report* (1999).
6. Heskett, "ServiceMaster," HBS Case Study N9-900-030.
7. Ibid.
8. *ServiceMaster Annual Report* (1998).
9. *ServiceMaster Annual Report* (2000).
10. Ibid.
11. Paul Bert in conversation with the author.
12. Pollard, *Tides of Life*, 137.
13. Ibid.
14. Around 2000, Jack Welch spoke at the Boeing Leadership Center, describing how he learned about technology from a young "mentor." He had recognized the changes coming to business from technology and had selected a "twenty-five year old kid" to meet with one day each month to learn about the "digitization of everything." He discussed some of this in his talk at Fairfield University, https://www.c-span.org/video/?c4601329 /jack-welch-fairfield-university.
15. See https://www.c-span.org/video/?c4601329/jack-welch-fairfield -university.
16. *ServiceMaster Annual Report* (1999).
17. Heskett, "ServiceMaster," HBS Case Study N9-900-030.
18. Roger Hallowell with David Kiron, "WeServeHomes.com," HBS Case Study 9-802-004 (December 13, 2001).
19. Ibid.
20. Ibid.
21. Chris Gutek, "ServiceMaster Announces Weservehomes.com," *Morgan Stanley Investment Report*, January 24, 2000. Reported by Hallowell.
22. Hallowell with Kiron, "WeServeHomes.com," HBS Case Study 9-802-004.
23. *ServiceMaster Annual Report* (2000), 8.
24. Ibid., 12.
25. Board members in conversation with the author.
26. *ServiceMaster Annual Report* (2000), 8.
27. Heskett, Sasser, and Hart, *Service Breakthroughs*, 201.
28. Pollard, *Soul of the Firm*, 74.
29. Pollard, *Tides of Life*, 169.
30. Ibid.
31. C. William Pollard, "The Awesome Responsibility of Leadership," Seattle Pacific University Library Collection, Seattle, WA, https://digital commons.spu.edu/pollard_papers/.
32. Pollard, *Tides of Life*, 193.
33. Ibid., 191.

34. Ibid.

35. David Packard, *The HP Way: How Bill Hewlett and I Built Our Company* (New York: HarperCollins, 1996).

36. "Lewis E. Platt: Sharing Insight from 33 Years at Hewlett-Packard," *Ethix* (April 1, 2000), https://ethix.org/2000/04/01/sharing-insight-from-33-years-at-hewlett-packard.

37. Ibid.

38. James Collins, *How the Mighty Fall* (New York: Harper Collins, 2009), 85.

39. *ServiceMaster Annual Report* (2000), 10.

Chapter 8

1. R. C. Sproul, *Stronger Than Steel* (New York: Harper Row, 1980).

2. "Wayne T. Alderson: Valuing People Helps Business of the Person," *Ethix* (October 1, 2009), https://ethix.org/2009/10/01/valuing-people-helps-business.

3. Ernie Mrozek in conversation with the author.

4. David Barboza, "In This Company's Struggles, God Has Many Proxies," *The New York Times*, November 21, 2001.

5. Six Sigma is a disciplined, statistical-based, data-driven approach and continuous improvement methodology for eliminating defects in a product, process, or service. It was developed by Motorola and Bill Smith in the early 1980s based on quality management fundamentals and then became a popular management approach at General Electric (GE) with Jack Welch in the early 1990s. The approach was based on the methods taught by W. Edwards Deming, Walter Shewhart, and Ronald Fisher, among many others. See http://leansixsigmadefinition.com/glossary/six-sigma/.

6. Solomon, *Evangelical Christian Executives*, 78.

7. A request for Jon's perspective on these issues led to the simple response, "I decline."

8. *ServiceMaster Annual Report* (2001).

9. Ibid., 17.

10. Mike Mack in conversation with the author.

11. Historical board members in conversation with the author.

12. Robert Manor, "ServiceMaster Management Unit to Be Sold," *Chicago Tribune*, October 5, 2001.

13. Barboza, "In This Company's Struggle, God Has Many Proxies."

14. Bill Bond in conversation with the author.

15. Patricia Asp in conversation with the author.

16. Manor, "ServiceMaster Management Unit to Be Sold."

17. *ServiceMaster Annual Report* (2001).

18. Rob Keith in conversation with the author.

19. Ibid.

20. See https://www.hpalumni.org/hp_way.htm. The website, demonstrating the continued passion of former HP employees, is a volunteer effort named "HP Alumni Association" and is not endorsed by the company.

21. Jocelyn Dong, "The Rise and Fall of the HP Way," April 10, 2002, https://www.scribd.com/document/136660697/The-Rise-and-Fall-of-the-HP-Way.

22. David Jacobson, "Founding Fathers," *Stanford Magazine* (July/August 1998).

23. Jim Collins, "The Ten Greatest CEOs of All Time: What These Extraordinary Leaders Can Teach Today's Troubled Executives," *Fortune* (July 21, 2003).

24. Mathew Ingram, "Fiorina Collides with 'the HP Way,'" *The Globe and Mail*, November 8, 2001, https://www.theglobeandmail.com/technology/ingram-fiorina-collides-with-the-hp-way/article20934686/.

25. *Slashdot*, "David Packard Writes HP Epitaph," May 9, 2002, https://slashdot.org/story/02/05/09/174228/david-packard-writes-hp-epitaph.

26. "Orin C. Smith: Managing Growth and Leadership Change at Starbucks," *Ethix* (April 1, 2005), https://ethix.org/2005/04/01/managing-growth-and-leadership-change-at-starbucks.

27. Ibid.

28. Jonathan Birchall, James Politi, and Francesco Guerrera, "Starbucks Schultz Returns as CEO," *Financial Times*, January 7, 2008, https://www.ft.com/content/e89a896e-bd6b-11dc-b7e6-0000779fd2ac.

29. John Ewoldt, "Did Someone Really Return a Set of Tires to Nordstrom?," *Point of Sale* (blog), October 2, 2015, http://www.startribune.com/did-someone-really-return-a-set-of-tires-to-nordstrom/330414071/.

30. Carol Tice, "Nordstrom Takes Street Beating," *Puget Sound Business Journal* (September 8, 2000).

31. Al Erisman, "Dealing with the Failure of the Shareholder Value Model," *Ethix* (June 1, 2003), https://ethix.org/2003/06/01/dealing-with-the-failure-of-the-shareholder-value-model.

32. Bill Pollard letter to Jon Ward and the board of directors, September 12, 2002.

33. Steve Preston in conversation with the author.

34. Heskett, Sassar, and Hart, *Service Breakthroughs*, 201.

35. Solomon, *Evangelical Christian Executives*, 10.

36. *ServiceMaster Annual Report* (2005).

37. Ibid.

38. *Industry News*, "ServiceMaster Reorganizes Management Team," January 11, 2005.

39. *The Contractor*, "ServiceMaster May Sell Plumbing, HVAC Operations," January 1, 2006, https://www.contractormag.com/plumbing/cm_newsarticle_803.

40. Ibid.

41. Bob Tita, "Cantu Out at ServiceMaster over Disagreement," *Craine's Chicago Business*, December 13, 2005.

42. Reuters News Service, "ServiceMaster CEO Ward Resigns," May 16, 2006.

43. Steve Preston in conversation with the author.

44. Bob Tita, "Albert Cantu Tops Early List to Be Next ServiceMaster CEO," *Craine's Chicago Business*, May 18, 2006.

45. Bob Tita, "ServiceMaster's New CEO to Get $900K Base Salary," *Craine's Chicago Business*, August 24, 2006.

46. Jonathan Maze, "ServiceMaster Goes Private with Buyout," *Franchise Times*, May 1, 2007.

47. Ibid.

48. Ernie Mrozek conversation with the author.

49. Chuck Bowen, "ServiceMaster CEO Resigns," *Lawn and Landscape Industry News*, April 12, 2013.

50. Rob Gillette in conversation with the author.

51. Palmer, "Whatever Happened to ChemLawn?"

52. Brian Horn, "Battered but Breathing," *Industry News*, May 23, 2014,https://www.lawnandlandscape.com/article/ll0514-top-100-trugreen -comeback/.

53. *ServiceMaster Annual Report* (2014).

54. Rob Gillette in conversation with the author.

55. *Marketwired*, "ServiceMaster to Relocate Headquarters to Downtown Memphis," June 3, 2016, https://finance.yahoo.com/news/service master-relocate-headquarters-downtown-memphis-170000259.html.

56. See https://news.servicemaster.com/press-release/servicemaster company-news/servicemaster-named-fortunes-2016-worlds-most-admired.

57. Bill Dries, "Gillette Out, ServiceMaster to Spin Off Unit," *Memphis Daily News*, July 27, 2017.

58. Rob Gillette in conversation with the author.

59. *ServiceMaster Annual Report* (2014–2018).

60. Ibid.

61. ServiceMaster history, https://servicemaster.com/company/about /history/.

62. ServiceMaster Clean, West Virginia and Maryland, http://www .yellowcleanteam.com/content/about_us.

63. ServiceMaster Clean, Yakima, WA, http://www.smcleanyakima.com /about/.

64. Meagan Nichols, "ServiceMaster Team Pilots Subscription Box as Innovation Becomes Core Company Value," *Memphis Business Journal* (May 17, 2019).

65. ServiceMaster Mission Statement and Vision, https://www.service master.com/company/about/vision.

66. Pollard, *Soul of the Firm*, 13.

Chapter 9

1. Pollard, *Serving Two Masters*, 27.

2. Mike Mack, president and owner of the Seattle Franchise for Service-Master Clean and ServiceMaster Restore, in conversation with the author, January 17, 2019.

3. Ibid.

4. Ibid.

5. Bob Smith in conversation with the author.

6. Ibid.

7. Ibid.

8. Ibid.

9. Dave Moore in conversation with the author.

10. Ibid.

11. Ibid.

12. Ibid.

13. Mike Isakson in conversation with the author.

14. Fitzpatrick, "The People We Touch: The Story of Mike and Jinny Isakson," *Believers in Business*, 205–16.

15. Mike Isakson in conversation with the author.

16. Ibid.

17. Matt Edwards, COO of Pine Cove Christian Camps, in conversation with the author.

18. Ibid.

19. Joy Flora in conversation with the author.

20. Dallen Peterson, *Rags, Riches, and Real Success* (Wheaton: Tyndale, 2000), 154.

21. Joy Flora in conversation with the author.

22. Hassan Moharrak in conversation with the author.

23. Ibid.

24. Bill Pollard in conversation with the author.

25. Pollard, *Tides of Life*, 243–44.

26. Ming Lo Shao, with interpreter Phillip Pan, in conversation with the author.

27. Mill with Skallerup, *Radical Redemption*.

28. Ibid., 90.

29. Ibid., 93.

30. Ibid., 94.

31. Manny Mill in conversation with the author.

32. Greg Leith in conversation with the author.

33. Fred Smith in conversation with the author, October 2017. He has subsequently retired from his work leading the Gathering.

34. Ibid.

Chapter 10

1. See Albert M. Erisman, *The Accidental Executive: Lessons on Business, Faith and Calling from the Life of Joseph* (Peabody, MA: Hendrickson, 2015).

2. Albert Erisman and David Gautschi, eds., *The Purpose of Business: Contemporary Perspectives from Many Walks of Life* (Hampshire, UK: Palgrave Macmillan, 2015).

3. Schuster, "The Gods of Retail."

4. Darren E. Grem, *The Blessings of Business: How Corporations Shaped Conservative Christianity* (New York: Oxford University Press, 2016).

5. Amanda Porterfield, Darren E. Grem, and John Corrigan, *The Business Turn in American Religious History* (New York: Oxford University Press, 2017).

6. Solomon, *Evangelical Christian Executives*, 10.

7. This visit was summarized in the story of Mike Mack in chapter 9.

8. Patricia Asp in conversation with the author.

Bibliography

Books

Catmull, Ed, with Amy Walker. *Creativity, Inc.: Overcoming the Unseen Forces that Stand in the Way of True Inspiration.* New York: Random House, 2014.

Collins, James. *How the Mighty Fall.* New York: Harper Collins, 2009.

Davenport, Thomas H. *Process Innovation: Reengineering Work through Information Technology.* Boston: Harvard Business School Press, 1993.

DePree, Max. *Leadership Is an Art.* New York: Doubleday Dell, 1989.

Emery, Allan C. *A Turtle on a Fencepost.* Waco: Word, 1979.

Erisman, Albert M. *The Accidental Executive: Lessons on Business, Faith, and Calling from the Life of Joseph.* Peabody, MA: Hendrickson, 2015.

Erisman, Albert, and David Gautschi, eds. *The Purpose of Business: Contemporary Perspectives from Different Walks of Life.* Hampshire, UK: Palgrave Macmillan, 2015.

Failde, Augusto, and William Doyle. *Latino Success: Insights from 100 of America's Most Powerful Latino Business Professionals.* New York: Fireside, 1996.

Fitzpatrick, Elyse. *Believers in Business: Stories from the ServiceMaster Family.* N.p.: ServiceMaster Clean, 2001.

Grem, Darren E. *The Blessings of Business: How Corporations Shaped Conservative Christianity.* New York: Oxford University Press, 2016.

Hammer, Michael, and James Champy. *Reengineering the Corporation: A Manifesto for Business Revolution.* New York: HarperCollins, 1993.

Hansen, Kenneth. *Reality: That Which Gives Purpose, Zest, and Motive Power to Life.* Foreword by Ken Wessner. Downers Grove, IL: ServiceMaster, 1984/1979.

Heskett, James. *The Culture Cycle: How to Shape the Unseen Force That Transforms Performance.* Upper Saddle River, NJ: FT Press, 2011.

Heskett, James L., W. Early Sasser Jr., and Christopher W. L. Hart. *Service Breakthroughs: Changing the Rules of the Game.* New York: The Free Press, 1990.

McCullough, David. *The Spirit of America: Who We Are and What We Stand For.* New York: Simon & Schuster, 2017.

Mill, Manny, with Jude Skallerup. *Radical Redemption: The Real Story of Manny Mill*. Chicago: Moody, 2003.

Nash, Laura. *Believers in Business*. Nashville: Thomas Nelson, 1994.

Packard, David. *The HP Way: How Bill Hewlett and I Built Our Company*. New York: Harper Collins, 1995.

Peterson, Dallen. *Rags, Riches, and Real Success*. Wheaton: Tyndale House, 2000.

Pollard, C. William. *Serving Two Masters? Reflections on God and Profit*. New York: Harper Collins, 2006.

———. *The Soul of the Firm*. New York: HarperBusiness, 1996.

———. *Tides of Life: Learning to Lead and Serve as You Navigate the Currents of Life*. Wheaton, IL: Crossway, 2014.

———, ed. *The Heart of a Business Ethic*. New York: University Press, 2005.

Porterfield, Amanda, Darren E. Grem, and John Corrigan. *The Business Turn in American Religious History*. New York: Oxford University Press, 2017.

Schwartz, Barry. *Why We Work*. New York: Simon and Schuster, 2015.

Solomon, Lewis D. *Evangelical Christian Executives: A New Model for Business Corporations*. New Brunswick, NJ: Transaction, 2004.

Sproul, R. C. *Stronger Than Steel*. New York: Harper Row, 1980.

Tichey, Noel H., with Eli Cohen. *The Leadership Engine: How Winning Companies Build Leaders at Every Level*. New York: Harper, 1997.

Van Dyke, Henry. *Now First Collected and Revised with Many Hitherto Unpublished*. New York: Charles Scribner's Sons, 1911.

Wade, Marion. *The Lord Is My Counsel: A Businessman's Experiences with the Bible*. New York: Prentice Hall, 1966.

Wessner, Kenneth T. Chapter 52 in *What My Parents Did Right*. Compiled by Gloria Gaither. West Monroe, LA: Howard, 1993.

Articles

Amadeo, Kimberly. "History of Recessions in the United States," *The Balance* (August 07, 2018). https://www.thebalance.com/the-history-of-recessions-in-the-united-states-3306011.

Ansoff, I. "Strategies for Diversification." *Harvard Business Review* 35, no. 5 (September–October 1957): 113–24.

Barboza, David. "In This Company's Struggles, God has Many Proxies." *New York Times*, November 21, 2001.

Birchall, Jonathan, James Politi, and Francesco Guerrera. "Starbucks Schultz returns as CEO." *Financial Times*, January 7, 2008. https://www.ft.com/content/e89a896e-bd6b-11dc-b7e6-0000779fd2ac.

Bowen, Chuck. "ServiceMaster CEO Resigns." *Lawn and Landscape Industry News*, April 12, 2013.

Brownsville Herald. "Carlos Cantu, retired senior chairman of The ServiceMaster Company, dies at age 69." September 22, 2003.

Burko, Casey, "WMX chief to become Vice Chairman of ServiceMaster."
Chicago Tribune, April 29, 1997.

Chavez, Donna. "No Challenge Has Been Too Great for Carlos Cantu." *Chicago Tribune,* May 19, 1996.

Collins, Jim. "The Ten Greatest CEOs of All Time: What these extraordinary leaders can teach today's troubled executives." *Fortune,* July
21, 2003.

Daniels, Steve. "At ServiceMaster, a Reformation for Phil Rooney." *Crain's
Chicago Business,* April 10, 1999.

Darby, Edwin. "ServiceMaster Cleans Up in a Big Way." *The Chicago Sun
Times,* October 2, 1986.

Dong, Jocelyn. "The Rise and Fall of the HP Way," April 10, 2002.

Dries, Bill. "Gillette Out, ServiceMaster to Spin Off Unit." *Memphis Daily
News,* July 27, 2017.

Ewoldt, John. "Did Someone Really Return a Set of Tires to Nordstrom?"
Point of Sale (blog), October 2, 2015. http://www.startribune.com/did
-someone-really-return-a-set-of-tires-to-nordstrom/330414071/.

Fortune. "Scrubbing Up for the Lord," January 1956.

Fuller, H. Howard. "My Pilgrimage in Mission," *International Bulletin of
Missionary Research* 34 (January 2010): 37–40.

Gelfand, Howard. "Growing ServiceMaster Industries, Inc. Thrives by Calling on God and Hospitals." *Wall Street Journal,* January 23, 1973.

Gunset, George. "William Pollard Returns to ServiceMaster Chief Executive Post." *Chicago Tribune,* July 27, 1999.

Gutek, Chris. "ServiceMaster Announces Weservehomes.com." *Morgan
Stanley Investment Report,* January 24, 2000.

Haanen, Jeff. "God of the Second Shift," *Christianity Today,* September
20, 2018.

Hall, Ron. "What Now TruGreen?: ServiceMaster is no longer the parent
company for TruGreen," *Turf,* December 6, 2013. https://www
.turfmagazine.com/viewpoints/what-now-trugreen/.

Harbison, Brad. "ServiceMaster's Carlos Cantu passes away at 69." *Pest
Control Technology,* September 22, 2003.

Healthcare Management Review. "HCMR Interview: Kenneth Wessner,
Bill Pollard and Alex Balc, Jr. of ServiceMaster Industries, Inc." Vol.
5, Issue 1 (1980): 93–100.

Horn, Brian. "Battered but Breathing." *Industry News,* May 23, 2014.
https://www.lawnandlandscape.com/article/ll0514-top-100
-trugreen-comeback/.

Industry News. "ServiceMaster Reorganizes Management Team." January 11, 2005.

Ingram, Mathew. "Fiorina Collides with 'the HP Way,'" November 8, 2001.

Jacobson, David. "Founding Fathers." *Stanford Magazine*, July/August 1998.

Loomis, Carol. "How the Service Stars Managed to Sparkle." *Fortune*, June 11, 1986.

Loomis, Carol J., with William Sheeline. "Stars of the Service 500: Strict attention to costs and a passion for satisfying the customer have kept profits blazing at nine standout companies." *Fortune*, June 5, 1989.

Manor, Robert. "ServiceMaster Management Unit to Be Sold." *Chicago Tribune*, October 5, 2001.

Marketwired. "ServiceMaster to Relocate Headquarters to Downtown Memphis." June 3, 2016. https://finance.yahoo.com/news/service master-relocate-headquarters-downtown-memphis-170000259 .html.

Maze, Jonathan. "ServiceMaster Goes Private with Buyout." *Franchise Times*, May 1, 2007.

McCormick, Jay. "Amazing Grace: ServiceMaster Industries, Inc." *Forbes*, June 17, 1985, 83.

Memphis Business Journal. "Cantu Center Dedicated in Chicago." October 1, 2007. https://www.bizjournals.com/memphis/stories/2007 /10/01/daily29.html.

Modern Healthcare Weekly Business News, September 14, 1992.

Murphy, H. Lee. "ServiceMaster Keys on Hospital Frugality." *Crain's Chicago Business*, May 12, 1986, 90.

Nichols, Meagan. "ServiceMaster Team Pilots Subscription Box as Innovation Becomes Core Company Value," *Memphis Business Journal*, May 17, 2019.

Palmer, Robert. "Whatever Happened to ChemLawn?" *WeedPro* (blog), February 27, 2015. https://www.weed-pro.com/blog/lawn-care -company-chemlawn.

Reuters News Service. "ServiceMaster CEO Ward Resigns." May 16, 2006.

Rudnitsky, Howard, and Christine Miles. "Who Help Themselves." *Forbes*, March 3, 1980, 56–57.

Schuster, Mike. "The Gods of Retail: ServiceMaster." *Minyanville* (blog), March 24, 2009. http://www.minyanville.com/investing/articles /ServiceMaster-retail/3/24/2009/id/21539#ixzz4qWqbN8a7.

Tice, Carol. "Nordstrom Takes Street Beating." *Puget Sound Business Journal*, September 8, 2000.

Tita, Bob. "Albert Cantu Tops Early List to Be Next ServiceMaster CEO." *Craine's Chicago Business*, May 18, 2006.

———. "Cantu Out at ServiceMaster over Disagreement." *Craine's Chicago Business*, December 13, 2005.

———. "ServiceMaster's New CEO to Get $900K Base Salary." *Craine's Chicago Business*, August 24, 2006.

Watt, Ken. "Values Take Company to the Top." *Daily Herald*, 1991.

Wessner, Ken. "Turning Crisis into Personal Growth," *CBMC Management Memo*, 1979.

Wessner, Kenneth T., R. Daniel Claud, and C. William Pollard. Service-Master Industries presentation to the New York Society of Security Analysts, October 16, 1978.

Young, David. "Flat Stock Makes a Convert out of ServiceMaster." *Chicago Tribune*, December 16, 1991.

———. "New Leader at ServiceMaster." *Chicago Tribune*, September 2, 1993. https://www.chicagotribune.com/news/ct-xpm-1993-09 -02-9309020125-story.html.

Ethix Resources

Alderson, Wayne T. "Wayne T. Alderson: Valuing People Helps Business of the Person." *Ethix*, October 1, 2009. https://ethix.org/2009 /10/01/valuing-people-helps-business.

Bakke, Dennis. "Dennis Bakke: Creating Real Fun at Work." *Ethix*, June 1, 2004. https://ethix.org/2004/06/01/creating-real-fun-at-work.

Broetje, Cheryl. "Cheryl Broetje: An Orchard with Fruit That Lasts." *Ethix*, December 1, 2005. https://ethix.org/2005/12/01/an-orchard-with -fruit-that-lasts.

Erisman, Al. "Dealing with the Failure of the Shareholder Value Model." *Ethix*, June 1, 2003. https://ethix.org/2003/06/01/dealing-with -the-failure-of-the-shareholder-value-model.

Flow, Don. "Don Flow: Ethics Flow at Flow Automotive." *Ethix*, April 1, 2004. https://ethix.org/2004/04/01/ethics-at-flow-automotive.

———. "Don Flow: Maintaining Ethics in a Downturn: Auto Sales, Real Estate, Home Building."*Ethix*, June 1, 2009. https://ethix.org /2009/06/01/maintaining-ethics-in-a-downturn-auto-sales.

Platt, Lewis E. "Lewis E. Platt: Sharing Insight from 33 Years at Hewlett-Packard." *Ethix*, April 1, 2000. https://ethix.org/2000/04/01 /sharing-insight-from-33-years-at-hewlett-packard.

Pollard, C. William. "C. William 'Bill' Pollard: Leading by Serving." *Ethix*, October 1, 2006. https://ethix.org/2006/10/01/684.

Rowan, Barry. "Barry Rowan: Bringing Meaning to Work." *Ethix*, July 27, 2011. https://ethix.org/2011/07/27/telecommunications-barry-rowan.

Sinegal, James D. "James D. Sinegal: A Long-Term Business Perspective in a Short-Term World."*Ethix*, April 1, 2003. https://ethix.org/2003/04/01 /a-long-term-business-perspective-in-a-short-term-world.

Smith, Orin C. "Orin C. Smith: Managing Growth and Leadership Change at Starbucks." *Ethix*, April 1, 2005. https://ethix.org/2005/04/01/managing-growth-and-leadership-change-at-starbucks.

Harvard Business School Case Studies

Hallowell, Roger, with David Kiron. "WeServeHomes.com." HBS Case Study 9–802–004. Harvard Business School (December 13, 2001).

Heskett, James. "ServiceMaster: We Serve." HBS Case Study N9–900–030. Harvard Business School (June 6, 2000).

"ServiceMaster Industries." HBS Case Study 9–388–064. Harvard Business School (rev. June 27, 1988).

Seattle Pacific University Library Collection

Donated papers from C. William Pollard's speeches over the years can be found in the SPU Library Collection, with online access through https://digitalcommons.spu.edu/pollard_papers/. Other private papers that are listed in this section (e.g., speeches from Ken Wessner, Pollard's extracts from the Ken Hansen memoirs) are contained in the Al Erisman Papers, which are physically part of the Seattle Pacific University Library's Work and Faith Collection.

Hansen, Bruce. CHC interview from handwritten notes, September 1993. SPU Library Collection, Seattle, WA.

Hattwick, Richard E. "Wade, Hansen, Wessner: ServiceMaster." American National Business Hall of Fame, October 24, 2014, http://anbhf.org/laureates/servicemaster/. SPU Library Collection, Seattle, WA.

———. "Vision and Control: Interview with Kenneth N. Hansen," September 16, 1990. Hattwick personal archives.

Nast, Tom, and Carl Wilke. A skit, written and performed in the 1980s for ServiceMaster leadership, provided by Scott Heise. SPU Library Collection, Seattle, WA.

Pollard, C. William. "The Awesome Responsibility of Leadership." SPU Library Collection, Seattle, WA. https://digitalcommons.spu.edu/pollard_papers/.

———. Kenneth Hansen Memorial Service, May 14, 1994, College Church, Wheaton, IL. SPU Library Collection, Seattle, WA.

———, ed. "Ken Hansen Memoirs" (selected). SPU Library Collection, Seattle, WA.

———. Kenneth T. Wessner Memorial Service, April 2, 1994, College Church, Wheaton, IL. SPU Library Collection, Seattle, WA.

———. "The Leader Who Serves." Speech, Windsor, England, April 23, 1994. SPU Library Collection, Seattle, WA. https://digitalcommons .spu.edu/pollard_papers/.

———. "The Servant Leader." Speech, August 18, 1994. https://digital commons.spu.edu/pollard_papers/.

———. William Pollard letter to Jon Ward and Board of Directors, September 12, 2002. SPU Library Collection, Seattle, WA.

Wessner, Ken. "Vitality Means Joy." Address to Delta Lambda Kappa, Lake of the Ozarks, MO, September 29, 1977. SPU Library Collection, Seattle, WA.

———. "Building a Winning Team." Address to Delta Lambda Kappa, White Sulphur Springs, WV, September 23, 1986. SPU Library Collection, Seattle, WA.

———. "On Such a Full Sea Are We Now." Address to Delta Group, September 28, 1978. SPU Library Collection, Seattle, WA.

ServiceMaster Annual Reports

1963, 1964, 1967, 1969, 1971, 1975 (plus a 25-year history supplement), 1983–2005.

Wheaton College Archives

Book of Remembrances, September 2001. The Marion E. Wade Center, Wheaton College, Wheaton, IL.

Chase, Richard, and Ken Hansen. Richard Chase and Ken Hansen correspondence, 1984. The Billy Graham Center Archives. Wheaton College, Wheaton, IL.

Gelfand, Howard. *Wall Street Journal*, January 23, 1973. The Billy Graham Center Archives. Wheaton College, Wheaton, IL.

Hansen, Ken. Ken Hansen application to Wheaton College, April 20, 1971. The Billy Graham Center Archives. Wheaton College, Wheaton, IL.

Wessner, Norma. Norma Wessner letter to *Wheaton College Alumni Magazine*, 3 June 1962. The Billy Graham Center Archives. Wheaton College, Wheaton, Illinois.

———. Norma Wessner letter to *Wheaton College Alumni News*, May 1979. Wheaton College Archives. Wheaton College, Wheaton, IL.

Wheaton College News Service (April 1993). Wheaton College, Wheaton, IL.

Wheaton College News Service (May 1966). The Billy Graham Center Archives. Wheaton College, Wheaton, IL.

Other Web Resources

C-Span. "Jack Welch at Fairfield University." April 9, 2001. https://www
.c-span.org/video/?c4601329/jack-welch-fairfield-university.

City of North Charleston. "Naval Base History." http://www.northcharleston
.org/visitors/attractions/greater-charleston-naval-base-memorial
/naval-base-history/.

The Contractor, January 1, 2006. https://www.contractormag.com
/plumbing/cm_newsarticle_803.

Cushing Memorial Library and Archives, Texas A&M University Libraries.
"Leaders in Business and Industry: Carlos H. Cantu." http://archive
exhibits.library.tamu.edu/siempre/index217f.html?pg=41&nav=5.

The Evangelical Beacon 59, no. 13 (June 23, 1986). http://collections
.carli.illinois.edu/cdm/ref/collection/tiu_beacon/id/273.

Funding Universe. "The ServiceMaster Company History." http://www.fund
inguniverse.com/company-histories/the-servicemaster-company
-history/.

Horatio Alger Association of Distinguished Americans, Inc. "Carlos H.
Cantú Member Profile." https://horatioalger.org/members/member
-detail/carlos-h-cantu/#.

HP Alumni. "The HP Way." https://www.hpalumni.org/hp_way.htm.

Ken and Jean Hansen Lectureship Series. The Marion E. Wade Center.
Wheaton College, Wheaton, IL. https://www.wheaton.edu/academics
/academic-centers/wadecenter/events/ken-and-jean-hansen
-lectureship/.

Memphis Business Journal. "Cantu Center Dedicated in Chicago." October
2007. https://www.bizjournals.com/memphis/stories/2007/10/01
/daily29.html.

ServiceMaster. "Defining the Residential and Commercial Service Industry
for 90 Years." https://servicemaster.com/company/about/history/.

ServiceMaster. "ServiceMaster Mission/Vision." https://www.service
master.com/company/about/vision.

ServiceMaster. "ServiceMaster Named to Fortune's 2016 World's
Most Admired Companies List." February 22, 2016. https://news
.servicemaster.com/press-release/servicemastercompany-news
/servicemaster-named-fortunes-2016-worlds-most-admired.

ServiceMaster Clean/ServiceMaster Restore. "The History of ServiceMaster Clean." http://www.smcleanyakima.com/about/.

Slashdot. "David Packard Writes HP Epitaph." May 9, 2002. https://slashdot
.org/story/02/05/09/174228/david-packard-writes-hp-epitaph.

Wessner, Ken. *Healthcare Hall of Fame,* 1992. https://www.modern
healthcare.com/awards/health-care-hall-fame-inductees
-kenneth-t-wessner.

INDEX

About the Hendrickson Publishers/Theology of Work Line of Books

There is an unprecedented interest today in the role of Christian faith in "ordinary" work, and Christians in every field are exploring what it means to work "as to the Lord" (Col. 3:22). Pastors and church leaders, and the scholars and teachers who support them, are asking what churches can do to equip their members in the workplace. There's a need for deep thinking, fresh perspectives, practical ideas, and mutual engagement between Christian faith and work in every sphere of human endeavor.

This Hendrickson Publishers/Theology of Work line of books seeks to bring significant new resources into this conversation. It began with Hendrickson's publication of the *Theology of Work Bible Commentary* and other Bible study materials written by the TOW Project. Soon we discovered a wealth of resources by other writers with a common heart for the meaning and value of everyday work. The HP/TOW line was formed to make the best of these resources available on the national and international stage.

Works in the HP/TOW line engage the practical issues of daily work through the lens of the Bible and the other resources of the Christian faith. They are biblically grounded, but their subjects are the work, workers, and workplaces of today. They employ contemporary arts and sciences, best practices, empirical research, and wisdom gained from experience, yet always in the service of Christ's redemptive work in the world, especially the world of work.

To a greater or lesser degree, all the books in this line make use of the scholarship of the *Theology of Work Bible Commentary*. The authors, however, are not limited to the TOW Project's perspectives, and they constantly expand the scope and application of the material. Publication of a book in the HP/TOW line does not necessarily imply endorsement by the Theology of Work Project, or that the author endorses the TOW Project. It does mean we recognize the work as an important contribution to the faith-work discussion, and we find a common footing that makes us glad to walk side-by-side in the dialogue.

We are proud to present the HP/TOW line together. We hope it helps readers expand their thinking, explore ideas worthy of deeper thought, and make sense of their own work in light of the Christian faith. We are grateful to the authors and all those whose labor has brought the HP/TOW line to life.

William Messenger, Executive Editor, Theology of Work Project
Sean McDonough, Biblical Editor, Theology of Work Project
Patricia Anders, Editorial Director, Hendrickson Publishers

www.theologyofwork.org
www.hendrickson.com

PHOTOS

Marion E. Wade, founder of ServiceMaster, who frequently had a big smile on his face. (Used by permission of the Marion E. Wade Center, Wheaton College, Wheaton, IL.)

Marion Wade (first CEO) and Ken Hansen (second CEO), who formed a unique arrangement called "shingles on a roof," working together and supporting each other as they established the foundations for ServiceMaster. (Photo of Marion Wade and Ken Hansen from the 1968 annual report. Used by permission of the Marion E. Wade Center, Wheaton College, Wheaton, IL.)

Marion Wade continued to be a part of leadership at ServiceMaster until he died in 1973 (photo taken 1960). (Used by permission of the Marion E. Wade Center, Wheaton College, Wheaton, IL.)

Portrait of Lil and Marion Wade. It was customary at ServiceMaster to recognize the wives with their husbands in portraits of the leaders. (Photo courtesy of Dave Baseler and used by permission.)

In 1968, Ken Hansen vacationed in Europe and began painting. For years, this painting hung in the ServiceMaster offices and appeared on the cover of his 1984 booklet *Reality*. See chapter 3 of this book for a description of the painting. (Photo by Bob McGuffee and provided by Dave Baseler. Used by permission.)

Portrait of Ken and Jean Hansen. (Photo courtesy of Dave Baseler and used by permission of Baseler and G. Walter Hansen.)

Kenny (far left) with Jean and Ken Hansen in 1988. (Used by permission of G. Walter Hansen.)

KENNETH T. WESSNER

A — Spectator Staff 4; Band 2, 3; Hi-Y 2, 3, 4, Chaplain 4; Basketball 2, 3, 4, Captain 4; Soccer 3, 4; Track 4
V — Academic
I — Summer vacations, sports
A — Business executive
T — Pitching a no-hit, no-run baseball game
I — Pessimists and chemistry tests
O — Handsome
N — Ken, Wes

Wessner's photo in the 1940 yearbook of Wilson High School in West Lawn, Pennsylvania. (Courtesy of Karen Troutman, director of public relations at Wilson High School, and used by permission.)

Ken Wessner and Ken Hansen, after Wessner became the third CEO and Hansen became chair of the board of directors. (Photo courtesy of Dave Baseler and used by permission.)

Portrait of Kenneth and Norma Wessner. (Photo courtesy of Mike Isakson. Used by permission of Isakson and David Wessner.)

Bill Pollard and Ken Wessner with ServiceMaster building and truck on the cover of *Fortune* magazine (June 5, 1989), when *Fortune* recognized ServiceMaster as the top service company. (Photo by Katherine Lambert. Used by permission of Lambert and *Fortune*.)

ServiceMaster and Ned Cook Industries sign the agreement with Cook Industries, allowing ServiceMaster to become the parent company of Terminix in 1986. Seated (left to right) Ned Cook, Cook chairman and CEO, and Bill Pollard and Carlos Cantu. Standing (second from left) Jim Holloway, Terminix CFO; (third from left) Everett Cook; and (second from right) Fred Slocum, Cook VP Administration. (Photo courtesy of Albert Cantu and used by permission.)

Paul Harvey was a noted broadcaster in the 1980s and a friend of Ken Wessner. ServiceMaster frequently advertised on his program, and he spoke at their events. Harvey pictured here with Wessner (center) and Pollard (right). (Photo courtesy of Dave Baseler and used by permission.)

Standing in front of Marion Wade's portrait are (from left to right) Ken Wessner, Chuck Stair, Ken Hansen, Bill Pollard, and Carlos Cantu. The first five CEOs are shown here with Stair, head of Management Services at the time. (Photo taken by Bruce Quist and provided by Bill Pollard. Used by permission.)

Portrait of Judy and Bill Pollard (fourth CEO). (Photo courtesy of Dave Baseler. Used by permission of Baseler and Bill Pollard.)

Portrait of Carlos (fifth CEO) and Gloria Cantu. (Photo courtesy of Dave Baseler. Used by permission of Baseler and Albert Cantu.)

Carlos Cantu ringing the opening bell at the NYSE on January 15, 1999. On July 17, 1998, ServiceMaster converted to a public company under the SVM name. (Photo courtesy of Albert Cantu and used by permission.)

Rob Gillette speaking at the opening of Groundfloor, a new ServiceMaster innovation center in Memphis. (Photo courtesy of *The Memphis Daily News*, where it appeared June 16, 2017. Used by permission.)

Dave Baseler joined ServiceMaster in 1980 and served through 2002. He worked in marketing communications, which included compiling and editing annual reports. He worked with Bill Pollard in his writing projects and was an enormous help to the author in gathering material for this book. (Photo courtesy of Dave Baseler and used by permission.)

Patricia Asp joined ServiceMaster in 1978 when ServiceMaster acquired the hospital food services company she was leading at the time. She enjoyed a twenty-five-year career at ServiceMaster and played a major role in People Services, which included supporting Carlos Cantu when he became CEO. She retired from ServiceMaster in 2003. (Photo courtesy of Patricia Asp and used by permission.)

The ServiceMaster Wall honors employees with the company for twenty-five years. Pollard's name appears in the group that started in 1977. (Used by permission of Dave Baseler.)

The balance beam, created in 1989, was used as a teaching tool to explore the balancing act needed to hold the four objectives together. (Photo courtesy of Dave Baseler and used by permission.)

Mike Mack's desk with Pollard's books and the bookends that depict the statue of Jesus washing the feet of the disciple. (Photo by Al Erisman. Used by permission of Michael Mack.)

In 1990, Esther Augsburger was commissioned to create this eleven-foot-tall sculpture of a disciple having his feet washed by Jesus. This was originally placed in front of the ServiceMaster "wall of service" as a "practical example of servant leadership" (as stated in the 1991 annual report that featured this image on the cover). When the company moved its headquarters to Memphis, the statue was placed in storage. It now finds a permanent home at Wheaton College. (Photo courtesy of Dave Baseler and used by permission.)